P9-DMS-392

WHITE GIRLS

WHITE GIRLS

HILTON ALS

MᶜSWEENEY'S
SAN FRANCISCO

MᶜSWEENEY'S
SAN FRANCISCO

www.mcsweeneys.net

Copyright © 2013 Hilton Als

Some of this work appeared in different form in the *New Yorker*,
the *New York Review of Books*, *Artforum*, *Studio Magazine*, *Grand Street*, the *Believer*,
McSweeney's Quarterly, and the collection *Malcolm X: In Our Own Image*.

McSweeney's and colophon are registered trademarks of McSweeney's,
a privately held company with wildly fluctuating resources.

ISBN: 978-1-936365-81-4

CONTENTS

One evening an actor asked me to write
a play for an all-black cast. But what exactly
is a black? First of all, what's his color?
                                        —Jean Genet

I know these girls they don't like me
But I am just like them.
                    —The Roches, "The Married Men"

TRISTES TROPIQUES

SIR OR LADY (as I shall call him) sits on the promontory in our village, deep in movie love. He's running the same old flick in his head again. In it, the stars kiss breathlessly, in true love. This is the kind of movie he enjoys: the movie guy kisses the movie girl and they are one. I listen to Sir or Lady detailing this or that movie scenario and look for myself in every word of it. I don't want to exist much outside his thinking and regard. I'm convinced Sir or Lady's movie tales are his way of telling me he and I are one; he's a romantic, but a silent one. He says: The movie girl overcomes her resistance to the movie guy and then we know they are in love forever. (He's never told me this part of the story before. He's never used that exact sequence of words before.) Who is the "we" Sir or Lady is referring to? And what do they "know"? I'm off his screen, apparently. When I can't find myself in what Sir or Lady says, the world as I know it is nearly washed away by wave after wave of ocean-gray fear: how can he have a thought, a feeling, without me? How can I be a we without him?

The truth is, I have not been myself lately, and for a long time. In the three decades or more since Sir or Lady—or SL—and I have been friends, I have felt myself becoming him, to a certain extent. I've adopted his vocal intonations, his vegetarianism, and his candor. He is my second but longer-running we. This did not come about without its share of relationship noise. I've spent a fair amount of time trying to apprehend—in the blind, awkward, and ultimately solipsistic way many of us strive to articulate why the beloved has become just that— how SL came to fill my mind like no one else on earth.

Metaphors sustain us. For some time before we were known as an "Oh, you two!" I felt SL was my corny and ancient "other half." Nearly from the first I wanted to "grow into one" with him, as Aristophanes sort of has it in Plato's *Symposium*. We are not lovers. It's almost as if I dreamed him—my lovely twin, the same as me, only different. I cling to that story in *The Symposium*, of the two halves coming together in "an amazement of love and friendship and intimacy, and one will not be out of the other's sight," because that's all I want to know. Like most people, I respond to stories that tell me something about who I am or wish to be, but as reflected in another character's eyes. With it all, though, I know I will lose sight of SL eventually. I have before. To the movies and movie kissing. To his love of women. To his interest— unlike me—in the plural aspects and manifestations of the world, from its vastness to its multitude of worms. To his politics. To his various subjects (he is a photographer and a filmmaker). To his migraines. To his social drinking. To his lack of interest—unlike me—in delineating who we are. To his lack of interest in speaking of our friendship—our twinship—to anyone at all. To his lack of interest—unlike me—in seeking anyone's validation for what he thinks or feels.

Nothing accounts for me and SL getting together, and everything does. Our respective biographies and hence personalities don't add up to us being a we. We were raised in different parts of the world, in different kinds of families. But we shared this: we each had a daddy, and that can send you packing, even from yourself. Still, SL and I met at a moment when we'd relaxed into that particular conundrum; it was just part of who we were. By the time we met we were anxious to share our black American maleness with another person who knew how flat and not descriptive those words were since they did not include how it had more than its share of Daisy Buchanan and Jordan Baker in it, women who passed their "white girlhood" together. We were also the first line of Joni Mitchell's autobiography: "I was the only black man in the room." We were also the the gorgeously corny complications one finds in Joni's 1976 song, "Black Crow": "There's a crow flying / black and ragged / tree to tree. / He's as black as the highway that's leading me. / Now he's diving down / to pick up on something shiny. / I feel like that black crow / flying / in a blue sky." We were Barbara Smith and her twin sister, Beverly, and their feminism and socialism, and we understood every word of what Barbara meant when she and her co-editors titled their 1982 anthology *All the Women are White, All the Blacks Are Men, But Some of Us Are Brave: Black Women's Studies*. We were the amused "sickness," that Eldridge Cleaver felt existed between white women and black men and he said so in his 1968 memoir, *Soul on Ice*. Our bodies could never forget how Louis Gossett's character goes mad in the 1970 film *The Landlord* upon discovering that his wife has taken the white title character as a lover: "Christ has never known the horror of nappy hair in America." In our lives we had been, variously, the landlord, Louis Gossett, and his wife. We were equal parts "butch realness" and "femme realness," as delineated in Jennie Livingston's essential 1990 film *Paris Is Burning.* We were every word of "Racism: The Sexism of the Family of Man" in Shulamith Firestone's seminal 1970 book, *The Dialectic of Sex: The Case for Feminist Revolution,* except when she said: "Just as the child begins with a bond of sympathy with the mother, and is soon required to transfer his identification from the mother to the father, thus to eradicate the female in himself, so too the black male, in order to 'be a man,' must untie himself from his bond with the white female, relating to her if at all in a degrading way." Part of our shared tragedy—we recognized it at once—was that we never separated from our mothers, which meant we liked girls more than the world liked them, which is to say more than they liked each other, let alone themselves. We were the twin boys— one dead, one not dead—in Thomas Tryon's fantastic 1971 novel *The Other.* We were, in short, colored male Americans, a not easily categorizable quantity that annoyed most of our countrymen, black and white, male and female alike, since America is nothing if not about categories. But despite the perplexity of the outside world we could not give the other up. Having finally found someone who spoke the other's language, we could name who we were, which was rare enough indeed, given the history others like us—fellow spectator bait—had with being named incorrectly, or not at all. But what galled our audience, really, is the fact that our friendship grew out of wanting to interest each other. We wanted the world to have no part in it.

SL had been a we before he met me. He says: What else is there but other people? He's taken his share of his previous other halves to the movies. There's hope at the movies. (As an army brat and an only child, SL moved with his parents a lot; movie palaces were the only homes he recognized as such.) While sitting in a movie theater on one of our first dates, I stole glimpses of SL in the dark. He's a lovely shade of brown. The silvery movie light and dark made him look more colored. I loved his profile, his long strong neck and perfect posture. He looked as authoritative as someone you might call Sir, and as beautiful and poised as someone you might call Lady. Watching him watch a movie, I noticed how his eyes would open and close slowly, like the folds in an accordion. The movies filled his eyes up.

Some movies and stars and scenes in movies we saw and loved on our first nights out together: the two actresses who look alike in the opening sequence of Ingmar Bergman's 1966 film, *Persona*. David Bowie and Candy Clark drawing our attention to how much they resemble one another in Nicolas Roeg's 1976 *The Man Who Fell to Earth*. Sissy Spacek as Pinky Rose and Shelley Duvall as Millie Lammoreaux in Robert Altman's brilliant 1977 movie, *3 Women*. In it, the two stars work as physical therapists, along with a set of blond twins. Driving in a car one dusty afternoon, Pinky asks: "I wonder what it's like to be twins?" Then, continuing: "Bet it'd be weird. You think they know which one they are?"

> Millie: Sure they do. They'd have to, wouldn't they?
> Pinky: I don't know. Maybe they'd switch back and forth. You know, one day, Peggy's Polly, the other day Polly's Peggy.

Pinky pauses. She smiles a small mysterious smile before saying:

Pinky: Who knows? Maybe they're the same all the time.

To SL, I was always Pinky. I don't know, I've never asked him, but maybe he knew that, like Pinky, I longed to be his other half long before I found him.

We met in 1982—I was twenty-two, he's seven years older—and the only time I effectively left our twinship for a time was in 1992. That year my beloved K died from AIDS. He was diagnosed in 1990, and I spent 1990, 1991, and 1992 in a kind of couple daze. I'd look on as old men walked down city streets arm in arm with their wives. I would watch babies resting on their mothers' bellies in patches of grass and sunlight in Central Park. I would watch cigarette-smoking teenagers glittering with meanness and youth, whispering and laughing as they shopped on lower Broadway. These exchanges of intimacy were all the same to me because they excluded me, that twin who somehow lost his better half. I was an I, an opera of feeling with a very small audience, a writer of articles about culture but with no real voice, living in a tiny one-bedroom apartment in the Crown Heights section of Brooklyn, a dream of love growing ever more expansive because it was impossible, especially in the gay bars I sometimes frequented in Manhattan, where AIDS loved everyone up the wrong way, or in a way some people weren't surprised by, particularly those gay men who were too indifferent to be sad—in any case night sweats were a part of the conversation people weren't having in those bars, in any case, taking your closest friend in because he was shunned by his family was part of the conversation people weren't having, still, there was this to contend with: that friend's shirt collars getting bigger; still, there was this to contend with: his coughing and wheezing in the little room off your bedroom in Brooklyn because TB was catching, your friends didn't want you to catch it, loving a man was catching, your friends didn't want you to get it; his skin was thin as onionskin, there was a lesion, he couldn't control his shit, not to mention the grief in his eyes, you didn't want to catch that; those blue eyes filled with why? Causing one's sphincter to contract, your heart to look away, a child's question you couldn't answer, what happened to our plans, why was the future happening so fast? You didn't want to catch that, nor the bitterness of the sufferer's family after the death, nor the friends competing for a bigger slice of the death pie after the sufferer's death, you certainly didn't want to catch what it left: night sweats, but in your head, and all day, the running to a pay phone to share a joke, but that number's disconnected, your body forgets, or rushes toward the love you remember, but it's too late, he's closer to the earth now than you are, and you certainly don't want to catch any of that. So. You search, like some latter-day Frankie Addams in Carson McCullers's *The Member of the Wedding*, for your "we of me," but at a distance. Your we could be dying, but so filled with love, all those couples in the park, dancers in the street, unlike you, so resentful of the romantic strain love engenders, the pulverizingly tedious self-absorption loss wraps you in: *I was subjected to that. This is what it meant to me.* The ego— what a racket. And what of the person who actually disintegrated, and the imprint of his sad eyes and rotten luck in your living atmosphere of air and buildings? He has only you to go by now. To stay awake to the memory of his toes, and small buttocks in those jeans, the sound of his heels on the floor, and what it sounded like when he said "we," as you lay in bed holding his dying in your now relatively well-ordered world of health and well-being.

Even though SL and I talked on a more or less daily basis from 1989 on, there were certain things I was never entirely comfortable discussing with him, such as AIDS, and my queerness. By the time I met him, I was so used to being on my own in the latter, and felt so alone in the former, that, even after my beloved K died, in 1992, I had no real language for that part of my life that dick transcended, and degraded.

I met K in 1981, in New York; we were students at the same college. He had the straightest back and longest neck—just like SL. Even though he was straight off the boat from Connecticut when we met and he resembled, then, a young Montgomery Clift—he looked like an older Montgomery Clift when he was dying—K's demeanor was as disciplined and colored as SL's, which is to say K's affect was not too far removed from how Flannery O'Connor might have described someone like SL when she wrote: "[The Negro] is a man of very elaborate manners and great formality which he uses superbly for his own protection and to insure his own privacy." In his privacy K often fell in love with his opposite—big men with big, expansive feelings; the turn-on for him was in trying to stitch them up and make them behave properly. We always failed him.

SL met K a few months after I met SL, who said, after meeting him: I watched you guys walk into the restaurant, and I thought: "Oh, they're married." We were. At college K studied art history, and I studied him. That's how you recognize love: you've never met it before. Even before I knew who K was he interested me. At first, he irritated me. Sitting behind him as a Tintoretto or a Gorky flashed across one art history course screen or another, I saw K's neck, his freshly laundered shirt, his neatly sharpened pencils, and his readiness to do well. I didn't recognize him because I didn't recognize any of that in myself. Our love was a confusion of non-twinning, that is, we didn't recognize anything of ourselves in the other. We were not lovers, or we were lovers in every way except one. I shall never forget how our lips felt when we'd kiss good-night. I shall never forget what his little body felt like, in sickness and in health. And I shall never forget him saying, "Oh, Bear," as he hugged me good-night. I'll never get over him, nor the fact that he understood how I was never able to grasp that, for most people, love and conflict were the same thing, and, if that was really the case, what did that say about their love? When it came to love, K was practical and traditional: for him, it was not separate from conflict and conflict was not separate from marriage. So when I would start to absent myself from a scene— the inevitable buildup that comes with getting close to anyone—K yelled, "Don't withdraw!" as I climbed into his little bed. (We did some of our best thinking together lying in his bed.) His anger could not beat my silence, though, and so, after a while, he gave up and climbed into bed with me. Another time—K had finished college by then, I never did; he was living in the East Village, I'd just gotten my little flat in Brooklyn—K was angry with me about one thing or another. This time I wouldn't take it. He stormed off to the super-market; there, a black woman accidentally bumped into K's cart with her own. K exploded—"I've had it with you people and your anger!"—a remark that not only made me laugh, but made me love him more. By then it was 1987 or 1988, and we weren't even thirty. K was thin and white and he loved and identified with white girls like Mariel Hemingway as she appeared in the 1979 motion picture *Manhattan*. I'd never felt like part of a couple before. We *did* things together. The only time I felt as though we'd separated was when we went to gay bars together. But when it comes to gay bars, it's every man for himself. K was one pretty white girl. As such, he had a certain currency in those bars that made me feel jealous: couldn't the world see he was mine? Couldn't the world see I was his universe, and he mine? While we each had boyfriends (K more than me; I couldn't physically take how much I wanted to be loved and how much I felt when I was; K was made of the world and, so, of much stronger stuff) they were animal-smart enough to know that the real connection was between K and myself. Inevitably, one of his boyfriends but more likely one of mine because that was the only real power they had in the relationship, threatening not to love me, they were men after all and getting there was always on their mind—anyway, more than one of these guys hit on K after they broke up with me. But I wouldn't have known about it had K not told me. Once, after he relayed that So and So had come on to him, K said: "I don't know why I told you that! I don't know why!" I didn't know why, either, but I knew who K was, and I knew he could and did fall in love with that which

I could not love: the blowhard boy, the taking-up-too-much-space boy, the hysterical boy, the consumerist boy, because they were as glamour-struck as K was struck by their surface glamour. I wanted to love K as a lover but I wanted him to get this kind of person out of his system first. But couldn't he see I loved him more than any of those horned-up lunkheads, and that he could sometimes be like them in that he wanted to get at some essential part of me that was my own and couldn't be touched, in the Flannery O'Connor sense? Were all white girls like that?

Of course, SL was more than aware, emotionally and otherwise, of what was happening as K began to leave. SL drove me to K's funeral in Connecticut. He even helped me walk K down the stairs in the tenement building K lived in before he died so he could get home to Connecticut to be with his family one last time. SL even had dinner with my beloved and me and another friend on K's last New Year's Eve on earth, December 1991, and then SL drove him home, trying hard not to look at K's body leaving his life—while sporting a cravat, even. For a time, after they first met, K would sometimes twitch in SL's presence. And while K could let his periodic impulse to hurt but not his jealousy show—"I don't know why I told you that!"—I wonder, now, if my twinship with SL flooded him with feelings he couldn't sort out. When K was growing up in Connecticut, the Black Panthers were on trial in New Haven. This was in 1970; he was eight. One day, his mother drove her children into New Haven to do a little shopping. Upon arriving, his mother told her kids to lock the car doors because "those Panthers were loose." And K remembered thinking: Oh, let them in, let them in. SL and I let him in. Sometimes things got even more confusing. Once, K's boyfriend threw me a birthday party. I was twenty-three and K was twenty. After the party, K found me in bed with a woman. Later, over breakfast, K was tight-lipped for a long time. I don't think I remember asking him what was wrong because I knew what was wrong. Finally, he exploded. "You were in bed with B!" Did K want to be my only white girl? It was a marriage.

SL listened to me sob on the telephone once, after my beloved was diagnosed: But he's only thirty. He doesn't even know who *he* is. SL stood by my side as the lid was placed on K's coffin and the dirt was being shoveled. There was a figurine on top of the coffin lid—a dark Jesus. Looking at that Christ, SL said, I bet K would like that black Jesus on top of him. And without hearing what SL said through his tears, I murmured through my own: I bet K will like that black Jesus on top of him. Then we said good-bye and SL became the only one for a long time.

SL and I met at an alternative weekly, where we both worked in the art department; I was the department assistant, SL a freelance graphic designer. By way of introduction he would shyly offer me things he thought might interest me: postcards, books, photographs. One of the first postcards he sent me was by the photographer Helen Levitt. It showed two colored boys on a street in New York, in the nineteen forties. One boy is facing the camera; the other boy's back faces the camera. Their arms are linked. They look like two sides of the same coin, like Janus. SL passed along a play: Ibsen's *John Gabriel Borkman*. In it, twin sisters long to be loved by or control the same man. He dies. In the end, the twins accept being "twin sisters…of one mind." Because of SL—he loved her work—I also read Gertrude Stein's *Ida: A Novel*. In it, Ida, the heroine, wishes for a twin. She writes letters to her imaginary twin, also named Ida. "Dear Ida my twin," one such letter begins. Then, continuing, "Are you beautiful as beautiful as I am dear twin Ida, are you, and if you are perhaps I am not." SL gave me a VHS tape: *Chained for Life* (1951). In it, real-life conjoined twins Daisy and Violet Hilton star in a fiction about their struggle for love, set against a show-business backdrop. No man can separate them, though; they're emotionally "chained for life." Then there was *Thought to Be Retarded*, written and designed by SL himself. It was based on a performance he'd done in collaboration with the photographer Daniel Lerner. Their piece was based on the story of Grace and Virginia Kennedy, the famous German American twins born in Georgia in the early nineteen seventies, who developed their own language and were "thought to be retarded" because their parents, social workers, and speech therapists alike couldn't understand them. (The Kennedy girls were themselves the subject of Jean-Pierre Gorin's exceptional 1980 documentary *Poto and Cabengo*.)

SL and I had both grown up feeling that the language we spoke was somehow incomprehensible or fuzzy to those around us. He'd spent his adolescence on army bases in England, France, and Germany, while I had no direct experience with white people until I was a teenager. SL's parents were middle-class American Negroes from the Midwest who went to work in Europe to escape, if it can be done, racism. (SL's father taught college-level chemistry on various army bases, while his mother worked as an administrator.)

But his father brought that racism with him. Like many men of his background, his racism was really counterphobic: he revered white people. That his only son couldn't assimilate enough for his angry, continually disappointed father—an impossible task; SL was a black kid in a white world; no matter how much he was lauded or fucked over in that world, he would always be black—was just one of the small crucifixions SL endured for his father's sake. Other nails and splinters: the irrefutable sense that he didn't really know why he was here, in the world, at all. He had no I because he had no country. He would not have his maleness because that was a sick and diseased and controlling thing—like his father.

In the late early nineteen seventies, SL, a tremendous reader, began to hear bits of himself not in Piri Thomas or Eldridge Cleaver but in Shulamith Firestone, and Ti-Grace Atkinson, and Carolee Schneemann, and Robin Morgan: women who were of SL's class, more or less, and had experienced, growing up, something akin to what he had known at the hands of a father: being subject to emotional violence because they owned you, you were their property. He and his mother had grown up in what Shulamith Firestone called "shared oppression." The difference between her and her son was that she believed it: Wasn't her pain the pain you suffered for family? Later SL would withstand mountains of pain for his family. But in the early nineteen-seventies he did two things: he got out, if only he could get out. That is, SL moved forward into his future, but his past resented it. He had boundless hope, but his past thought otherwise. Leaving home, he would kiss white women, or they would kiss him, with no expectation and every expectation, and then—sometimes—he would turn to me and love me as he had been loved in his past, walking in the Black Forest or wherever, tagging along behind his parents in his Eton cap, wondering about the forest worms as he served as an audience for his parents' follies, their seemingly endless marital drama of acceptance and rejection, a form of theater many mothers, for instance, try to justify by saying, We're staying together for the kids' sake. That's the first lie of family. It's never for the kids' sake. Why has no mother, including Hamlet's own, not admitted to her libidinal impulses, saying this crazy-ass dick or uncontrollable freak works for me, I could never do what *he* does in the world, be so out of control, terrible and boundaryless, I'm a woman, confined by my sex, prohibited from acting out because other lives, my children's lives, depend on me, but still there's my husband acting out for me, what a thrill as he crashes against the cage of my propriety. What no mother in history, including Hamlet's own, has ever been able to entirely process, let alone admit: My husband may not actually be our child's type.

From the first, SL and I were each other's hall of mirrors, and is this me currently looking at my parents, or SL looking at his parents? Was it my mother's competitive desire to make a kind of glued-together, unforgettable art out of her marriage, all the while saying: Who could make a better thing out of it? Me or your father? Wait. Who said that? My mother, or SL's mother? Was it SL's mother or my mother whom we loved beyond her comprehension, hating that she treated her own body as a thing to be manipulated by male hands, something that reinforced her idea of male authority, which she admired even as she did and did not admire her son's repudiation of it, a rejection that made her ashamed of her need for it, and so there was nothing for it but to reject the son as weak, poetic, a loving pussy to be tolerated and sometimes reviled. Who could love her for having such thoughts? Who could say? SL and I were each other's hall of mirrors, each a kind of Marvin Gaye in relation to our respective fathers, but SL got away, and left Europe for the United States. I can't bear this part of the story, the he-got-away part, even if it was the best thing for him, and it was, because it presages his getting away from me, the very embodiment of his boyhood isolation.

I ate dirt until he came along. I had what they called the ringworm. I picked my scalp and there it was, underneath my fingernails, piles of sick. I was a preteen Caliban deformed by flaky skin; I had pus on my mind. My head was a compost heap. My fingernails dug into what they, the older people, called the ringworm, or eczema, and I sent shivers down my own spine—an erotic "pain" I could not wait to get my hands on. My gray woolen Eton cap was lousy with me. There was SL in his Eton cap and his forest of worms, and there I was in my cap, waiting until he came along. My contemporaries—other children— risked contagion if they touched my cap, let alone my diseased spot, which, come to think of it, looked a little like a woman's private parts; boys spitballed it.

My infirmity sat on the back of my head, just above my neck. My ringworm was my cruddy friend; it had no other friends and so many enzymes, a dark flower could be forced in it. My ringworm was philosophical. It had certain ideas about the world, about me. One thing that made my ringworm sick was my interest in myself— an interest I almost never uttered in the company of the well. My self-interest was not founded on self-love but on fury over my scabby presence, which no amount of love, from my parents or siblings, could cure. Self-interest ran in my family. They could see me only as the cute extension of what they felt to be cute about themselves. If I expressed, let's say, a dislike of marigolds, that shocked them: I was too cute to contradict flowers. I shut up early on and let my imagination run wild, or as concentrated as my patch of sick.

My ringworm was as infested with longing as I was. My body and soul were a sewer, briny and foul with sexiness. Daddy doesn't like that about me, and I don't like him, but my body craves him.

Daddy says that I am strange, that he never knows what I am talking about. When he comes to call on my mother, he says, Goddammit-what-the-hell-Jesus-Christ-aw-shit-for-fuck's-sake, and Huh? whenever I open my mouth to speak; consequently, I rarely do. Daddy turns me on because he doesn't think I'm cute; he makes me work for his admiration.

He knows that I spend a lot of my time at the big lending library at Grand Army Plaza in Brooklyn, reading books. What he doesn't know is that while there, I also listen to recordings by grand actors reading famous poetry, prose, and plays as a way of learning how to speak in an authoritative, genteel way meant to captivate my father, like a pus-y siren. I listen to white girls such as Glenda Jackson as Charlotte Corday in Peter Weiss's play *Marat/Sade*, because she is not genteel or cute in the role of the knife-wielding anarchist: she is a gorgeous hysteric, as loud as the worst flower. She contradicts my family for me. One of Charlotte's interlocutors begs her to turn away from her various hatreds and "look at the trees / look at the rose-colored evening sky / and let those horrible things pass you by / feel the warmth and the gentle breeze / in which your lovely bosom heaves." Charlotte cannot. "What kind of town is this?" she asks. "I saw peddlers / at every corner / they're selling little guillotines / with tiny sharp blades / and dolls filled with red liquid / which spurts from the neck / when the sentence is carried out / What kind of children are these / who can play / with this toy so efficiently / and who sits in judgment / who sits in judgment?"

As Charlotte Corday, I can hate marigolds. Glenda Jackson's ferocious tone encourages me to imagine Daddy dragging his big Daddy body toward me because I want him to, because I am, finally, all he could ever need: a person capable of screeching, How I hate the marigolds! He bites into my ringworm and eats the red, pused-out bits in the way my older sister ate the petals she pulled from red flowers: with relish. I am not a child. I am a judge. I have been made older through cultivating need, which feeds my imagination, the one thing Daddy does not have access to, the one thing I can make him a lovesick prisoner of.

But SL got out. In 1975, he returned to America on his own, ostensibly to attend college, although he never went. Instead he fell in with New York–based feminists, some of whom roamed the Berkshire woods naked with bow and arrow, looking for men to kill, while others stepped on the accelerator when they saw men crossing the road. In this world, SL became a wife, supporting a number of friends' and lovers' work while his own work took a backseat; it was the least he could do: he had had a father, and he would have no further truck with that. By the time I met him and longed to be his wife, SL sometimes described himself as a lesbian separatist. No man could have him.

I was attracted to him from the first because I am always attracted to people who are not myself but are. It was less clear why he was interested in me. I made him laugh, I suppose. Perhaps he enjoyed the fact that, in those days, I always looked like an old-school bull dagger, what with my thick neck, little gold earrings, no makeup, and hair cut short and shaved on the sides. Also, he knew, and chuckled over the fact, that I was a gay man who did not suck white dick: I refused on the grounds that the world sucked them off well enough. Most certainly he liked the fact that I came from an enormous family of women. He definitely liked hearing about my first-generation West Indian–American parents, who hadn't been raised to be professional Negroes, and who didn't know the first thing about how to keep up appearances: they'd never married, let alone lived together.

But, like SL's father, my father disliked men, less because he wanted to control me—that would require a closeness he wasn't in the least interested in—but because he found them to be invasive, childish, loutish tit grabbers—the very thing he was, and accused his sons of being without knowing much about them. Once, after I'd won some prize in elementary school for writing a poem, my mother encouraged me to hug my visiting father; she knew he could not do it but she also knew I could not write that poem without him on some level; Daddy and his incessant on-the-phone language was one source for my "art." While I stood before him, rigid and blank, he took me in his great arms—my father was a big man; I would grow up to be a big man; I wanted a bigger man to hold me so I could feel, as a grown-up, what my father's embrace made me feel: that I didn't want to grow up to be a big man—and whispered: When I was your age, I didn't like my father to hug me, either. SL understood all that. Or, rather, what it set up in me: a horror of my I, since that meant being a him—my father.

On one of our first dates together, SL and I took a walk. It was early spring; we had just finished work. SL was costumed in his usual striking manner: a stiff, ankle-length motorist's jumper, blue-and-white-polka-dot tie, brown spectators, and a brown fedora. I loved his entirely adult attire; it relieved me of the responsibility of being an adult; in his company I got smaller and smaller, hungry for his protection. SL was a wit you didn't want to cross. As we walked along, we started to talk about all the places we'd ever visited, or hoped to visit. In fact, in a few days' time, I would be off to Amsterdam to visit a friend. Rather offhandedly, I asked SL if he'd like to join me, have a lark, and to my horror he said yes. It was as if he were cursing me in a baroque, foreign language. What could it mean—his acceptance? Where was this: my father offering me a ride downtown—I was a teenager taking a summer-school class in mathematics—but before I could get in the car, he jumped in and slammed the door, called out, *So long, sucker!* as the cab drove off. Where was this: my father telling me I'd go from "Shakespeare to shit" if I didn't stop hanging out with my teenage friends, indeed, if I had any friends. Where was my father doing this:

refusing to stand up, let alone look at any friends I might bring home, especially if they were white, sometimes if they were women.

In retrospect, how could my father love me? I was that part of his self that wanted to write and would write but did not. I was that part of his self that wanted to love and would love but did not. Here was evidence of that: SL. He would go to Amsterdam with me. O Amsterdam, city of canals! SL would listen to what I would write about even if it was derivative, or boring, and find something of me in it to support and praise. He would look for me in every part of Amsterdam because I loved it so, in every canal, in the city's flatness, and in the waves that came up from Haarlem, and the city's famous tolerance, its clouds and herring. But how did he find me now, on lower Broadway? I was short-circuiting because of this information, so casually offered: he would go with me, and he would love me. Would he die because of this love? Would I? Would I have to eventually mourn this memory on lower Broadway, his scratchy-sounding duster, and should we travel to Amsterdam together, him and an entire country? His existence was too much. I fumbled and made an excuse: oh, the place I'd be staying in was a friend's, it was too small, maybe the next time, with better preparation? SL smiled. He knew enough about love—or, more specifically, about its offers and denials—to back off, say nothing, and smile.

After I returned from Amsterdam, he continued to connect to me through metaphor, which is how he approached me in the first place. He would explain our "us," not through direct touch or communication but through artifacts, all those books and films, postcards and films, with "we" or "us" as the subject, as if there is any other. SL gave me those gifts—the movies and books and so on—because he knew, too, that I was like everyone else, except him: I identified with other people. His gifts were road maps to our love, the valley of the unconditional.

As we became friends, the strangest thing happened: most of our acquaintances abused adverbs in their rush to condemn—violently, passionately—our becoming a we. We were something dark and unforeseen: two colored gentlemen who moved through the largely white social world we inhabited in New York (the world where art and fashion and journalism converged) who did not exploit each other or our obvious physical traits—their coloredness and maleness—for political sympathy or social gain. People looked at us and thought we were really evil. That we had pointy heads and forked tongues. That we wore furs and had no animal rights. That we knew the twelve steps but skipped intimacy. That we betrayed every confidence and judged without impunity. That we lauded women and then denigrated them. That we mentored young boys only to corrupt them. That we borrowed money with no thought of returning it. That we were indolent and crackled with ambition. That we were gluttons who drank from a bottomless well of envy. That we were gay and couldn't admit we were straight. That we were faithless Jesus freaks who had forsaken Him for tight pussy, credit cards we abused, and loose shoes. That we had lockjaw once but still managed to feed off our enemies. That we sold children down the river and watched then suffocate in an ocean of adult bitterness. That we were racists, especially against our own kind. That we were matricidal, especially toward our own mothers.

That we were nothing like the "we," or "just us," in songs, lovely moments of togetherness we drowned out whenever we walked into a room, given our "loud" apparel, our conversation.

We faced these faces so many times: white women who had been denied nothing most of their lives feeling bitter about me and SL because they could not be part of "us," but continuing to be attracted to us past the point of reason since they lived to be disappointed; white guys who wanted to fuck me for sport and who resented SL's presence because he was perceived to be the embodiment of my conscience, which could not be defiled; black women who called us freaks since we somehow represented their twisted relationship to their own bodies and other black women; ambitious black male artists who resented our presence, largely because SL and I did not play by the rules they followed in their quest for success—a sad game James Baldwin describes in his 1961 essay "Alas, Poor Richard," which concerns his intellectual twin or father, and occasional nemesis, novelist Richard Wright:

> [O]ne of my dearest friends, a Negro writer now living in Spain, circled around me and I around him for months before we spoke. One Negro meeting another at an all-white cocktail party...cannot but wonder how the other got there. The question is: Is he for real? or is he kissing ass?...Negroes know about each other what can here be called family secrets, and this means that one Negro, if he wishes, can "knock" the other's "hustle"—can give his game away... Therefore, one "exceptional" Negro watches another "exceptional" Negro in order to find out if he knows how vastly successful and bitterly funny the hoax has been. Alliances, in the great cocktail

party of the white man's world, are formed, almost purely, on this basis, for if both of you can laugh, you have a lot to laugh about. On the other hand, if only one of you can laugh, one of you, inevitably, is laughing at the other.

We felt sad when all those Negroes couldn't look us in the eye at parties. But we understood. No narrative preceded us. We were not "menchildren" in a promised land, as Claude Brown would have it. We did not consider ourselves as having "no name in the street," as James Baldwin did himself. We did not suffer the existential crisis that afflicts some male Negro intellectuals, as Harold Cruse presumed. We did not have "hot" souls that needed to be put on ice, as Eldridge Cleaver might have said. We were not escapees from Langston Hughes's "Simple" stories. We were nothing like Richard Wright's Bigger Thomas, nor did we wear white masks, as Frantz Fanon might have deduced, incorrectly. We saw no point of reference in *The Life and Loves of Mr. Jiveass Nigger*, by Cecil Brown. We did not see the point of Sammy Davis Jr.'s need to be loved by not one but thousands, as detailed in his autobiography, *Yes I Can*. We were colored but not noirish enough to have been interesting to Iceberg Slim. We were not homies in the manner of John Edgar Wideman's young proles floating around Homewood. We were not borne of anything Nathan McCall or Ishmael Reed, in his recent books, certainly, might deem worthy of talking about. In short, we were not your standard Negro story, or usual Negro story. We did not feel isolated because we were colored. We did not want to join the larger world through violence or manipulation.

We were not interested in the sentimental tale that's attached itself to the Negro male body by now: the embodiment of isolation. We had each other, another kind of story worth telling.

No one seemed to understand what we were talking about most of the time. There was no context for them to understand us, other than their fear and incomprehension in the presence of two colored men who were together and not lovers, not bums, not mad. Sometimes, as a joke, I'd wonder aloud to SL if we sounded like this to them: *Ooogga booga. Wittgenstein. Mumbo jumbo oogga booga, too, Freud, Djuna Barnes, a hatchi! Mumbo lachiniki jumbo Ishmael Reed and Audrey Hepburn.* And because the others couldn't understand us, meaning was ascribed to us. We couldn't be trusted. We should see a shrink. We should not spend so much time together; we were only hurting ourselves. We should spend more time in the art world, separately, so that SL could have more of a career as an artist. We should get on with our lives, separately, since there was no such thing as fidelity anymore.

I would be lying if I didn't say these various opinions—or really one opinion—didn't affect me: I've lived in New York long enough to know that any kind of failure is considered contagious. But something else overrode my fears: once I was with SL, once we were a we, I wanted to house myself in SL's thinking. It was so big and well lit, like a large house sitting solid on the bank of a river.

We tell each other stories in that house, largely unencumbered by the sound of other people's fear, and for the most part that was true until our we began to disintegrate, in 2007, a parting that killed the world for us. But that was later. Just now the world is whole. It's 2000, and I'm forty, and I have a real home at last. I've dropped my bags at SL's door. The house itself is composed of his skin and thought. Nearby, lilacs bloom in the garden door. Or are they hyacinths? "My mind forgets / The persons I have been along the way," Borges said. And yet it's those persons—in addition to my I—SL wants to hear about; he says they're a part of who I was. Oh, Lord, don't ever let this end: he smells like no one else on earth, and he sounds like no one else on earth. (SL's voice is so deep that people often ask him to speak up, but he is always speaking up.) I love listening to what he says as I have loved listening to no one else talk. Once, after I'd written a piece SL enjoyed, he said: "Mama likes." Once, while crossing a street in the East Village with a friend, she said, with a sigh: "Lord love a duck," and SL added: "And other homilies." Once, after a white girl insulted me about my weight, SL said of her: "I know how Daisy can lose seven pounds. Cut off her head." And another time, when I described running into a white girl we both admired, SL, always starved for style, said: "Was she wearing anything at all?" About another person I longed to trust—I was always longing to trust someone; I was making life a fiction, or writing fiction; I longed for people to not be who they were, another thing SL forgives me for, and shall always forgive me for, even when he has to deal with the fallout, which is often, God bless him—SL said: "I'd trust her with about five dollars." SL is a bullshit detector par excellence. His inability to fictionalize the truth—a habit I picked up from my mother, who was always hoping for a better day, she died hoping for a better day; I suspect SL doesn't want me to die with similar hope flakes on my lips—is what makes me cleave to him, my protector, my truth.

I love listening to his stories. In his early, back-to-America days, SL hung out with some white lesbian separatists on a farm; there, he planted burdock, and ate cold griddle cakes, and read *Our Bodies, Ourselves*. It was the times. Everyone in his world was wearing plastic jellies except SL; his feet were too flat. One night, one of the girls approached SL; she wanted to be intimate with him; it would feel like part of his fabulous conversation. SL turned her down; she wanted to know why. They talked about it for hours, they processed and processed. The next day, SL left. He didn't want to besmirch his utopia with his own presence. He repressed his heterosexuality to save women from it.

Once, in his house—a house of many embarrassing corridors that sometimes made one think something about a mother, I don't know why—I asked SL what his life among the lesbians had been like. He said: "You mean women?" SL has a way of removing one category— lesbian—by getting at its root. It's 2000 or something, and I'm on my way to SL's. He has a studio in Chelsea; there, he photographs any number of women for queer magazines and the odd album cover. I love his pictures; they look like a cartographer trying to approximate a dream. Sitting on the subway, the lights go by but the people don't. Standing above me and around me I see how we are all the same, that none of us are white women or black men; rather, we're a series of mouths, and that every mouth needs filling: with something wet or dry, like love, or unfamiliar and savory, like love. And there's my mouth, too, and it's filled with SL, so to speak, including his idea that race doesn't make much of a difference at all in his world of—aside from me—women.

But that's not really true. It's impossible to say whether or not the women SL has been involved with would have loved him as they did had he not been black, but I'd hazard a guess they probably wouldn't, just as SL had his type, too. In the words of one academic: there are no neutral narratives. Of course, all this contradicted SL's everyman approach to life, its sidewalks and greasy diner countertops, just as SL's object choices contradicted his tenderness. What SL's women shared was this: they found other people's misfortunes funny. SL and I did not find anyone's misfortunes funny, but here comes another SL axiom: people do not sleep together because they're similar. SL loved being an educator. He was hilarious and sage. Once he said about a number of women he knew: They're fucking multiorgasmic, but what *really* gets them off is a cheap rent. His gargantuan patience had an enormous influence on any number of young women who lacked home training, and who leaned mightily on attitude to get them by. This was interesting to me: SL's lovers had, in abundance, the very things he wanted to tame, which was the stuff he was attracted to in the movie stars he loved most, too. SL on Bette Davis: "Ugly and with attitude? Fabulous." SL on Elizabeth Taylor: "I love her in almost any movie. It's like she's always saying, 'Are you too fucking stupid to understand what I'm saying?'" He also loved Janet Shaw, who played the laconic, don't-careish waitress in the sleazy bar in Alfred Hitchcock's 1943 film *Shadow of a Doubt*, and anything featuring Grace Zabriskie. In fact, one of SL's early video pieces featured images of Zabriskie taken from Gus Van Sant's fabulous 1991 film *My Own Private Idaho*. In the clip SL used, Zabriskie stands in a room looking over a trick (River Phoenix) with a cold, appraising eye. She walks around Phoenix slowly and, as she does so, she pulls her robe closer about her. Overwhelmed by the presence of this woman—and the memory of the first woman: his mother—Phoenix collapses. What boy doesn't understand that moment? And it's part of SL's genius that he doesn't know where those moments come from in his work, just as he doesn't understand why he's attracted to women he wants to school when they will not be schooled.

In 1999 or so, SL's mother came to visit her son. She lived in a small town in the Midwest. Mrs. SL was handsome and small; she looked the way the director Robert Wilson described his mother in an interview: "My mother was a beautiful, intelligent, cold, and distant woman...She sat beautifully in chairs." Sitting with the beautiful Mrs. SL in a restaurant, one was reminded that one of SL's favorite movie scenes involving a mother occurred in *The Grifters*. In that 1990 film, Anjelica Huston plays a mother and con artist who loves her only son, but not at the expense of herself. The scene that amused SL most in that film takes place in a diner. Huston lays a fresh dude out by cuffing him in the throat. Then she complains to the management: Isn't it a shame a lady can't feel safe eating out on her own?

SL's mother looked at me across the dinner table with don't-care-ish-was-I-stupid-I'm-pulling-on-my-Grace-Zabriskie-robe attitudinal eyes. But we had another dinner together, and she saw how much her son loved me, and she did what most women do in similar situations: she adapted. I was her best friend until she didn't need me to be her best friend. And in a bid to be included in what turned her on, which is to say what she perceived as a boys' club—she didn't have much truck with women—Mrs. SL pretended to understand what we were talking about, but I know she didn't. How could she? How could any girl? We were better mothers than any of them.

It's a measure of SL's difference in most ways that he didn't fuck me up after I expressed—silently and sometimes not so silently—my occasional reservations about his family. (Typically, he was more concerned with what he called my "terrible need to confess," as opposed to what I expressed.) Most colored men can't deal with anyone talking about their mama. But it was a measure of SL's trust in me—and his interest in the *philosophy* of language; why take it personally when you didn't have to?—that allowed for those moments when I felt out of control because people of color were out of control toward me. The issue of racial loyalty is a tricky one, and largely specious if you knew the colored people we knew. Vis-à-vis that whole endlessly fascinating and tiresome race subject, SL and I lived for the actor Morgan Freeman when he said he didn't play black, he *was* black. And it broke SL's heart when I assumed fraternity with other black writers because, for the most part, they could care less what I felt. What interested them was how much of the black pie would I get. Or take away from them. Literature was a market. For instance: a black gay woman I was friends with at the weekly newspaper where SL and I met had a brother who was dying of AIDS just as my beloved K was dying of AIDS. In fact, they had the same name. I used to go to one hospital to cut her brother's hair, and then to my friend's hospital, so he could kiss me good-night. Both those young men died, and it was some months later, to win her white straight male boss's approval, that that black gay woman took me out to lunch to ask if I would give my health insurance up—someone else needed it. SL liked to die as he watched me try to fill that dry fallacy of brotherhood with the Botox of faith. He turned his face away as those people behaved badly toward me because they could: they saw that I believed in them because I felt I should.

Of course, when things turned bad, SL was the beneficiary of my angry sadness. Once, at a party, when I felt he was ignoring me, I threw chairs at him. I, too, could be unschooled. But I could not do what I saw white women do to him, which included everything I did to him. I belittled him because, upon occasion, his empathy and stoicism annoyed me even as it turned me on; I complained about him to other people—white women mostly—because I just knew he didn't love me, and wasn't it always going to be about some other bitch, but when I had lunch with a white girl who knew us both, and she compared SL to her ne'er-do-well black lover, I said, SL doesn't hurt people like that, even when they want it, and I never really spoke to her again. And where was the love I wanted to scream as SL held my hand through my mother's death, in 1993, and where was the love and when will I see you again I wanted to plead as SL held my hand and heart up in Barbados two years later, it'll always be one of the sadder islands to me because my mother died there, and, while SL and I traveled around visiting several of her relatives, trying to feel what she must have felt in her ancestral home, her relatives expressed a dry lack of concern over the fact she'd gone home to die, I think that was important to her, but where was the love, stand by me, I wanted to sputter when I felt as though I would collapse between the army of words I had to produce in exchange for shelter, and the army of words

I wanted to produce in exchange for myself. And where was the love, when will I see you again, I belong to you, I hissed through gritted teeth even as SL read our book of days—smiling.

In SL's house there are many mirrors. We don't get in their way. What would be the point? Our eyes are monstrous, reflective, and loving enough. "My mind forgets / the persons I have been along the way." And yet SL wants to know each and every one of those persons who had gone into the making of my *me*. How dare he stand there waiting for my I of selves? No one can have them, or me. But he counters with: How can we be a we, if I don't know your I? Edna St. Vincent put my rejoinder best: "Why do you follow me?— / Any moment I can be / Nothing but a laurel-tree." Still, SL's love wanted every bit of me while I ate secrets in order to formulate a self; those selves were more interesting to me than my I. No one else can have those selves. Or me, who's not nearly as interesting as those other stories—about Marlene in her white dress standing near a tree, or one of my sisters walking into a room and changing everything. How dare SL stand there waiting for my I. Is this what love gets up to, one person demanding self-exposure so there's more to love, a feeling best described as the devil eating you alive, from the toes up? About that toe. In SL's house, I read Vladimir Nabokov's novel *Despair* (1936). In that book, a Russian émigré businessman named Hermann Karlovich meets his doppelgänger—a German word I've just learned means "double goer." (The French words for "pairs," or "some pairs," is *des paires*. Marvelous.) *Despair* doesn't tell much of a story—I should talk if my I did talk—but at the heart of the book is the story of love. Hermann is always looking for it, and it's always out of reach because he's looking for it, like any number of us. His first double is his brother. Hermann recalls talking to his shallow wife, Lydia:

> I told her about my younger brother. He was a student in Germany when the war broke out; was recruited there and fought against the Russians. I had always remembered him as a quiet, despondent little fellow. My parents used to thrash *me* and spoil *him*; he did not show them any affection, however, but in regard to me he developed an incredibly, more than brotherly adoration, followed me everywhere, looked into my eyes, loved everything that came into contact with me, loved to smell my pocket handkerchief, to put on my shirt when still warm from my body, to clean his teeth with my brush. At first we shared a bed with a pillow at each end until it was discovered he could not go to sleep without sucking my big toe.

And if I were not SL's younger brother, what was I? I could not bear to be alone knowing he was in the room. I sucked his figurative toe because its sweat acted as a kind of poultice on my tongue; I would say who I was if he would not take it away from me, that sandy-colored digit, as stimulating as anything, curling up at the tip as his flat foot tapped the day away as he waited for me as he stood in his house, braver than any memory.

In his house, we tell each other stories largely unencumbered by the sound of other people's fear that surrounds us in New York. Or so we wanted to believe. Upon moving in, our neighbors phoned the police. It must have looked strange: two colored gentlemen moving furniture into a house. As a result, we become more isolated. Our isolation—like all isolation—breeds a certain amount of discontent, and it takes the form of questions about who we are, as twins and not. Twinship, SL says, is the archetype for closeness; it is also the archetype for difference: in one's other half, one sees both who one is and who one isn't. Here we are on Wuthering Heights. Our neighbors eat bitter black bread and look bitter when they see us coming. The rain falls. The birds fall in the rain.

Most days, or most nights in SL's house, it is I who asks SL to tell me a movie story. He loves movies so, maybe he'll love me so. But why is it that when he tells a movie story, or any kind of story at all, he tells it from the point of view of the eye and heart that is following the white girl in the tale? Does he identify with them? Feel "like" them next to my not–Liz Taylor skin and crinkly pubes? How can I change his mind—get him to see me—when, like the rest of us, he is a slave in relation to his overbearing past, shackled to these memories that he has not shared with me but I know just the same because we're twins: young white girls rolling their stockings down on a beach in Corsica, near the Bosphorus, and SL, shunned because of his color or being profoundly without family, sitting nearby, barely aware of his body, other than his eyes, which are filled with such longing. They're the same eyes that find such pathos whenever Laura Nyro sat down at the piano, or humor and concern when Sigourney Weaver fought off aliens, especially in suburban Connecticut, or familiarity when Nico stood flickering in an Andy Warhol film, disassociated from and connected to her child as she cut her bangs, later to amuse SL ruefully when Nico delivered her rendition of "*Deutschland Über Alles*," in her own way, what a strange song for a colored boy to know by heart. In Europe, SL became a white woman. He felt no separation between himself and the women rolling their stockings down. When I knew him, we both stopped dead in our tracks when we saw the Benetton ad that showed an albino African girl standing in a group with black Africans who didn't have that issue. SL identified with that ad for his reasons, and I identified with it for my own.

SL would sometimes leave me alone in his house when he had to work, that is, deal with freelance graphic-design jobs. When he returns after a day or two, he usually brings a gift—photographs, a book—that's very much in keeping with the generosity he exhibited when we met fifteen or twenty years ago. He also brings stories. About one new movie, or the next. Like the books and photographs he shares with me, the parts of the movie stories he tells make indirect reference to us, and our story, and then the whole world is not otherwise.

But around 2006 SL became less available to the telling. For several years before that I could feel him becoming an I. And like a photographic negative in reverse, I watched as he began to fade away from our image bit by bit. He'd spend less time listening to me laugh while standing under a door frame smoking a cigarette in the rain; he became less present to the anxiety I have around writing; he wouldn't touch those hyacinths for days. The truth is what I imagine: he's met a woman who would benefit from his touch. That same woman will be welcoming to me socially. She will look on my friendship with SL with great admiration. She will be pale-skinned and blush, charmingly, when

I make some not-at-all-veiled reference to how loving and difficult SL can be, a shared joke of love. She will have worked with SL on some project, maybe she's an art director, or a stylist, that's how they met. She will have noticed SL for a while before he began giving her books and photographs. She will phone me, not exactly with SL's permission, but he will not resist our going around together, this is his dream of love, me and a woman loving him, and our loving each other, and that will happen for a little while, but then she will become annoyed by the way I can make SL laugh, and she will eventually be vexed by my ability to listen to her everlasting love for him, and how that love has created a hole in her heart, why does he need other people, wasn't she enough, the implication being that I was other people, another "we" altogether, a foreign body that was something less and something more than her white body, which would not see as such, in any case, only the shape of her wounded love. She will wonder, before long, what he sees in me. She will make scenes on any public occasion that I host—a birthday party, say—because that means she's passionate about him. She will hire me to do some freelance work for her, but that has nothing to do with what I can or cannot do; it's just an opportunity for her to tell me what to do, to criticize my work and denigrate me in the process, because it's one way to attach my we with SL. But he will go home with her, despite or because of her movie drama. He will kneel and wash her feet despite or because of her movie bloodletting. He will try to open her flesh by beating at the door of it with his flesh, just like the movie guy who kisses the movie girl. And he will be all in love because he's done this before, with any number of white girls. But the difference in 2012 is, I'm not central to it.

*   *   *

In all those years in the house I used to wonder: If a man touched me in the way that I imagined SL touched white women, would I die? A friend told me once that his first brush with intimacy during the height of the dying epoch was with an older man who would rub my friend's facial cheek with his own while saying, *I like you*. No kissing. *I like you*. No close hearts. *I like you*. No grabbing. *I like you*. No shared saliva. *I like you*. That was the way it was not just for my friend, but for so many people, including myself: love not fully expressed physically wasn't true love; they wouldn't die if you didn't touch them. Before, I touched SL through white girls. And I got him back, always, because I offered what they could not: love that was free of their quest for "liberation," and thus egoless. Or so it seemed. After a few months away in that world of women, SL would come back to our play, and the cast of characters in our village, the backdrop of sea spray. But by 2006, neither of us verbalized what we felt: my I, and his you, and the ever-widening gulf in our twinship. Look at that empty door frame, look at that unhappy hyacinth. But I cannot look at the days SL spends away as *those days*. That is, I cannot see them for what they are, and what I am now: unjoined, without pattern, some meaning, a series of questions, untwinned. I cannot look at myself as myself and not see him, or the feeling of him, not SL, but the first we, and feel our unjoining because of death, but he couldn't help it and SL can, he couldn't help his jawline becoming sharper above the checked shirt that was disappearing him, I didn't want to look, I couldn't help it.

But SL wasn't dead. He was with a white woman. How could

I compete and keep him near me forever? By becoming a white girl, too? And what kind? One white girl we loved: Adèle Hugo. We so loved Isabelle Adjani's portrayal of her in François Truffaut's 1975 film *The Story of Adele H.* Born in 1830, Adèle was the youngest daughter of Adèle and Victor Hugo. Hugo's other daughter, and his favorite of the two, was named Léopoldine; she was Adèle's elder by some six years. (The Hugos also had three boys, one of whom, Leopold, died in infancy.) In 1843, when Léopoldine was boating on the Seine in Villequier with her new husband, Charles Vacquerie, the couple's boat capsized, and they were drowned. Victor Hugo mourned his daughter's loss for the rest of his life; in fact, as a result of that loss, he became interested in the occult, séances and the like: he wanted to contact Léopoldine in the beyond, often consulting with Madame Delphine de Girardin, Hugo's "spiritist." Adèle would follow suit, eventually believing that Léopoldine was a kind of twin; the young girl would sit at the "table" in whatever room or house she lived in and call on her dead sister's spirit. Adèle could love the dead because of what they meant to her imagination. How did I love my dead? Did my love for them cut me off from the living? Adèle could not love her fiancé because he was not absent enough. Was I the same with SL? In her famous diary, Adèle wrote about her fiancé:

> August 21 Auguste left me. He said to me: I've decided that I'm not like you; I don't use my self-love to *not* love; I use it to love. I'm the one who loves more. For eight years, I—me, a man of genius—used my genius to make you love me. I failed. I'm giving it up for lost; Pygmalion had only one love, his marble statue; Galatea, me, I had

more to do: I had you to love. I'm not the one leaving you; it's you who's leaving me.

I, you, me, us, words let alone concepts I struggled with as well. Did SL have his own we? Was I his Auguste, or was he mine? In the midst of her rejecting Auguste in favor of the unattainable, Adèle Hugo wrote:

August 27 The spirits' advice has helped me; my good humor has prevailed, miraculously. Yet my heart was in despair. The spirits told me: Drink; I drank. And when I told them: I won't have the courage to kiss him, they answered: Kissing makes love. Indeed, throughout the night I felt a happiness without a name; I loved him. His foot on mine awoke a thousand desires in my blood.

Lessons of the Heart: Kissing makes love.

I did not kiss SL but that which was not my body—my spirit— did. Did he feel it? Did my kissing help continue to make our love? Would my kissing make the love that would make him stay? I was Adèle. But before I could manage that transformation—would I end up as she did? Living for a time in Barbados, searching for a love she could not see when it passed her on the street because it was so solidly in her imagination what did reality have to do with it? So tristes, so tristes—SL and I had many years of unrealized kisses folded into conversation.

*   *   *

In our home that is his body I said something like this once: I have always thought of twinship, by birth or choice, as a kind of marriage: another metaphor that sustains some of us. And as metaphors go, marriage—twins joined by a ring and flesh—has always been attractive to me, the pomp and circumstance, the illusion veil and orange blossom, the rice landing on sanctioned heads like a hard rain as I and I become we, if they weren't born that way.

Call me what you like, but I cannot marry myself; there is no story there. If I lift my illusion veil—but just for a moment—and put away the songs I've planned to play at my nuptials, songs such as the Talking Heads' "Thank You for Sending Me an Angel" ("Oh, baby, you can walk…just like me! With a little practice, you can…talk just like me!") and Hole's "She Walks on Me" ("We look the same! We talk the same! We are the same! We are the same!")—if I stop all that, I can see that any such celebration is completely driven by my writerly self, like so many things. I need an audience to tell me how my love story is playing.

SL abhors weddings, all that "O thou / to whom from whom, / without whom nothing" stuff Marianne Moore eviscerates in her great poem "Marriage." SL is bemused by all the conventions I cling to, like dopey trimmings on a Christmas tree. What SL believes: no wedding ring can cast a golden light on anyone's we. No we is without friction. The exchange that takes place between I and thou is essentially private—like the intuitive language of twins. Like the vivid language marriage-crazy Nijinsky employs in his 1919 *Diary* to describe life with his first wife, his first twin, the ballet impresario Diaghilev:

Diaghilev has two false front teeth. I noticed this because when he is nervous he touches them with his tongue. They move, and I can see them...I began to hate him quite openly, and once I pushed him on a street in Paris. I pushed him because I wanted to show him that I was not afraid of him. Diaghilev hit me with his cane because I wanted to leave him. He felt that I wanted to go away, and therefore he ran after me. I half ran, half walked. I was afraid of being noticed...I felt a pain in my leg and pushed Diaghilev.

I pushed him only slightly because I felt not anger against Diaghilev but tears. I wept. Diaghilev scolded me...I could no longer control myself and began to walk slowly. Diaghilev too began to walk slowly. We both walked slowly...I was walking. He was walking. We went, and we arrived. We lived together for a long time.

Like dancers, none of us gets over that figure we see in the practice mirror: ourselves. Choosing your twin gives you that reflection forever— or as long as it lasts. Perhaps SL will leave me for one reason or another, but he will never go away: I see myself in him and he in me, except that for him our twinship is essentially private and silent. So how do I justify putting our we-ness out in the world by writing about it? I can't. It's something I've always done; SL accepts this in me: half living life so I can get down to really living it by writing about it. I wrote about my first kiss more fully than I lived it. I wouldn't know what I looked like in relation to SL, my twin, if I didn't describe it on the page.

*   *   *

It's 2002, and we're twenty years into our twinship. Little has changed, except for our age. We're both over forty. Our bodies remain what they always were. SL is thin and I am not. I tried to grow a great beard like his. It didn't happen. Not that I know what I look like at all—with or without a twin. Over the years we've shared, I have tried to see myself, the better to see him. To that end, SL made a gift of the novel *Immortality* by Milan Kundera (1990). In it, I read: "Without the faith that our face expresses our self, without that basic illusion, that arch-illusion, we cannot live or at least we cannot take life seriously." In a way, that basic illusion is beyond me. I wrote the following on the corridor walls leading to SL's great room to describe that feeling:

I have always been one half of a whole. The first Hilton was stillborn. His little wet head and arms and feet were dragged out of a mother who did not want him. That mother was my mother's closest friend. She told my mother, during her pregnancy, that if her child turned out to be male, she wanted him dead, given how despicable she thought men were, especially her husband. So she willed Hilton's death. She had named her child Hilton—a boy's name—even before he was born. Perhaps she'd always wanted a boy to kill.

A year or two after that, my mother gave birth to Hilton again: myself. My mother named me Hilton for her friend's stillborn baby. The minute I was born, I was not just myself, but the memory of someone else. And I belonged to two women who identified with one another for any number of reasons, my mother and her friend, the one who bore death and the one who bore the rest.

As boys, we went everywhere together, Hilton and I, my ghostly twin, my nearly perfect other half. He was perfect because he never seemed to need anything, even though we grew up in the same family.

We lived in Brooklyn then, in a two-story house in East New York. It was a place of spindly trees. We had four older sisters who dressed like the Pointer Sisters on the cover of their debut album. We knew we'd never get over them, or our younger brother, whom we adored. And our Ma, who raised us all. We never knew what any of those people were talking about when they used *I* as a pronoun—they were all the same. They were annoyed by anything they perceived as the catalyst for separation. Evil forces from the outside world included: boyfriends, anyone else at all. (They didn't know I had a twin. They would have resented him.)

Our Ma. We were all the same to her. We were her we, a mass of need always in need of feeding. Standing over a pot of boiling some-thing, waiting for what she called "the last straggler" to straggle in to dinner—our brother Derrick, say—she would call out each of her children's names, as if naming off all the parts on one body: "Sandra! Diana! Louise! Yvonne! Hilton! Derrick!"—before giving up and giggling and saying, "Whoever you are, whoever I'm calling, come in and eat."

I was fat and drank so much soda and Kool-Aid, you wouldn't believe it. By the time I was thirteen, I had enough fat to make one thin perfect Hilton, so I did. I was the stronger twin. I was a little smug because I had a twin, not unlike Ramona, the smart glutton who invents a thin twin for herself in Jean Stafford's brilliant 1950 short story "The Echo and the Nemesis." At the end of the story, after Ramona's been found out as the mythomaniac and hoarder of food she is by her classmate Sue, Ramona still feels she has reason to gloat. Glittering with malice, she tells Sue she will "never know the divine joy of being twins," and ends by calling Sue "provincial one." Sue is a "one" and Ramona is not and a double is more, in every way. Exactly. Exactly. For Hilton and me, knowing each other made us feel exalted. Everyone else was a plebe. We knew so much about so many things! We read about identical twins, two beings split in one egg. We looked at pictures of twins by marriage—our favorite being Eleanor and Franklin Roosevelt. We loved pictures of them by the sea, standing close together, split from the same romantic egg, one pretty, one not so pretty. We looked at art books, at the work of Gilbert and George. We read astrology books. We knew how to look at clothes. We knew how to write short stories.

At the end of our thirteenth year, there were many changes outside our control. We moved to an apartment in Crown Heights, among other West Indians who called themselves a we, one political body, proud of their association by birth with former congresswoman Shirley Chisholm. By the time we moved into that apartment, a lot of our sisters had moved into their own homes. Another change was Hilton and I went to a predominately white high school in "the city." It was the first time we had ever been around white people much, so it was strange to consider our own bodies next to theirs and it made us hate each other for the first time—Hilton and I. If only we could be rid of one another, we would be the one that another one could love. But since there was two of us, there was two of everything no one seemed to want, including, or specifically, our coloredness, our double lovesickness. How strange we must have looked, walking down the street! Like thieves in wait for someone to give up something we could not demand, because we could not speak. Our demand for love felt cruel, even to ourselves; to speak it would be a crime.

We followed the white people we liked home. They lived, most of them, in tall apartment buildings with doormen. We couldn't stand in front of those buildings for long without being glared at by those doormen, so we had to imagine the person we had a crush on, on the long subway ride home, to Brooklyn. We imagined them going up to their beautiful home in an elevator and going into their bedroom (their own bedroom!) and turning on their desk light and putting on a record by some singer we had overheard them talk about in the school cafeteria (Bob Dylan, Van Morrison), and then taking off their jeans, their leg hair lying flat on their legs like stockings. Our imaginings split us up—Hilton and I. We wanted to be a we with one or another of the people we followed home, so we split up to make room for those other people, who were never coming and sometimes there and whom we always partially imagined. And in this way, years passed, until I met SL and became a we with someone entirely different.

But we never actually lived together, not really. About twenty years into our friendship—this was in 1998 or so—I still lived in the Brooklyn apartment I'd rented since before I met SL. It was less a home than a place I could say I was going home to. What it was, really, was a stage set, as provisional as that, and one I longed to strike at a moment's notice, but that moment never came. Besides, where would

I go? SL lived somewhere else and frequently with someone else.

I rarely had guests. How can you host in a theater? But if you looked behind the flats where, variously, my double bed had been sketched, along with a tea cup, shower curtains, and a stove, you'd find the same dull isolated crud you'd see in any number of apartments occupied by men who could not move on from AIDS. In any case, moving on was a ridiculous phrase, given the enormous physical memory of your loved one being stuffed in a black garbage bag; that's how the city's health-care workers dealt with the first AIDS victims, stuck them in garbage bags like imperfect pieces of couture. So much time and effort had gone into creating this dress or that person, but it was imperfect, and its imperfections could contaminate the rest of the line, bag it up fast, seal it off, and move on.

In any case, "moving on" was a ridiculous phrase in this context, as was the trite idea of closure, and yet I was supposed to be alive, moving on, and what was that? Sometimes I moved on to a few boys who looked like the trashed and bagged loved one—especially around the eyes and feet—but they didn't lie on my stage set's double bed without getting paid: actors for hire.

I did not want SL to die remembering the look of a thousand garbage bags in my eyes. I loved him more than grief. So, periodically, I pushed him away into the world of living white women. The ostensible reason was ecology. Our twinship wouldn't be a living thing without other living things. He needed to live for us because he could. (No one he loved had ever died, including the people he didn't like very much.) SL's favorite religious group was the Stoics. He had grown up watching two people not take love—least of all from him—and so he knew people in general could not take love; other people are always our parents. And so his self-appointed job, his brilliance, really, was in staying, and taking what you threw at him, and not engaging the crap, because that had been his job, ever since he was little: staying. That's what made SL such a turn-on, especially to white girls who lived inside and outside the privilege of their skin, and their horror about what they shared with their white male oppressors: their skin. White girls could rant, weep, treat him like a servant, like the girlfriend in the Prince song he loved so ("If I was your girlfriend… / would u let me dress u… / If I was your one and only friend / would you run 2 me if somebody hurt u / even if that somebody was me"), and he could take it and more while styling what you should wear on a night on the town, with or without him, but there was always this unspoken, distinctly male caveat in the air: he could leave when he wanted to. That's one reason those girls and queens loved him. His authority. He could put on his boots and leave. Even when he didn't, he could. (When his girlfriends were annoyed with him they'd telephone and yell at me; they were too frightened of him to talk shit to him directly. One of SL's former partners said, vis-à-vis his various strengths and enviable stoicism and love of other ladies: "What is this? Fucking *Ivanhoe?*")

I remember standing on the corner of Eighth Avenue and Nineteenth Street with SL once, chatting. It was a sweltering summer day in 2000, and SL had on a dark blue jacket, silk knickers, and boots that went up to his knees. He was bareheaded and bare chested. As we chatted, a man rode up to us on his bike. He made a pit stop in front of SL, looked him up and down, and exclaimed, "Cute!" before riding off. SL didn't blink an eye.

That was a large part of SL's fabulous allure: his resistance to his audience's self-dramatization, especially when it came to their desire for him, a single twin who did and did not want to be wanted. As a husband who longed to be a wife, one of SL's favorite movies was Rainer Werner Fassbinder's 1972 film *The Bitter Tears of Petra von Kant*. Petra is a German fashion designer who falls in love with Karin, a young model. Karin torments the besotted Petra with tales of her other lovers, specifically a black man with a large penis. While all of this is going on, Petra's assistant, Marlene, who never speaks, goes about the business of running her abusive boss's life, down to coming up with the designs that have made Petra famous. One thing and another happens, Karin leaves Petra in a cloud of degradation—the tormentor is tormented—and, thus chastened, Petra turns to Marlene, longing to treat the woman who was in effect her slave as an equal. But Marlene will not have it. Moments after Petra reaches out to her in a human and humanizing way, Marlene packs her bags. She doesn't want freedom and equality. She's gone.

SL said a number of things about himself through his movie stories; that's how he talked his desire. (SL on sex: "If you have to talk about it, it's not happening.") Marlene: was she part of SL's love, or identification? For SL, those two things weren't mutually exclusive; he loved Marlene because he felt he was, or wanted to be, Marlene: a silent wife to other wives, a wife who could play what looked like degradation because he could not be degraded more than any woman, including his mother, whose marriage had degraded him.

But I could not be Petra. I had learned about love at home, too, but in a different way than SL; despite my parents to say the least interesting ideas about intimacy, I never felt they equated it with brutality, or lies. My parents didn't stay together for the sake of the children because they weren't together, not in any traditional way; mundane daily closeness would have hurt their mutually lonely skin too much and encroached on their independence of mind. This was light stuff compared to what SL observed of love at home—he called me, somewhat condescendingly, a brilliant normal person; oh, what hadn't he survived! Oh, what had I not survived!—an experience that prompted him to say to married friends who were intent on teaching their children how wrong love could be by staying together when they shouldn't, but their vanity said otherwise: Don't stay together for the sake of the children. Look at me.

I loved looking at him. I loved listening to him. In 1999 he said about me to me: "You have infant schema. Children and animals will always love you." In 2000 he said: "The downside about what you've written is the special pleading angle. You're not greater than the subject." In 2001 he said: "Are we codependent? Beyond." He also said: "I don't care." In fact, "I don't care" was his most frequently spoken phrase. That was the worst kiss ever, I don't care. I'm so glad you like my pictures, maybe the world at large will never see them, I don't care. From 1999 on I wondered how I could make him care. I saw our twinship dissolving in words I could not control, words that stressed SL's Billie Holiday, don't-careish attitude, even as my I stressed itself on page after page. Neither of us could stop himself: by 2002 we were breaking out of our we casing through an explosion of self-expression, and the disavowal of self-expression the world would not look at his pictures, and his love, the world, would see me no matter how much I tried to hide in my universe of stage sets and the crud behind it. I would not leave him, and yet he felt I had already left him, the words were going out into the world more and more frequently from 2003 on, even as I loved SL's pictures, body, and voice, more than my words, and always more and more; but that wasn't the point, the attention I received wasn't happening to him, and in any case, SL implied, as our talk went on, even as it dried up, that, as an unreconstructed seventies lesbian, the commercial world of magazines and praise was corrupt, why would I want any part of that, why care, I don't care.

Blame it on capitalism. Despite SL's Laura Nyro–like abhorrence of business and his utterly touching and captivating struggle with modesty, he tied himself up—as he tied himself up in a Comme des Garçons shirt, or lovely turban—in a debate about the meaning of his I, the ego as a form of aggression. He would not put that fellow— his I—forward; he gave SL the spiritual creeps. And yet there was his I, who was a superior artist, and art must be seen for it to matter to other people. In any case, what colored person has ever handled attention well? For years there was no Michelle Obama. And the colored people we saw become famous—Jean-Michel Basquiat and the like—could not reconcile all that love with their former degra-dation. I could not handle the attention I received for my writing; it was not separate from SL's relative invisibility on the art market. Despite the fact that SL always married stars who knew he was a star, the world can absorb only the obvious, and for whatever reason I was more obvious to the world at that time than my twin, the same as me, only different.

SL's struggle for recognition became my own. I didn't mind. In fact, I loved the process. It all felt like an Earth, Wind & Fire song, full of effort and hope. One helps, and there is sometimes less of oneself, or one's I in the effort. SL and I were comrades, we would get through it, the world would love him as much as I did. But the world would not. Once, after we became friends and SL moved on from the weekly where we met to a magazine that was part of a big, lady-centered corporation—they published magazines whose major themes were weddings, eyebrows, and the like—SL would describe how few black men worked there, and how they never talked to one another. Some time later, I got a job at the same company—by then, SL had quit to pursue his own work—and as he waited in the lobby for me one day, SL looked on as I talked to two black men who worked in fashion. As we walked away, SL exclaimed: "Oh, my God, when I saw that, I couldn't believe the building didn't explode!" Presumably the city's cultural life—which, after 1980 or so, was dominated by white female gallerists, curators, critics, and the like—would have exploded if it had accepted SL's photographs and video work along with my praise, and that is how they treated him: as being too much. In 2001 his pictures were too much. In 2002 his appearance was too much. In 2003 his morals showed people up too much. Where was this man of high principles supposed to fit in the highly unprincipled worlds of art and fashion that he aspired to and disdained, a world where success was based as much on personality, body type, and eye color as it was on any recognizable skill (sometimes more so)? And by aspiring to those worlds, was SL not returning to Europe in a way, hankering to love that which he could not be, which is to say a white woman?

Since I have always preferred to live in the next generation of hope, it was the children of those art-world ladies who worried me. Living in their male-identified world of having it all, the mothers who toiled in the corridors of photography and literature and the like couldn't be bothered with feminism because what is feminism but humanism; they didn't want their children—particularly their girl children—to make the mistake they'd made at Brown or Yale or Berkeley or whatever, which is to say believing feminism and thus humanism had any value at all, and would get them anywhere in this stinking world. So they let their daughters say whatever they wanted under the guise of free "self-expression," but what amused those mothers—the same mothers who would not mother SL's longed-for career—was listening to, and watching, their daughters' aggression. One such little girl told me that if I shaved my beard, I'd look like CeeLo Green. Another little girl told her mother that she didn't like the way I smelled. Another asked how I could be happy, considering that I looked like a gay Unabomber? These were the children of the mothers SL longed to kiss, and protect, even as my wounds would not heal and shall never heal because now I have the hatred of a white woman and if SL doesn't think his unconditional love of them and ultimately wary love of me didn't contribute to the immense loss of our love, he's crazy.

*   *   *

But by 2006 my pain was becoming less real to SL; he was struggling
for his own survival, but how do you do that when you're a twin? Or
what I believed to be a twin? That was one reason I encouraged SL
to leave occasionally, and join the world of living white women: our
twinship not only needed other blood to survive, but, until the end,
and even now, we believed our twinship could take it. Our we could
survive anything, including this fact: that SL knew perfectly well that
my I liked skating on the edge of abandonment, it had always been
that way, there was my father in one direction, and my mother in
another, and it was their coming together at certain times—to protect
me from a homophobic teacher when I was in elementary school,
taking turns rubbing me with witch hazel as they tried to bring one
of my childhood fevers down—that I relished more than anything
else. But there had to be a split first so I could feel the full power of
their subsequent Socratic fusion. I loved smelling the glue. I believed
in destroying a home to make a more powerful, integrated home. So
from 2000 on, and maybe once a year or twice, until 2006, when we
parted, I would encourage SL to leave by introducing him to someone
else. He was reluctant and obliging: surely he could meet white girls
on his own? But that wasn't the point: the ones he could meet on his
own had nothing to do with me, just as SL saying that one reason he
loved me was that I was such a respite from his normal life, why get
all mixed up with his desire to begin with? But who doesn't long to
be mundane? To say who they are through domestic complaint? To
have love every day? (SL laughed and loved me more than he could

say when, early on in our relationship, I said how marvelous it must be to be married; you could have sex whenever you wanted it. What did I know? I didn't grow up with anyone who had been married in any conventional sense.) Having not grown up hearing complaints about the old ball and chain, I longed to be one; what a novelty, to be a source of love and irritation, all at once.

But I must have been, especially when SL, to accommodate me more than anything else, went out into the world of living women; he did it for me, our we, and yet it was my I who stood at the threshold of our imaginary house with blood in my eyes when I saw, upon his return, the long hairs across his teeth, and toes.

One thing that occurs to me now: perhaps SL left so he could return home to the happy news of my desire. Because in all the years I loved him, I did not say I loved him, or, more specifically, how I loved him. If I did, wouldn't that end up in a garbage bag, too? My love for SL: this wasn't the yearning one finds in early and bad Gore Vidal, or Edmund White, or James Baldwin novels; that is, I did not worshipfully suffer at the altar of SL's love of women. If anything, SL was a supplicant at the prie-dieu of my queerness. As such, he was beyond heterosexual. Let's call him something else. And it occurs to me now that the vengeful queen in me—the queen who wanted to extract his revenge for all he'd felt reading all that early self-pitying or romanticized or both Gore Vidal and James Baldwin—did have a subconscious interest in his pain for loving other kinds of people more than he could love me, but that wasn't true, and yet I wanted it to be because it justified my not saying what SL longed to be said, despite the hair across his toe: that I could not name my desire because he knew he was my desire and how can you describe yourself to yourself?

I think SL felt a very great sadness over my inability—my unwillingness—to express my desire, to say I want you, do you want me, such a basic thing, and, potentially, so beautifully expressed, as it was, for instance, by Diane Keaton, another white girl we loved, when she asks the Woody Allen character in 1977's *Annie Hall* whether he likes her or not, but I just couldn't do it, that meant everything was at stake, and wouldn't someone leave or die because of it?

But in 2007 someone did die. She was one of my first I's, and integral to all the years I've described. I've waited until now to talk about her because that's the way she would have wanted it. She was a great believer in traditional story structure, and would say, apropos her appearance here, what readers crave most, what fills them up, is the story of love, and how it ends. As a spoken-word critic—one of the very best—she knew what was real when she read it because she trusted her gut. Indeed, she had a great interest in her gut; she was always thin, but she ate more food than any human I have ever known. (Even after she got sick she longed for me to describe a dinner party I'd attended. She licked her lips. "I'm always hungry," she said.) She came to the first reading I ever gave, at my college, and while I read she sat in the front row with her then boyfriend, eating a hoagie. After the reading, she said that I needed more stuff behind me while I read, to lively things up. Lights? A video? But I am getting ahead of my story.

She was our first home, no, she was our tree, and we hung in her young branches, our bodies swinging like flags in a permanent sweet chill, then a little sunshine through the branches, some bird sounds and maybe Jesus floating beyond the birds. No, she was our ground, and we would die to be closer to her. No, she was a white girl, whatever that means. No, she was colored because she preferred colored men to most white people. No, she was words, and they always came up short against her presence, and if you were a poet whose vocation it is to take the words out from in between other words, and relish white space, then you would be more suited to the task of relaying who she was, as Wallace Stevens seemed to do when he wrote, in 1947, twelve years before she was born, and sixty years before she died, in his poem "So-and-So Reclining on Her Couch": "She floats in air at the level of / The eye, completely anonymous, / Born, as she was, at twenty-one, / Without lineage or language, only / The curving of her hip, as motionless gesture, / Eyes dripping blue, so much to learn." What can I tell you about her that might not sound trite by comparison, well, there are mundane details that don't diminish her, she loved proper storytelling, the details and hidden meanings and facts and all, but let me just say that the details—how we met, how she and SL met, how she died, how SL and I died—diminish me, or, rather, the whole storytelling enterprise does, words limit things, that's what I told her once, we were sitting in her little house near a pond on Long Island, she had said good-bye to Manhattan years before but she was made for New York, she was beautiful and made no sense and made perfect sense, just like Greenwich Village, or the Bronx. We were sitting in her little house, and she was so sick, Jesus help her, and I was saying how much

I loved her without telling her that because that's how we talked—by not talking. We didn't want speech to limit us. Instead we did things, like making a chicken, or, the first time we had SL come over to her place in New York, and to accommodate his vegetarianism, a gratin dauphinois. Sitting in her house, I could not say how much I loved her even though time and her body were saying I wouldn't have many more opportunities to do so but we never talked much and as SL said during that time: Why start now? SL understood, intuitively, which is the best way to understand anything, my thoughts on that particular subject: if I said I loved her, it would limit her to my love just as a tree, once described, becomes just a tree, or your tree. I always wanted others to know her and cherish their perspective of her; that would mean there was more of her in the world, how marvelous, and other men aside from SL and myself who felt as one of my boyfriends felt when he said, after meeting her: Whatever that girl has, someone should bottle it.

Let me just say one reason I can talk about this at all is because of SL and Mrs. Vreeland—as I called her. They wanted my I, more than most other things, and what is writing but an I insisting on its point of view, fuck them for making me do it, fuck them and love them for making me do it. Let me just say, I never wanted my love or language to limit her and relegate her vibrancy, but that's what time and illness did anyway, confine her body to a wheelchair, such sadness, I can't even tell you. Imagine Holly Golightly or Sally Bowles or Maxine Faulk or Vera Cicero in the 1984 film *The Cotton Club*, infirm, not walking down the street or swimming with their boys in the sea, sick and feeling useless to themselves after all those years of creating such lasting, vibrant images in someone else's mind, artists and writers for the most part, images that might include this one: a city girl walking somewhere, sometimes with a purse in hand, her fur wrap pulled tightly around her, a little snow falling, the memory of a lover's kiss somewhere on her person, so many opportunities; sometimes life offered a quick, synthetic fix that felt like a million roses smothering them but then nothing, and that remarkable white girl rose from that temporary death to soldier on, and then her body struck down by some uncontrollable internal malady and tell me, SL, or someone, what's left of that body and its own memories, the beautiful things artists who admired her made out of her? Wallace Stevens got it right when he said, in "So-and-So Reclining on Her Couch," that his white girl was actually "This mechanism, this apparition, / Suppose we call it Projection A." I can't write one complete sentence about her because she was her own complete sentence, and her sentence about herself was better than anyone else's because she uttered it sort of without thinking while thinking too much, I can't tell you how unusual that is in a world where, nowadays, no one leaves the house without some kind of script. Still, her brilliance was in part contingent on knowing how the New York City script—a story of youth and ambition and race and blood and money—works and needs to work in order to be a story and therefore of value to other people; the human mind cleaves to details and what-happened-next so it can imagine what happened next, and I haven't even told you enough of the story so you can imagine who she was and take it from there. She was a white girl who, while growing up in New Jersey, read Kurt Vonnegut and listened to punk music, and jazz. In high school, she sported a beret à la Rickie

Lee Jones. She was a newspaper freak and, as a young woman, wrote letters in support of Rajneeshpuram despite the facts. She wanted to protect the faithful from the faithless. She regarded SL's vegetarianism as a kind of faith, and she admired it, but how could she give up her belief in bacon? Her attraction to men who had language was profound. Sometimes she'd visit me at the weekly newspaper I worked at back in the day because she was also drawn to a pasty gay journalist who spread his body anywhere there was available space. She called him the Answer Grape because he looked like a grape, and he had all the answers. She was the daughter of Europeans, immigrants who'd survived a world war to find something like stability in North America, and their survivalist instincts may have contributed to her own, which included being very protective of her fun. When she was up to no good you could see it on her face, so, to some extent, she was always an innocent, albeit one who thought: You could consider doing the right thing, but you could consider doing the wrong thing, too. For as long as I knew her, she walked a moral balance beam in high heels without chalking up her hands; she was as interested in sometimes falling off that beam on a friend's bad side as well as their good.

The first time I saw her she was a waitress in a gay bar, were we even twenty-one years old? She was the lovely, ebullient, practical mind artists always love having around to remind them that the world exists, and Con Edison would like to hear from you—all while they painted her portrait. She worked in that bar in 1980, or 1981, and she was close to Jean-Michel Basquiat, who died in 1988, the summer she went to Europe with her first husband, a beautiful Berber boxer who was so kind to me, and when she got back from Europe we drove out to Brooklyn in her little car to visit Jean's grave, just me and her, SL didn't even know about that pilgrimage until after 2007, and at Jean-Michel's grave in that Brooklyn cemetery, she kept saying, Poor baby, poor baby, as she toed the dead leaves away from his grave's mouth. Standing there, looking down at her looking down, I remembered that Jean-Michel was indeed a baby when I met him; he was seventeen and I was sixteen. We were introduced by a fat and funny white girl who had an apartment in Brooklyn Heights. But is it an introduction if one of the two people won't say hello and just stared? Because that's what Jean-Michel did when he met me. We stood in that girl's attic room in Brooklyn Heights; Jean-Michel had a Mohawk—I had never seen a black man with hair like that—and he was wearing a green mechanic's jumper. He was so vibrant and hungry, *predatory* might be the word, he wanted to get somewhere, and he kept staring at me and it wasn't until years later that I heard he liked black boys as much as he liked white girls. So I wonder what it was like for him when I showed up with Mrs. Vreeland—I called her Mrs. Vreeland from the first because she was stylish, and everything she wore was unfussy and the opposite of fashion and what did the first Mrs. Vreeland say about style? "It helps you get down the stairs." My Mrs. Vreeland got down the stairs all right, but sometimes she tripped or stumbled, which is a form of being graceful, too, since what is grace but the desire to forget one's body, or share it with others? She did both; I saw it all at one of Jean-Michel's first big exhibitions. He was part of a group show called *New York/New Wave*, and oh my God I just looked it up—the show took place at PS1 in 1981. Like an Adrienne Kennedy heroine I would give anything just now if I could talk to Jesus that night, and just once. I would tell Jesus what I remember about that night. I would tell him what I remember about that night. Were we even twenty-one? Yes, we were, just, and I don't think I even put the Jean who wouldn't take my hand in Mrs. Vreeland's presence together with the artist whose work I saw in a show I had admired tremendously some time before—*The Times Square Show*, a show that combined the refined and the dissolute: how perfect was that, since New York was a disaster area then so why couldn't an exhibition be a disaster area, too? I don't think I took much notice of Jean-Michel's paintings at PS1, though, since what was interesting to me that night was watching and not watching as the artist sometimes watched me and looked at Mrs. Vreeland; I'd give anything to talk to Jesus about it just once because it was one of those moments when life was changing me and she was life, a skinny white girl talking to an existentially freaked black man and already I was in love with Mrs. Vreeland's bravery: how many white girls do you know, Jesus, who didn't grow up around colored people, and who step outside of what life is supposed to look like for them—which is to say, white—and put on a party dress to look pretty for, and try to please, a black man who almost never has any power at all? Those impulses are rarer than you think. I seem to remember the dress, if not the material, then the shape she wore that evening at PS1. The skirt was reinforced with a little, not much, crinoline. The artist and his muse talked to one another as lovers do; he was living with another woman by then, but I'm not sure if that was a heartbreak for Mrs. Vreeland because other people interested her as well. Besides, she liked her heart's desires being a secret, a story only she could tell when she wanted to tell it. She was so intelligent about men and had realized at an early age that, despite the bluster, they were essentially passive creatures; you could get one if you wanted one, no problem. She was Fitzgerald's Jordan Baker in that she was aware that it took two to have an accident, but she was herself when she said to me, once, as I tried to learn how to drive a car and was too frightened of other people: They have brakes, too. As Mrs. Vreeland and Jean talked to each other in a conspiratorial way at that opening, I became what I would always be, later, in her and SL's presence, a kid loving the smell of their adhesion. How did people talk the way that Jean-Michel was talking to Mrs. Vreeland now, in the utter privacy of their souls, and yet in public, for all the world to see? To talk to myself, even, I had to turn off the lights, as in a cinema.

I met her through some queens I didn't like but thought I should like, because they were queens. It was also the summer I met—through the same queens—a Dutchman who was spending time in New York; he had swapped his apartment in Amsterdam for a small place on East Fourteenth Street. (That's the same Dutch guy I visited early on in my friendship with SL, when SL offered to come along to Amsterdam with me and I freaked out, early love will freak you out.) Eventually Mrs. Vreeland took the flat above him, he found her the place, and that was one of the things I never noticed about her until sort of late in our friendship: part of what her love demanded was to live in or near your actual home, I never understood what that meant other than the obvious. She was her very own crew on her very own Flying Dutchman. I fell in love with the Dutchman who ended up suffering a variation on a garbage-bag death, but in those years I was really much more in love with K, my college friend, the guy I would mourn in my stage-set apartment, sometimes with boys I paid to look like him. K was my heart's desire, I took him to the bar where Mrs. Vreeland worked maybe a week or two after I met her because I loved her and I loved him, and the world was amazing! Amazing! Amazing! including Mrs. Vreeland's willingness to be a Projection C as Wallace Stevens defined it. "She is half who made her. / This is the final Projection, C. / The arrangement contains the desire of / The artist." Mrs. Vreeland not only affected this writer's vision but the visual artist's vision, too, Jean-Michel aside, there was SL remarking, soon after he met her, in 1988, referring to her carefully applied makeup: I've never known a white girl to use such colors, plus she doesn't even like the Beatles! Later, looking at family photographs, SL pointed to a Modigliani reproduction that hung in his family dining room and said: I knew you before I knew you. SL also discussed, with a Japanese friend of Mrs. Vreeland's, how her facial proportions resembled those in eighteenth-century ukiyo-e, or Japanese woodcuts. Also, curators who worked in the art field got her, too. One such curator said about Mrs. Vreeland once: I get it. She's an old black man. Yes, I can see a little old Bojangles in her, why not, I saw everything else in her, she was one of life's last great journeymen not to turn that experience into a career, she traveled from house to house learning from what was in her way but even though she longed for someone to make her a home I can't ever remember her bringing a suitcase to that wish, she was always moving on, looking for a friend or a family, sometimes leaving whatever she'd acquired on her travels but more likely just throwing it away to stay light and keep everything moving, and it's okay, Mrs. Vreeland, I'll keep it with mine, like old Bob Dylan said, I'll keep it with mine. But would she let anyone keep her but herself? She used to joke with SL and say that he was married to himself but Mrs. Vreeland you were like every human being on the planet in that what you saw in the person you loved most was the person you were frightened of most, which is to say yourself, and so I guess the world is full of twins, beings who are attracted to themselves even as they're repelled by and drawn to that same-only-different equation. You spoke our language even before SL and I became a we. In the bar where we met I heard your tone before I heard what you were saying; each was interesting but let me just say I find nothing more charming than a white girl who speaks with a slightly black syntax. Then I heard you say: I looked up at the sky and booga oog fletmarx Karen Horney exstasis! Then you worked in a clothing store or somewhere else and you said: Aeghtakeeywow! Then you got married and went to Europe and Jean died and you said: OoopfmaniklyatranonicpooReich! You said: Eeegarwooootick! Radicalismoooggamindfloatchic! after you looked at SL for the first time, or maybe it was the third time. That was in 1988. You lived in a small walk-up in the West Village with your husband, who had a number of business concerns in the East Village. Life was just chugging along, and we weren't even thirty. Suddenly, there was new love. What I recall of that new love was its beginning, which included SL and me escorting you to Jean-Michel's memorial, and I could see as you sat close to both of us—we were your sentries, silent and stalwart—how you were moving away from one marriage to be married to SL, and did you ever know how that completed my we with SL? From the first you were necessary to his body and thus soul, and his loving you was one way for me to love you, too, without thinking my body would reduce you to a garbage bag. Jean-Michel died in August 1988, I can't remember the day exactly but when I think of it the memorial service was in the fall, and by that winter you and SL were together, and I never told you how bereft I felt when you and SL would go off together to be married in your way and I just waited for my heart's desire to return and then there you were again with the curl of your hip. But I don't want to make a romance of their romance, which feels like such a slight word compared to marriage, which doesn't do it, either. Shall I call it as I saw it? A twinship? In all our years together, I don't think Mrs. Vreeland had much interest in people who weren't romantically connected to other people she loved. And because she loved you, she wanted to have your experience not in a purely selfish way, but in an empathetically selfish way. She wanted to wear your heart on her sleeve. I can't say she wanted to be me as I was in my we with SL, but I will say that she found our us as interesting as her considerable I. (One reason SL was attracted to the women he was attracted to, he said, was their self-interest; they weren't ambivalent about his love and strengths, except when he wouldn't let them have their way. From the first I was greedy for SL, too. I was always starving for him. I loved to learn, and he had so much to teach, ranging from his interest in graphic design to the world, with its multitude of worms. I know I loved SL, too, because he was an artist. My mother—my soul's twin— somehow communicated to all her children that artists were exalted beings, and some of us fell in love with them over and over again. The world and the times she grew up in prevented my mother from being the dancer and artist she longed to be; she wore too-tight shoes for years to disfigure her feet so she would and would not remember that she had wanted to be a dancer in her youth. She wanted to prevent her children from going through any of this.) SL's attachment to me wasn't divisible from what she found such a turn-on about SL, which included his language, his authoritative, circuitous sentences and unimpeachable logic. Once, just for fun, I read to my friends from a story Veronica Geng published in 1978 called "James at an Awkward Age." The piece sounded the way SL's beautiful Negro speak sounded, and made Mrs. Vreeland feel. Maybe Mrs. Vreeland loved SL so because her soul felt like the way he sounded. Geng wrote:

> The NBC-TV sitcom "James at 16," canceled in 1978, will inevitably resume in a new format. Episode One, "Pop Quiz":
>
> Segment 1: Interior, the Berkeley Institute, a boys' school in Newport, Rhode Island. The Reverend William Leverett has just finished lecturing on "Cicero As Such." Boys stream from the classroom into the hall. JAMES and his only friend, SARGY, meet in front of James's locker.
>
> SARGY: James, my man! (They shake hands.) Isn't Leverett something else?
> JAMES: As to what, don't you know? else he is—! Leverett is of a weirdness.
> SARGY: Say, my man, what's going down?

JAMES: Anything, you mean, different from what is usually up? But one's just where one *is*—isn't one? I don't mean so much in the being by one's locker—for it does, doesn't it? lock and unlock and yet all unalterably, stainlessly, steelily glitter—as in one's head and what vibes one picks up and the sort of deal one perceives as big.

SARGY: Oh, I wouldn't sweat it.

Once, as another kind of joke, the always formally attired and layered SL—being colored, clothes were his other complicated language; trying to be "normal," or white for a minute, I complained to him at one point about the layers black men wore, even in the summer, and he said: Son, we didn't wear bikinis in the desert—put on a pair of Mrs. Vreeland's blue jeans and walked around a parking lot. On Mrs. Vreeland's videotape of the occasion, you can hear her husky laugh. But the truth is we were both enthralled by SL's irreducible visual sense and language. There was nothing like it. We tried to imitate his photographs when he gave us cameras or lent us his own. We tried to sport hats as jauntily as he did, but our heads seemed to miss the point. We tried to go to as many movies as he did, but fell asleep in them. We tried to do with as little sleep as SL seemed to live off, but had to dream and be hurt or happy in our dreams. We tried to speak with his authority, but could only manage to blow baby bubbles. Once, by way of illustrating Mrs. Vreeland's frustration and fascination with SL's powerful linguistics (he enjoyed frightening people with his speech, sometimes, or putting them to sleep), SL told me that they were having an argument and he used a word she didn't know and she said so. He suggested she look it up in the dictionary and she cried: You have all the dictionaries! In 1988 and 1989 and 1990, as their love grew—they didn't officially break up until Mrs. Vreeland, per her usual program, found someone else in the mid-nineties; in any case, none of us broke up, really, until 2007, when she died; I haven't seen SL in a long time now, but he never broke up with her, even after she died; I knew there was no way he couldn't identify with her until the end, and beyond: she was a white girl—my happiness for their fate and *in* their fate was often marred by the way they sounded. For a time, their language was indistinguishable; they used the same words and phrases—"Did that feel well?"; "Yikes"; "I love you"—that drove me mad: they were becoming twins. Did that preclude my twinship with SL? My twinship with Mrs. Vreeland? It was maybe a year or two after they got together, and Mrs. Vreeland and I went to a record store near her home to ask after a recent release. We were living in an rpm world then. And if this was 1989, we were probably looking for De La Soul's first album, *3 Feet High and Rising*. Or if it was 1991, we were probably looking for De La Soul's second album, *De La Soul Is Dead*, because without articulating it, we loved those boys best because of their SL-like language, particularly when, on 1989's "D.A.I.S.Y. Age," we heard this:

This is Posdnuos
The president of a paragraph
Paragraph, president
President preachin' 'bout the on-tech
Known for the new step

Stop and take a bow…
Fill you with my vocab
Hope you have a spoon…

We ate any version of SL up. At the store, and for no apparent reason, a group of teenage boys of color, three or four at the most, started to circle me. I didn't feel threatened so much as I felt the energy of an exchange with them I didn't understand; they were animals responding to another animal while Mrs. Vreeland, a white girl, stood outside the circle. The whole event was profound, inexplicable, and silent. Afterward, as Mrs. Vreeland related the experience to SL on the phone, I felt myself in her: those boys looked at me not as one of their own, but as something as familiar and foreign as a white girl. And in terms of how people responded to us—they either wanted to fuck or fight us, someone said—Mrs. Vreeland and I were the same and even though I thought it was impossible for SL to love us the same, he did until he didn't.

I was away on a reporting trip in 2006 when Mrs. Vreeland's body started to fail her. She was as conscious of her body as she was fearful of it; in short, she was a woman. In the letter she wrote me about her condition—tumors, she would not say cancer, she would cure it all homeopathically, homeopathic medicine was her faith—she sounded just like SL in his letters; even though they hadn't been together in about eight years when Mrs. Vreeland left to find another house, and leave her suitcase someplace else, the body of his language was in her.

Which was the feeling I had when they were together: they were more themselves together than they were apart. They were twins. And, as such, SL was equally interested in Mrs. Vreeland's language. Indeed, he loved her literal transcriptions. He had her write words out on pieces of paper and he then put those pieces of paper in his films, and in his photographs. Looking at Jean-Michel's paintings, SL swore he saw Mrs. Vreeland's distinctive handwriting in some of the work. I could believe it. Just because she was SL's twin doesn't mean she hadn't been someone else's.

In 1981 Jean-Michel Basquiat painted *Arroz Con Pollo*, a big picture, dominated by yellow and white. The artist made the work when he and Mrs. Vreeland took a holiday together in Puerto Rico, she had to pull the canvas in off the balcony of their rented house because after Jean finished it he left it outdoors, and it began to rain. I love art the artist wouldn't mind getting disappeared. But *Arroz Con Pollo* exists still; it's outlived both subject and artist. The painting is a kind of double portrait about aesthetic and political twinship; both Jean and Mrs. Vreeland were Projection A's: Jean was a black man in America, let alone the primarily white art world, and Mrs. Vreeland was interested in men of color as much as "ordinary" white girls pursued white men with real power. It was only recently that I noticed in the painting that Mrs. Vreeland is baking a chicken. Later the same year—the year she went to Puerto Rico—Mrs. Vreeland spent the summer on Martha's Vineyard. This was after she left her job at the bar, and after that Dutchman left New York to return to Amsterdam. It was 1981 and

I was living with relatives in Brooklyn, ostensibly finishing college, but mostly what I was doing was mourning a first love that wasn't really love, which turned out to be the only kind of love I knew for a number of years. The phone rang, and everything changed; Mrs. Vreeland was on the line. Why not come to Martha's Vineyard? Why sit there more or less by yourself? The sky here is ooggboogasensationalughalicDe-Kooning! And unlike myself because she was unlike anyone else and sometimes one is enough of a person, I found myself on a boat within a few days after her call and then there she was on the other end of that journey wearing a white shift, her dark hair darker still under her straw hat; the shadows made her face dark but not her arms, and they were reaching up and up and everything was amazing! Amazing! Amazing! And I got off the boat and she said, by way of greeting: Come on, let's go to the supermarket and get a chicken.

Mrs. Vreeland didn't love white girls. And she let a colored girl live in part because she was colored. But, as a rule, Mrs. Vreeland spent her time with boys, most of whom I did not like in part because they were the gatekeepers at the arsenal of culture that would not let SL in. But perhaps *gatekeeper* is too strong or butch a word. Handbag carriers standing near the arsenal of culture? With no talent of their own save a talent for survival, those boys, some white and some black, became the nastier version of their female superiors, a variation on this old, tired theme: We hate white girls because we are white girls and that's what white girls do. That Mrs. Vreeland lived somewhere in that milieu let alone mind-set was a great sadness to SL and me, and to our we. But whereas SL, the unreconstructed nineteen-seventies lesbian, would trudge further into Mrs. Vreeland's consciousness around her various female-related "issues," while calling her on her shit and she on his, it was a marriage—once I lived in a perpetual state of disbelief: How could one be a white girl and hate it? Wasn't she—whoever she was—everything the world saw and wanted? When I was in high school I fell in love with a white girl. Her name was Marie. She wasn't technically white—her mother was Puerto Rican and her father Jewish—but she looked the part: camellia-white skin and blond hair. Looking back, I think of the Dorothy Parker line "the assisted gold of her hair" when recalling Marie's beauty. And then I think of Prince and his love of Dorothy Parker, another white girl, in his 1987 song "The Ballad of Dorothy Parker": "Dorothy was a waitress on the promenade. / She worked the night shift. / Dishwater blond, tall and fine, / she got a lot of tips… / (Dorothy Parker was cool)." Marie wasn't tall but she was fine. We met in our "specialized" arts high school in 1974 (we graduated in 1977). At that school we studied acting. Reading a script, Marie's skin would look translucent; as she read, she was becoming porous, letting the character in, whereas I could never find myself in another character; I liked to improvise, which was a form of writing. Marie wrote with her body.

She was my first real we, or my first real we, desire. My heart was always so filled to bursting with love for her. Would she leave me? She lived in a big building on the Upper West Side of Manhattan. Her father was a celebrity of sorts: he broadcast the news on a local television station; Marie adored him. Her relationship with her mother was somewhat more complicated; Marie wasn't free of the feelings Mrs.

Vreeland had toward other women. What I saw: Marie's very beautiful and hardworking mother, an excellent social worker who was prone to weeping, and to laughter.

Because Marie saw herself in her mother she couldn't see who her mother was, Marie made herself a character, the eldest of four kids with a commanding presence and assisted golden hair who could create drama just by sitting down at the dinner table and, oh, the tears. She came from a family of women—the same family I came from, with one less kid. After Marie was born, in 1960, her mother had two other girls, and then, finally, a boy of great beauty. Marie lied to get what she wanted in the midst of all those sibling limbs and bodies. One of her lies included pretending she was an only child. This was easy enough since she was the only one who had her own room in that long, messy, not sprawling and delicious-smelling apartment. Marie was a child of privilege because she felt that was the least she was entitled to. She alone could charge makeup at the family drugstore. I felt so much about her. She wore ropes of white beads a Santeria had given her. In her room: flickering candles, prayers for the dead, Santeria-blessed waters. Sometimes she sprinkled the waters on me. She made my soul happen. In the movie of my life, just out from SL productions, she could have been cast as one of the obeah women I had grown up with if audiences weren't so narrow, seeing white for white, even when that person's feeling colored. Marie felt every cell of her Jewishness, and every cell of her Rican. Her family celebrated Passover, and I with them. After someone opened the door for Elijah, Marie's mother would serve a pork roast.

*   *   *

Outside her apartment building on a summer's day in 1976 or 1977 or 1975, Marie smoked a Newport. Her white-blond hair, styled to look like Dorothy Hamill's, was made whiter in the white sunlight. In that world, Marie's whiteness was a kind of decoy. The Puerto Rican and Dominican men who leaned against their cars that lined the avenue in front of her apartment building, listening to merengue, to salsa, to Latin disco, waited for her to walk by so they could make rude comments in Spanish as she passed. And those same men fake fainted against their cars when she said, flashing her flat Jewish ass, something equally rude in *boriqua* Spanish. Did I love her or want to be her? Is there a difference?

What Wallace Stevens taught us in "So-and-So Reclining on Her Couch": the muse is as open to suggestion as the artist who learns from the muse's receptivity, her no-big-deal willingness to be available to whatever you, the artist, might feel. (I wonder if SL felt this about me. I certainly felt it about him.) The first writing I ever did for an actress was for Marie. It was a play, very much influenced by Jane Bowles's piece about two sister puppets, "A Quarrelling Pair." In my play, a brother and sister sat in separate rooms and expressed their innermost thoughts and feelings about the other to the audience. The part I concentrated on most, or the part I loved best in that script, was the sister's. She was Marie—her hopes, fears, judgments—but as seen by someone else. Not to dwell too long here in the thick woods of metaphor-land, but would my love for Marie have existed had she and other white girls not existed, and had they existed would I have learned what I knew about love by the time I met SL, who had loved and been disgraced by and fed and nurtured and disgraced and loved white girls? They were everywhere. We thought the world of Diane Keaton in the 1977 film *Looking for Mr. Goodbar,* and I especially identified with her when her character asks the married professor she's in love with why he doesn't like her anymore, was her sex too rough, or too soft, did she use the wrong deodorant, what was it? And I especially identified with Diane Keaton in that role (and so many others!) when, looking for love, she took a backseat to the professor's wife and let him make a mess of her body with his nonlove, and then abandoned her, unceremoniously. I knew something about that, and the yearning she felt for him, and I understood, too, the hatred and despair she felt for wanting, a despair so great that Teresa gets her tubes tied, no future generations of this, what was the point of hoping? Taking the subway back to Brooklyn, a day or two days spent on the Upper West Side with Marie—I could not smell her enough; eventually my mother would call, insisting I come home and attend to her own life, oh, I meant to write *mine,* come home and attend to my life, we were that close, twins after a fashion—I'd read what mattered to me then: Paule Marshall, the *Village Voice,* J. R. Ackerley. As I read, three or more things filled me up at the same time: the subway rattle and lights—the lights felt like another set of sounds, rising up, then fading—before going on to someplace else—and then there was the book or newspaper story I was reading, and then the memory of being close to Marie's body. I wanted her more than anything; her whiteness or, more accurately, her misleading whiteness—the blond mistaken for a gringo by Latin men; the Jewish girl mistaken for a shiksa by Jewish men; a white girl mistaken for a white girl in my colored world—felt not unlike myself and not like myself all at the same time. Marie's visual outsiderness was the corollary to how freaked she felt in the world, and even though it never occurred to me then that what I looked like let alone felt like might incite something more than catcalls, I couldn't see it. I saw the subway lights, and the words on the page, and what Marie went through in the world, but not my I. She—whoever she was at that time and later—was more important. SL was the same way, but to an even more dramatic degree; part of his art was his Negro self-abnegation. Or so it seemed to me, since others said the same thing about me. Once, as we were walking down a street on the Lower East Side, we thought it might be fun to stop by the home of a woman SL was seeing. This was in 1999 or so, we were walkers in the city, especially at night when the world's ills got mixed up with darkness, and we couldn't see the world very well and it couldn't see us so couldn't hurt us very well. We got to the woman's house late, around midnight, but she wasn't alone, she was in bed with another man, and instead of getting angry about this, SL sat down and had a measured and sweet conversation with them both. Walking away from that scene, I berated SL: Why did he do that? Why didn't he lay those guys out with his exceptional tongue? Why didn't he claim that white girl as his own? Nothing had ever been his, including my unconditional friendship. As I continued to berate him, SL went more and more silent; I knew he would not and could not take what I considered his—that white girl—because to his heart that would mean there was the possibility that people were to have and to hold, the marrying kind, and that would mean he was complicit in that, that he wanted to be a wife because he wanted to be a husband, a coupling that could, conceivably, lead to a child, one who, like his father before him, would stand on European soil considering the worms while his parents fought, like two howlers barking at the moon. SL couldn't bear to imagine any of that, and as my stupid language of possession rose in the black-man dark of night, SL looked like every white boy, or nearly every white boy I had ever loved because they weren't me, they were white boys, and different, among other things. Catching a glimpse of SL at my side, he looked like Andy, an elementary-school friend who had black hair and pale skin. I loved looking at him, particularly during nap time, oh, the flush of his cheek, that boy sleeping spittle. Then there was Brad Dourif as Billy Bibbit in *One Flew over the Cuckoo's Nest.* (Once, SL said I looked like Louise Fletcher's Nurse Ratched. Given SL's proclivities, I considered this a compliment.) More love: Timothy Bottoms in *The Last Picture Show*, particularly in that film's final moments, when he returns to the woman he's loved and left once before and she can't believe it, he's turned up again, why did he leave, did he hate her because she was old and ugly? Timothy Bottoms's character says nothing as his face says it all: this is life, this is resignation. And who could forget Bud Cort in *Harold and Maude*, but especially toward the end when, after Harold learns Maude's died, the actor turns away from the camera and faces a wall. Has any contemporary male performer expressed grief more beautifully? Probably Robert Downey Jr. in almost anything.

*   *   *

I berated SL about his girl that night-thick night because that's what twins do, we were just the same: I could never claim anyone outright. At fourteen, at thirty, at forty, I felt I didn't have the right to say I treasured Marie most, or SL, or Mrs. Vreeland, or the boy they almost put in a garbage bag because, swear to God, it never occurred to me that I was an I in Marie's presence. Her presence—that was the thing. SL and Mrs. Vreeland's presence—that was the thing. But human beings are put on God's green earth for at least one reason: to consume and be taken up and consume other people. (SL said it best when he said, early on in our friendship: What is there but other people?) What kept me from joining the reapers? Not being a white girl, a black man, a Chinese longshoreman? To claim my object of choice with a kiss, or a hand on a thigh during a film's end credits, was impossible. During the Marie years and for some time after, I looked at physical love like an anorexic looking at food: I did not understand how to consume it while I wanted nothing more than to consume it. Like everyone else, I required love's nutrients—its touch—but didn't that spoil love? To put one's body in it? To not claim it—to not grab it by the short of the hair, or by its wit—was, to this Simone Weil of the ghetto at least, the greater good: why could we not rise up out of the world of bodies? Rise up and be holy, holy, holy, in the oneness of love. "I love and I must," Purcell wrote. By the time I met SL, I still retained some of this attitude. And it killed him. After all, he had grown up with his parents. But my resistance to my I had something to do with the times as well—"I" was a game I would not play. SL and I met during the heyday of racial and gender politics, when black women with bad hairdos or turbans were telling us how he felt, and dwarves with splintered toenails were telling us how they felt, and the world was full of complaint about dead white men, all masquerading as "practice," or "conversation." That was the fashion. But SL saw that shit for what it was: shit. Just pitiful, egomaniacal folk trying to get more: more stage time, more TV time, more time with publishers. The noise of the marginal and the marginalized rising up because they believed what white people had to say about them in the first place. The fact that they were rising up for a primarily white audience—the gatekeepers were opening the doors, but just a smidge—was especially so. For a while, I refused to accept SL's point of view. All I heard in that rising up was that we were all alone until one or two of us wasn't. But that was my problem. As I've said before, for a long time I felt every black woman writer should be my sister, and every gay black male artist should be my brother. Was the colored world not my twin? It killed SL to watch me try to make those feelings true for other people. (SL was, in effect, a European, and didn't have such blatant feelings about anyone, let alone black people. In any case, SL felt that, in his life, white people had been kinder to him than most blacks. Upon hearing that, I wanted to ask: Had I not been nicer to him than any white woman? But I didn't. I was always so desperate for his approval I feared contradicting him most of the time, but sometimes there was anger there because I didn't, and sometimes there was anger on his part, too, because I did. But being colored, neither of us could admit any of this.)

What happened was this: it was already too late for the colored people I wrote about and celebrated in alternative weeklies and art magazines to feel the pitiful connection I offered on the page, partly out of obligation, and partly out of hope: their careers came first. Why would they want love to strip them bare via my words, or anyone else's? That didn't make sense, but when did need ever make sense? Perhaps Marie was similarly confused by the script I wrote for her, a world that had been her world but reimagined by me, the lover who didn't want to spoil her presence with his own. I'm trying to remember now how she responded to those pages. I remember that, as she read, she lit a Newport—another ethnic giveaway—and I remember sitting at her feet on the floor, looking up at her as she read those pages, wondering if this girl only New York could have produced felt as Holly Golightly, patron saint of so many of Manhattan's bachelor white girls, felt as Holly listened to the narrator of Truman Capote's novel *Breakfast at Tiffany's* read one of his stories aloud:

> As I read, each glimpse I stole of Holly made my heart contract. She fidgeted. She picked apart the butts in an ashtray, she mooned over her fingernails, as though longing for a file; worse, when I did seem to have her interest, there was actually a telltale frost over her eyes, as if she were wondering whether to buy a pair of shoes she'd seen in some window.

It was not inconceivable that, like Holly, Marie would unintentionally try to upstage my efforts by affecting boredom with my script; after all, she was a great actress, but only in real life, and in real life it was all about providing Marie with attention. But I didn't find that effortful. Maybe one day she would like my play. Maybe one day I would love her the way SL loved Mrs. V. Maybe. During my Marie time, I felt as though I would live in the fairyland of possibility forever. In that land love would happen and wholeness would happen and trust would happen and bodies would be kind and fathers would be kind and flowers would grow out of our eyes.

As Marie read my story, I watched her toes; her feet were curled near the edge of her bed. Her toenails were all chipped red varnish and dirt. I wanted to put them in my mouth, all of it. But to want any of it was to allow the witch of need to enter Marie's bedroom and frighten us half to death. That witch was scary and white, spoiled and terrible; she was a fire draft over my world of possibility, mowing all those Technicolor hearts and flowers down, burning all that hope down and for what, for something called the truth, erotic and otherwise, okay, how would that help anyone, okay, I wanted Marie's peeling varnish and white dirt in my mouth, what was the truth of that and what would be the truth of Marie's reaction if she suddenly found herself in my mouth? Would she hate it? She would hate it. Would she consider herself defiled? She would consider herself defiled. So said the witch of need. She knew everything about me, including the fact that I would not impose on another body what I felt about my own body, or believed had been imposed on me, which is to say my own body. By the time I knew Marie, I already had my mother's body, with its rounded shoulders shaped by too much tenderness and defeat and bewilderment over the world's cruelties and anger that this happened the way it happened. But my twin during my Marie time was different. His name was Vincent and he was beautiful, not a pound of fish scales. He went to our high school, and there was nothing he wanted more than to be an actor. His approach to acting was less cinematic, which is to say less internal, than Marie's. He liked making a show of his blondness—of everything. Vincent was my first white-boy twin outside the movies. He lived in Queens with his patient mother. He loved A *Chorus Line*, Barbra Streisand, spandex, Shirley MacLaine, high kicks, and a chorus boy named Kevin. In our junior year of high school Vincent kept taking me to a bad Broadway musical, I can't remember what it was called, because he was in love with a strawberry-blond boy in the chorus. That boy had a hard, fixed smile, and after the show Vincent would wait at the stage door with so much hope for that older boy dancer, and they always talked and as I watched them do so one afternoon, I saw Vincent looking at everything he wanted to be—his twin. Later, Vincent slept with that dancer, and I blushed when he told me the news because how was that beauty possible, but there was a baffled look around Vincent's eyes when he told me about that boy. He wasn't as white as he looked. The dude was into some fairly dark shit, and Vincent had obliged him because he loved him. Vincent died of AIDS, baffled by the fact that Broadway never made a home for him as a chorus boy let alone a star. He was always looking for what show business would not give him, which is to say love, as well as the drama or show business in love. Which is one reason I introduced him to Marie after that chorus boy showed Vincent things he did not want to see: here was Marie, and here was my self, and here was our love, which I could not subject her to, thus exposing her to the witch of need. But there's no keeping a bad woman down; that witch would not shut up. Two or three months after I introduced them, Vincent and Marie were kissing on the fire escape outside our school—a half-Jewish Maria with a gay, Polish Tony. And it seemed to me it was the least I could do to myself.

For years, I didn't think SL and Mrs. Vreeland was something I had "done" to myself, so much as their story of love was something they accomplished. I thought of their love as one of the things the world needed, and, when it comes to love, is the world not oneself? Love makes a home and what was I doing in their home after they built it slowly and fast? Still, they made a place for me there; they didn't take my no for an answer, they lifted me away from my world of garbage bags and stage sets, how could they offer me love like that, as Björk, another white girl sang, once, and Mrs. Vreeland, despite or because of all the push and pull she liked engaging in—like many people, tension defined her—she made room for my twinship with SL, God bless her, I'll love him eternally she said on her deathbed, cervical cancer, she wasn't even forty-seven when she diagnosed her own symptoms in 2006, reports said many women who had grown up in or near Toms River, New Jersey, where she was from, suffered the same fate, Jesus help the women of Toms River, New Jersey. In 2007 she asked me to help her with her medical stuff once she backed down and got the Western doctors involved, but I couldn't do it without SL even though we were all drifting apart, the world had not loved him enough and I could not love him enough but together we could do it, make her well. We stayed in her little house by the sea, actually it was her then boyfriend's, one of the relatively few white men she could ever bear to look at even though I couldn't. In that house, SL made me become an I, he was renting the fabric of our frayed we, by saying in response to me saying, At least we're not alone, But I want to be alone. He was leaving as she was leaving. I knew he couldn't do it any differently. Oh, Marlene! Most nights I didn't stay with them in that house. I stayed at a friend's house, it was near the bay and, at night, not sleeping, I could hear the waves, it was as Virginia Woolf corny as that, they lapped up to the shore of Mrs. Vreeland's illness, one after another, becoming myself as the world inevitably becomes yourself as you lay there in love, and your love is dying.

There were other people, Mrs. Vreeland's friends, they came to help me and SL. To them we were really very evil. We had loved her and then abandoned her. We were black and she had been martyred by blackness. We had been among the black men who offended her body, leaving it with illness. We really hated women and were probably okay with her dying. We really despised white women in particular and we didn't even know it. We were as terrible and vengeful as August Snow standing near the catafalque where a white woman lies in state, covered in flowers, some of them marigolds, in Jean Genet's 1959 play *The Blacks.* We heard the waves lap on Long Island as Mrs. Vreeland prepared to die and SL and I were as big and lonely as the bay and the shore, and we remembered the feel of Mrs. Vreeland sitting on the left or right of us at St. Peter's Church where Arto Lindsay sang for Jean-Michel Basquiat and later Mrs. Vreeland and I stood at Jean's grave and she said, "Poor baby, poor baby." We sat on either side of her dying bed, and what I remember then, before we were more or less asked to leave because our presence was considered disruptive, and I left, and SL tried to see her and then he disappeared himself because he felt he was a burden to me, our love, there was no way he wouldn't identify with her leaving, what I remembered sitting on one side of her bed was sitting with her in the center of a cab, SL on one side of her, me on the other, and Mrs. Vreeland trembling for no reason we understood but feeling protected for every reason she couldn't explain but wanted us to understand. We tricked children like this into loving us, despite the fact that, as the years went on, SL and I took, each now in his own I, in different parts of the country, other white women to movies like *The Central Park Five*, featuring Linda Fairstein and Elizabeth Lederer, two white women who, during the 1989 Central Park jogger case, worked in Manhattan's criminal justice system as the head of the district attorney's sex-crime unit and the prosecutor who handled the trials, respectively, two white women sanctioned by God and law, but who trafficked in lies that helped destroy a number of lives, all in an effort to prove their twinship with Lady Justice.

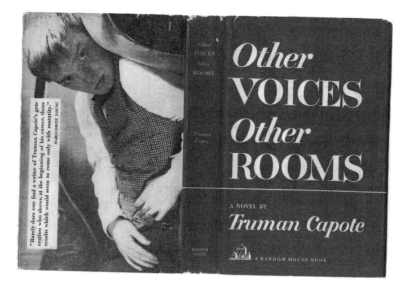

THE WOMEN

TRUMAN CAPOTE BECAME a woman in 1947, the year this photograph was taken. Much has been made of it since its appearance on the dust jacket on Capote's first novel, 1948's *Other Voices, Other Rooms*.

Actually, it is not a photograph, but a shadow ground through publicity, coming out the other side as something else. The mind cannot be blank in the face of it. It is an image that is an assertion, a point, asserting this: I am a woman.

In 1947, women did not publish books. So determined to be authors were they—Jean Stafford, Carson McCullers, Marguerite Young, say—that they buttoned themselves up on dust jackets in some Hemingway influenced image of a male American author. Truman Capote became a woman in 1947 just when "real" women would not or could not. And the woman he became in this photograph—itself better written than *Other Voices, Other Rooms*—wanted to be fucked by you and by any idea of femininity that had fucked you up.

In his writing, Capote addressed this issue only once—in the "factual" short story "Dazzle," which appeared in his last collection of writings, *Music for Chameleons* (1980). The story is sentimental because Capote could never write of himself—of what he wanted rather than what he imagined for others—without being sentimental. Another form of lying. In "Dazzle" he wrote, "I had a secret, something that was bothering me, something that was really worrying me very much...'I don't want to be a boy. I want to be a girl.'"

By becoming the most famous woman author—not writer, an important distinction—of his generation, Truman Capote sought to limit or cock block other women writers in their quest to be popular, admired, celebrated. He did not want to share the female stage. At the same time, he thought of himself as the model of potential for women who wrote, and an image of what they might become if they continued to write: popular, admired, celebrated.

The *Other Voices, Other Rooms* photograph, which also shows Capote as an American woman of style—the vest as opposed to a jacket, his translucent, flat fingernails, the watered or greased hair flattening the top of his head with the light hitting it just so, his eyebrows plucked or raised in mild astonishment, something to be fucked somehow—was too much for a number of his peers who did not possess the kind of will it took to deconstruct their bodies and make them thought-fodder for the camera.

Capote's career as a woman author made a more interesting narrative than *Other Voices, Other Rooms*. And his generally male writer friends realized that what separated them from Truman Capote was his drive to create a self that existed apart from the isolated, nowhere world of writing, the better to become an image accessible to publicity, a story in himself. Donald Windham's peevish response to this: "The publishing world is what I was aware of Capote's being in. We were both writers. Still, although I was twenty-seven and he was only twenty-three, he was in the publishing world and I was not."

We were both writers. A sentence that beats against Capote's concept of what the author's body means in the world—a narrative for other writers to write about. Windham again: "His defense in person was never camouflage; it was always boldness. Once, on a New York street, when he was telling me an anecdote in a high voice accompanied by expansive gestures and saw a burly truck driver glowering at him, he sassed, 'What are you looking at? I wouldn't kiss you for a dollar.'"

Truman Capote lied about this photograph in which he appears to be a woman. He lied about the photograph's intent, claiming in some instances that it had been sent to his publishers upon request by a friend while he was away, or that he was unaware of what he projected in the image. This was the first instance of the disjunction between Capote's image of himself and the meaning he ascribed to images of himself. It was also the first instance of Capote refusing to hear the weight of his affect as he effected it, a trope he would repeat within subsequent identities.

Perhaps he was aware of this: how images effect words in the contemporary world of publishing. "This subject [publishing] fascinates me, and I know so much about it I could talk for seven hours.

Nonstop. About how publishers work and why you should do this and why you should do that."

As he wrote less and less from 1966 until his death, in 1984, women authors—images of the new feminism—began to be packaged as such and, as such, they became the publishing world's new custodians of "other" language. (Elizabeth Hardwick "confirms her stature…[and] has as much to say about women in the world as…women on the page," reads part of the jacket copy of her book *Seduction and Betrayal* [1974].) Capote was left no other recourse than to become a man.

He became a man with the publication of his "big" book, *In Cold Blood* (1966), a book that focuses on one man, Perry Smith, a murderer consumed by vanity like the woman Capote believed he had been once. Which is to say that *In Cold Blood* set out to prove, in part, that Truman Capote was no longer a lyrical authoress (of *Other Voices, Other Rooms*, he explained: "What [I] had done has the enigmatic shine of a strangely colored prism held to the light—that, and a certain anguished, pleading intensity like the message of a shipwrecked sailor stuffed into a bottle and thrown into the sea"), but a writer validated by his experience in the world of fact—*In Cold Blood: A True Account of a Multiple Murder and Its Consequences*—a primarily male literary tradition.

In Cold Blood means a number of things to any number of people; by adopting the non-fiction novel as a form, Capote also wanted to usurp male authority, or at least one man's authority: non-fiction novelist Norman Mailer's. In the nineteen fifties Mailer had called Capote "as tart as a grand aunt." This statement, a caricature and a diminishment of Capote's role as a powerful woman author, marked how Capote's self-perception, and hence the public perception of him, would have to change. While grand aunts can be powerful, they are not generally perceived as such in the world of publishing. And as women writers eventually became what publishers could sell, albeit with reservations and marginally, Capote could, if asked, advise them why they "should do this and why [they] should do that." (Of course, Capote spent a great deal of his time advising significant women on how to become themselves, or his image of themselves. There was, for instance, Katharine Graham, publisher of the *Washington Post*, in whose honor he threw his famous Black and White ball. And, to a greater degree, he advised, molded, resented and loved Barbara "Babe" Paley—"She was the most important person in my life and I the most important in hers"—a woman made powerful through her association with her husband, media chief and CBS chairman William S. Paley.)

The image (or reality) of the maiden aunt is one that male power revolts against or finds revolting. Masculinity defines itself against such images, let alone realities. Capote was not a maiden aunt in the presence of male power; he was, however, a fashionable person in his attraction to, and fear of it. In a letter to John Malcolm Brinnin, Capote wrote, as he started to try on the role of the male writer: "Maybe I ought to...get drunk and play Prometheus like Norman." Which is to say that Truman Capote the woman realized that Truman Capote the man would eventually have to adhere to the publishing world's perception of the male writer if he were to occupy a place in it and be of continued interest to the press.

Capote identified this apparatus—the cultural press, media power—as male and Jewish. "The truth of the matter about it is, the

entire cultural press, publishing...criticism...television...is almost
ninety percent Jewish-oriented. I mean, I can't even count on one
hand five people of any importance—of real importance—in the
media who aren't Jewish." Two Jews at whom he leveled his sentimental anti-Semitism were Norman Mailer and William S. Paley,
men, who, by all accounts, did not want to be fucked by any idea of
femininity that had fucked them up but to fuck their idea of femininity.
The determination that Mailer and Pailey demonstrated in their work
and lives, their absorption and accumulation of power, was in part to
dispel the stereotypical image of the Jewish male, described again and
again by Philip Roth and others—Yeshiva boys paralyzed by reflection,
powerless to function, a Jewish mother's stooge. But Mailer and Paley
were, ultimately, far enough removed from Capote's sexuality (whatever that was) to be sexual for him. In *Answered Prayers* (1986), his
unfinished novel, the character widely believed to be based on Paley,
Sidney Dillon, "Conglomateur, advisor to presidents," is described by
Capote's fictitious alter ego, P.B. Jones, as a "wiry well-constructed man
with a hairy chest and a twinkle-grinning tough-Jew face." Looking at
a Polaroid of Dillon, Jones recalls that Dillon's trunks were "rolled to
his knees, one hand rested sexily on a hip, and with the other hand he
was pumping a dark fat mouth-watering dick."

That dick—as strong as any symbol—stretched across Truman
Capote's consciousness less because he identified it as being attached
to power than because he saw it as an object of desire for women.
In *Answered Prayers*, the act of romantic love is always recounted in
spoken language, not described as an act, let alone of love. P.B. Jones's
introduction to the formidable woman author Alice Lee Langman,

whom he sleeps with and whose protégé he subsequently becomes, is followed by: "Miss Langman was often, in interviews, described as a witty conversationalist; how can a woman be witty when she hasn't a sense of humor?—and she had none, which was her central flaw as a person and as an artist. But she was indeed a talker, a relentless bedroom back-seat driver: …'That's better better and better Billy let me have billy now that's uh uh uh it that's *it* only slower slower and slower now hard hard hit it hard ay ay *los cojones* let me hear them ring now slower slower dradraaaaagdrag it out now hit hard hard ay ay daddy Jesus have mercy Jesus Jesus goddamdaddyamighty come with me Billy come! Come!'"

Capote wrote: "Norman Mailer described [*In Cold Blood*] as a 'failure of the imagination'…Norman Mailer, who has made a lot of money and won a lot of prizes writing nonfiction novels…although he has always been careful never to describe them as 'nonfiction novels.' No matter, he is a good writer and a fine fellow and I'm grateful to have been of some small service to him."

The operative words here are "small" and "service"—"small" Truman "servicing" Norman on the altar of the non-fiction novel. Even as he published *In Cold Blood*, Capote lost any claim to male authorship by presuming that his factual account of a multiple murder would create him too—in Mailer's image. It is hard to garner privilege when you begin with none—for those who have to reach for it, it remains perpetually out of reach. Mailer would always have it and Capote would not, because Mailer assumed that he did and Capote, the perennial aunty-man no matter how hard he wrote, assumed he did not.

For several years before 1947 Capote had been a man (a state defined by uninflected ambition) in his pursuit of authorship and his appropriation of the style, syntax, and voice of women authors generally perceived as maiden aunts (Eudora Welty) or maiden aunts in code (lesbian Carson McCullers)—women with careers less powerful than Capote's would eventually be, but powerful in this: before Truman Capote became Truman Capote, they were themselves. Capote was not himself as a writer until *Answered Prayers*, a novel that grew out of his isolation and self-realization, a novel that remained unfinished.

As an ultimately fashionable author, which is to say a person who wrote but also felt uncomfortable with the responsibility of being only a writer, he rode the wave of fashion too, observing power and trends as established by others, change as established by others. Capote was a distinctly American author, one who spoke, read, thought in no other language than American and was, therefore, parochial in his knowledge. He could respond intellectually only to those things he responded to emotionally. There was no other referent for thought. What he responded to before 1947 and thereafter, in a different way, was himself (a man) in relationship to women. Since he spoke no other language than his own ("My voice had been described as high and childish, *among* other things"), he had to learn to become an American writer by appropriating the language of other American writers, and what he mostly responded to intellectually was written by women authors. But his reverence for them was always tempered. (On Flannery O'Connor: "She has some fine moments, that girl." On Carson McCullers: "She was a devil, but I respected her.") He strove to be the ultimate version of them that, as women, they would never be for themselves.

This was also true of Capote becoming a man. He could not simply admire William S. Paley, he had to surpass him in Babe's affection. He had to become a more powerful media figure by becoming recognizably famous. What Truman Capote could not do was reorder Babe Paley's ideas of her own femininity. He only did women on the page. And instead of attempting to reveal their secrets as women, he competed for an understanding of their identity as such. This was the only form of exchange he had with them, and it was different from the other exchanges these women had (or the only other exchanges Capote acknowledged them as having): being with "real" men who fucked them.

Capote's resentment of what these women did without him was based, as was his education as a writer, on an emotional response to two things: the ultimate impossibility of knowing or understanding women's sexual movements (up and down, in, out, around, what, when: the gossip's grid of information versus the writer's nongrid of reflection), and the heterosexual male's desire for them. Capote could not forgive his writing for obfuscating this interest. "My effects prior to *Answered Prayers* seemed overdone," he complained. The writing before *Answered Prayers* lied by taking the (public) fag's easy way out. It was filtered through a skein of perplexity about male and female relations.

Truman Capote could not have become a woman without women authors and editors being interested in him. (Let us leave aside early biographical data for now—how he was abandoned by his alcoholic mother, how he was taken in by maiden aunts and cousins, etc. These facts, while interesting, have more to do with his process of self-creation than with the moment he created himself as Truman Capote, the writer and the photograph).

The women Capote interested and those in whom he was interested were women who were interested in language. Perhaps he saw women as a form of language. Certainly those he was interested in before he became one himself had faces like words. "Not plain, not pretty, arresting rather, with an expression deliberately haunted rather than haunting," Capote wrote of portraits of two women published in Richard Avedon's *Observations* in 1959, a sentence interesting in its insistence on the word *deliberately*. Perhaps, even as he used the language of separation to describe them, Capote resented women separating from him.

One of the first women to be interested in Capote was Rita Smith, a fiction editor at *Mademoiselle*, who, in 1945, published "Miriam," the story, ostensibly, of a girl who can't grow up because she exists only in the mind of an old woman who has not. This fiction can be read as a foreshadowing of Capote's knowledge that he would become a woman, the floor plan, in a sense, of the image Truman Capote would eventually project on the dust jacket for *Other Voices, Other Rooms*:

[Miriam] was thin and fragilely constructed. There was a simple, special elegance in the way she stood…Mrs. Miller decided the truly distinctive feature was not her hair, but her eyes; they were hazel, steady, lacking any childlike quality whatsoever.

"Miriam" was the story that garnered Truman Capote—then twenty years old—a great deal of attention; after it appeared, the publisher Bennett Cerf signed Capote up at Random house; Random House published *Other Voices, Other Rooms*, and most of his subsequent work.

It was Rita Smith who introduced Capote to her famous sibling, Carson McCullers. McCullers's biographer states, "Never before had Carson been so enthusiastic about promoting another young writer… who many people thought served as a model for her final concept of John Henry West," a character in her novel *The Member of the Wedding*. In writing about Capote, Rita Smith all but disappears after he became friends with McCullers. In order to become a woman more famous than the older, established author, Capote needed to build himself on her model and then destroy that model to prevent any subsequent excavation of the genesis of Truman Capote.

While McCullers remained steeped in regionalism (the American South, of which Capote was a native, too), Capote went on to become a woman of the world, or enough of one to describe, in 1959, McCullers, once more famous than he, rather condescendingly as "not plain, not pretty, arresting rather"—words that also describe the exact effect of McCullers's writing on Capote, whom McCullers eventually suspected of having "poached on my literary preserves."

Once certain women artists became interested in Capote, he understood how to take from their work. What he stole was more syntax than complete style. Take, for instance, the the tone of Eudora Welty's 1941 "Why I Live at the P.O." (a story written during her literary apprenticeship to another woman author, Katherine Anne Porter):

I was getting along fine with Mama, Papa-Daddy and Uncle Rondo until my sister Stella-Rondo just separated from her husband and came back home again…Came home from one of those towns up in Illinois and to our complete surprise brought this child of two.

And Capote's 1945 story, "My Side of the Matter":

I know what is being said about me and you can take my side or theirs, that's your own business. It's my word against Eunice's and Olivia-Ann's, and it should be plain enough to anyone with two good eyes which one of us has their wits about them. I just want the citizens of the U.S.A. to know the facts, that's all.

Truman Capote knew—with the insightfulness of the writer who wishes not to be one sometimes and can step aside and see what his or her function as a writer means to others—that photographs were more immediate and vital than words and would eventually be more attractive to the general reading audience. And as a fashionable person, he saw attractiveness as the barometer of morality. (Recall his on-the-air feud with Jacqueline Susann, author of *Valley of the Dolls*. Capote described her appearance as not unlike that of "a truck driver in drag," a curious statement, layered like an onion. The truck driver as some-time homosexual erotic artifact; drag as part of the [then] homosexual code or underground; a truck driver in drag being, perhaps, of interest to Truman Capote only as an image of humor. With this comment he was spitting in the face of America for its acceptance of what he could not see as a "real" woman—someone successful as an author—and its rejec-tion of the "real" one—himself. His joke empowered him, made him greater than the woman America seemed to prefer, Jacqueline Susann.)

Truman Capote's travel book, *Local Color* (1950), with accom-panying photographs by Karl Bissinger, Cecil Beaton, and so on, was an attempt to conjoin his writing with the photographic demands of publicity. "My prettiest book, inside and out," he wrote to John Malcolm Brinnin.

Before 1947, illustrations in the form of watercolors by Eugene Berman, Christian Berard, and the like were used, mostly, to represent authors. Truman Capote single-handedly created a new interpretation of photography for his audience. Thereafter, photographs—of the bodies that created the words—were used to sell words.

Eudora Welty, who, in the thirties and forties, took photographs for the WPA project, also photographed Katherine Anne Porter (on whom Capote modeled Alice Lee Langman in *Answered Prayers*). The difference between the photographs of Katherine Anne Porter and Capote's authoress photograph on the jacket for *Other Voices, Other Rooms* is this: Porter is beautiful and therefore a removed object; Capote is sexual and simply embodies the subtext of his first book. *Other Voices, Other Rooms* is an idea about femininity made palatable by Capote's shallow interpretation.

Only one woman author—not as famous as Capote—equaled the power of his 1947 photograph: Jane Bowles in Karl Bissinger's portrait, taken in 1946 to accompany a story of hers that appeared in *Harper's Bazaar*. Bowles's photograph is a reinterpretation of what Capote projected in 1947. It illustrates the idea that femininity, as an idea, *does* fuck you up.

Jane Bowles, "that genius imp, that laughing, hilarious, tortured elf," was one woman author—a Jew, a lesbian, not a maiden aunt— from whom Capote tried to steal but could not. He attempted to retranslate her aesthetic—language and speech as unrepresentative of a woman's internal life in general—in his script for John Huston's film *Beat the Devil*. In it, Jennifer Jones plays Bowles (under the name

Gwendolyn) and speaks with Bowles's syntax. "Isn't that what we're most interested in: sin?" she inquires, just as Bowles had written to a friend, "There's nothing original about me but a little original sin."

Gwendolyn's loopy rationale ("I told him that I was in love with you when I thought you were dead…It made you seem less dead") is also reminiscent of Bowles's fiction; Christina Goering in *Two Serious Ladies*, for example: "'Oh, I can't tell you, my dear, how sorry I am,' said Miss Goering, taking both his hands in hers and pressing them to her lips…'I can't tell you how these gloves remind me of my childhood,' Miss Goering continued."

Jane Bowles wrote of Capote in a letter to her husband, Paul: "Alice T[oklas] was delighted that you didn't really care for him very much… She doesn't seem to worry in the least, however, about my liking him. So I'm insulted…again." Bowles did not consider Capote a woman. Her interest in the female body specifically precluded her complicity in Capote's self-delusion. Her very noncomplicity may explain why one of the few truly laudatory pieces Capote ever wrote about a woman was his introduction to her *Collected Works*, which came out in 1966, shortly after the publication of *In Cold Blood* and Capote's reversion to manhood: "Mrs. Bowles, by virtue of her talent and the strange visions it enclose[s], and because of her personality's startling blend of playful-puppy candor and feline sophistication, [is] an imposing, stage-front presence."

Realizing the authenticity behind Jane Bowles's "feline sophistication" was the end, too, of Capote's career as a woman author. There was no way into that sophistication without being literally exposed to women. Jane Bowles's physical proximity to women was not something Capote could experience. And his anger, fear, and resentment of this fact led to the self-caricature he projected in the film *Murder by Death*, and his unforgiving descriptions of any man he did not consider one— like Rusty Trawler, the millionaire, in *Breakfast at Tiffany's* (1958), who was also a portrait of the physically confused woman Truman Capote eventually became.

> [Rusty] was a middle-aged child that had never shed its baby fat, though some gifted tailor had almost succeeded in camouflaging his plump and spankable bottom. There wasn't a suspicion of bone in his body; his face, a zero filled in with pretty miniature features, had an unused, a virginal quality: it was as if he'd been born, then expanded, his skin remaining unlined as a blown-up balloon, and his mouth, though ready for squalls and tantrums, a spoiled sweet puckering.

The above description presaged the familiar television image of Truman Capote in later years: a series of circles to be filled in by the imagination. Although his distinct, inimitable voice interfered with this imaginative process, Capote, like Rusty Trawler, could not, eventually, commit to what he had become. As Holly Golightly said, "Can't you see it's just that Rusty feels safer in diapers than he would in a skirt?...He tried to stab me with a butter knife because I told him to grow up and face the issue, settle down and play house with a nice fatherly truck driver," a statement that recalls Jacqueline Susann, the truck driver with whom Truman Capote could not play at all.

Writing of a woman (Janes Bowles) without malice, Truman Capote saw himself, in comparison, as a man: the author of a book (*In Cold Blood*) about vanity turned to pain and grief and the taking of life, life lived as a man. *In Cold Blood* is, above all, Truman Capote's expression of his sadness at being a man, at the juncture writing creates between the self we see and the self we cannot know, that neither words nor photographs can ever accurately record. *In Cold Blood* is a book replete with this image question. Perry Smith is consumed by the idea of his face's meaning, construction, and story; it is like language to him and to Capote. *In Cold Blood* is an examination of the way in which the traditional values associated with women—concern with appearance as it tells a story to the world—are adopted "naturally" by a man:

> Time rarely weighed upon [Perry] for he had many ways of passing it— among them, mirror gazing…His own face enthralled him. Each angle of it induced a different impression. It was a changeling's face, and mirror-guided experiments had taught him how to ring the changes, how to look ominous, now impish, now soulful; a tilt of the head, a twist of the lips, and the corrupt gypsy became the gentle romantic.

In 1948, Capote went to Paris: "My book's succès fou there," he told John Malcolm Brinnin. "Why shouldn't I be?" In 1949, he also went to North Africa, where he became reacquainted with "that modern legend," Jane Bowles. A photograph was taken of them somewhere in Tangier. Capote is heavier than he was in 1947. Bowles is already whatever she was meant to be. She is directing her smile, her complete attention, which she equated with affection, toward Capote, who seems to be considering whether or not to accept this attention. In that moment, which appears to be a long one, Truman Capote began making his long move away from women, becoming closer still.

THIS LONESOME PLACE

THE TWO NIGGERS, a man and a woman, cutting across the field are looking for a little moonshine when they spot the white boy, Francis Marion Tarwater—the teenage antihero of Flannery O'Connor's startling second novel, *The Violent Bear It Away*—who is digging a grave for his great-uncle Mason. Mason, a self-titled prophet who spent his life denouncing the world for having forsaken its Savior, believed that Tarwater might have the calling, too, but the boy is not feeling his religion right now, standing in the dirt, just this side of death. O'Connor writes:

> The woman, tall and Indianlike, had on a green sun hat. She stooped under the fence without pausing and came on across the yard toward the grave; the man held the wire down and swung his leg over and followed at her elbow. They kept their eyes on the hole and stopped at the edge of it, looking down into the raw ground with shocked satisfied expressions. The man, Buford, had a crinkled face, darker

than his hat. "Old man passed," he said.

The woman lifted her head and let out a slow sustained wail, piercing and formal. She…crossed her arms and then lifted them in the air and wailed again.

"Tell her to shut up that," Tarwater said. "I'm in charge here now and I don't want no nigger-mourning."

"I seen his spirit for two nights," she said. "Seen him two nights and he was unrested."

"He ain't been dead but since this morning," Tarwater said…

"He'd been predicting his passing for many years," Buford said. "She seen him in her dream several nights and he wasn't rested…"

"Poor sweet sugar boy," the woman said to Tarwater, "what you going to do here now by yourself in this lonesome place?"

Published in 1960, *The Violent Bear It Away* appeared just as Martin Luther King Jr. was cutting a large revolutionary swath through the Old South, and only six years after *Brown v. Board of Education*, when that little black girl in sunglasses had her face dotted with the spittle of her white countrymen in Little Rock. The South may indeed have seemed like a "lonesome place" to whites then. Integration was not going slow, as William Faulkner had said it should (to which Thurgood Marshall responded, "They don't mean go slow, they mean don't go"). And, in order to move into a modern South, whites would need to be less encumbered by the old ways: by manners, by the Christian charity and moral rectitude of colored life—the "nigger-mourning" that cut to the soul.

Race and faith and their attendant hierarchies and delusions are O'Connor's great themes. She was hailed for her artistic and social independence, but readings of this American master often overlook the originality and honesty of her portrayal of Southern whiteness. Or, rather, Southern whiteness as it chafed under its biggest cultural influence—Southern blackness. It's remarkable to consider that O'Connor started writing less than a hundred years after Harriet Beecher Stowe published *Uncle Tom's Cabin*, and just a decade after Margaret Mitchell's *Gone with the Wind*, two books whose imagined black worlds had more to do with their authors' patronizing sentimentality than with the complicated intertwining of black and white, rich and poor, mundane and sublime that characterized real Southern life—and O'Connor's portrait of it. Her black characters are not symbols defined in opposition to whiteness; they are the living people who were, physically at least, on the periphery of O'Connor's own world. She was not romantic enough to take Faulkner's Dilsey view of blacks—as the fulcrum of integrity and compassion. She didn't use them as vessels of sympathy or scorn; she simply—and complexly—drew from life.

Flannery O'Connor's electric vision is still surprising enough, nearly ninety years after her birth, to have inspired five critical studies in the year 2000 alone—the most compelling of which are Richard Giannone's *Flannery O'Connor, Hermit Novelist* and Lorine M. Getz's *Flannery O'Connor, Literary Theologian*. But one hesitates to read her fiction autobiographically; it was not an approach O'Connor had much patience for. "I know some folks that don't mind their own bisnis," she wrote when she was twelve. Eighteen years later, she elaborated, in a letter to a friend, explaining why she had no interest in representing herself in writing:

To say that any complete denudation of the writer occurs in the successful work is, according to me, a romantic exaggeration. A great part of the art of it is precisely in seeing that this does not happen... Everything has to be subordinated to a whole which is not you. Any story I reveal myself completely in will be a bad story.

From the beginning, O'Connor worked to alchemize her background into something beyond mere anecdote and eccentricity. Born in 1925 in Savannah, Georgia, she was baptized Mary Flannery O'Connor at the Catholic Cathedral of St. John the Baptist. The Church's sanctioning of mysticism would later have a profound influence on O'Connor's writing, but Catholicism was a faith that had little sway in the "Christ-haunted" South O'Connor grew up in—a place where Jesus was God. Savannah had been settled first by Episcopalians and Lutherans, then by Baptists and Methodists; Catholics were excluded from the state's charter until 1794, and were thereafter rarely regarded as anything but an itinerant non-Reformed sect, as alien a presence as the Jews. ("That must be Jew singing," someone scoffs when two Catholic girls sing psalms in the 1954 O'Connor short story "A Temple of the Holy Ghost.")

O'Connor was the only child of Regina Cline and Edward O'Connor, a real estate agent who aspired to be a writer. Both parents were descended from Irish Catholic immigrants, and Mary Flannery began her studies at the St. Vincent's Grammar School for Girls. Even as a child, she had a merciless view of things, and her plain speech won her unwelcome attention from the Sisters of Mercy who provided her instruction. She grew up loving birds and she favored chickens with mismatched eyes or crooked combs. When she was five, she raised a "frizzled" chicken (its feathers grew backward), which she taught to walk backward. A New York-based newsreel company that specialized in natural phenomena heard about the bird and sent a crew to O'Connor's home to film it—"an experience that marked me for life," she said later. The crew's visit provided her with the first approval of her obsession with the grotesque as it lives beside the normal: a frizzled chicken striding backward in the yard while Mother airs out a tablecloth and Father closes the shed door, ax in one hand, wiping the sweat from the back of his neck with the other.

American genius often feeds on its own environs, and O'Connor was no exception. "I'm pleased to live in Baldwin County in the sovereign state of Georgia, and to see what I can from here," she told one interviewer. She knew where her material was, and had known it since she was twelve. By then she had discovered the tone of her voice, too, its lyrical flatness and its wildly leaping humor. ("If I... tried to write a story about the Japanese, the characters would all talk like Herman Talmadge," she once said.) O'Connor was already slipping verse under her father's napkin at the table and rejecting books that didn't satisfy her interest in the heretical. "Awful. I wouldn't read this book," she wrote in her copy of *Alice's Adventures in Wonderland*. In a copy of *Georgina Finds Herself*, by Shirley Watkins: "This is the worst book I ever read next to Pinocchio." About her early reading, O'Connor wrote to a friend in 1955:

The only good things I read when I was a child were the Greek and Roman myths which I got out of a set of a child's encyclopedia...

The rest of what I read was Slop with a capital S. The Slop period was followed by the Edgar Allan Poe period which lasted for years and consisted chiefly in a volume called *The Humerous Tales of E.A. Poe*. These were mighty humerous—one about a young man who was too vain to wear his glasses and consequently married his grandmother by accident; another about a fine figure of a man who in his room removed wooden arms, wooden legs, hair piece, artificial teeth, voice box, etc. etc.

From the beginning of her reading life, O'Connor preferred stories that were direct in their telling and mysterious only in their subtexts. She clearly despised the lack of clarity which she believed came with Northern liberalism, and which she lampoons with her intellectual characters, who always function in a kind of godless oligarchy. In many of her stories, intellectuals are depicted as grumpy poseurs, mean and homely failures who can't get on with life and are often driven into the ground by its brutality. O'Connor was like her chicken, walking backward, staring at others as she removed herself from them.

In 1938, after Edward O'Connor was appointed a zone real estate appraiser for the Federal Housing Administration in Atlanta, Regina and Flannery moved into the Cline family house in the nearby town of Milledgeville, where Edward could visit on the weekends. There was no parochial education for Flannery in Milledgeville, the home of the state insane asylum. (She eventually graduated from the experimental Peabody High School.) And, soon after the move, Edward's health began to deteriorate. He was suffering from lupus, a disease in which the body attacks its own tissues, destroying itself. Fifteen years after her father's death, in 1941, O'Connor wrote to her friend Elizabeth Hester, a clerk at a credit bureau in Atlanta and a frequent correspondent during the last nine years of O'Connor's life, whose identity was only recently revealed:

> My father wanted to write but had not the time or money or training or any of the opportunities I have had…Anyway, whatever I do in the way of writing makes me extra happy in the thought that it is a fulfillment of what he wanted to do himself.

That fulfillment came relatively quickly. In 1945, shortly before completing her A.B. at the Georgia State College for Women, O'Connor was admitted to the State University of Iowa with a scholarship in journalism. O'Connor had clear, pale skin, a heart-shaped face, lively eyes, and a thick Georgia accent. In a letter to the editor Robert Giroux, Paul Engle, then the director of the Iowa Writers' Workshop, recalls meeting her that fall and being unable to understand her speech: "Embarrassed, I asked her to write down what she had just said on a pad. She wrote: 'My name is Flannery O'Connor. I am not a journalist. Can I come to the Writers' Workshop?'" Engle continued:

> Like Keats, who spoke Cockney but wrote the purest sounds in English, Flannery spoke a dialect beyond instant comprehension but on the page her prose was imaginative, tough, alive…Sitting at the back of the room silent, Flannery was more of a presence than the exuberant talkers who serenade every writing class with their loudness.

O'Connor rarely if ever discussed her "bisnis"—her religion, her writing, her Southernness—with her peers in Iowa. One classmate claims not to have realized that O'Connor "really did believe in evil and damnation and redemption" until she produced a story that showed insight into a character's fall. O'Connor's parochialism might have been a defense, the armor she used to shield herself from other people, but she also seemed to view it as someone else's problem; she knew who she was and where she was going. Iowa, at least, provided her with a new perspective on the cryptic idea of home.

At the end of her first year at Iowa, O'Connor published her first story, "The Geranium," in *Accent*. The story focuses on an enfeebled man named Old Dudley who is living up North with his daughter and her family but wants to go back home to the South to die, near the "niggers" who are kinder to the old man than his own children. O'Connor reworked the story several times after its first publication, but already, at twenty-one, she had found many of her mature themes: the skewering of tradition, the erosion of one world that, disastrously, comically, is the weak foundation of the next, and the spectacle of blacks and whites regarding each other across a divide of mutual outsiderness. O'Connor was not a polemicist, but her work is implicitly political given the environment she drew from—the South during its second failed attempt at Reconstruction, otherwise known as Integration. As she wrote in an essay titled "The Regional Writer," "Southern identity is not really connected with mocking birds and beaten biscuits and white columns any more than it is with hookworm and bare feet and muddy clay roads." Indeed, she was at times violently critical of Tennessee Williams's and Carson McCullers's work, because she felt that they played on clichéd images of the region. "An identity is not to be found on the surface," she wrote.

O'Connor's vision of the postindustrial South—with its Winn-Dixie stores, its automobiles piled up in the junkyard of the Lord—as a modern version of the fall was all her own. But what fall? What loss of innocence? That of the slaves who became indentured servants and then "niggers," and who dot her pages like flies? No: in O'Connor's fictional universe, the whites in power are the only ones who can afford to be innocent of their surroundings. O'Connor's most profound gift was her ability to describe impartially the bourgeoisie she was born into, to depict with humor and without judgment her rapidly crumbling social order. In "Revelation," a 1964 story, she described Mrs. Turpin, a woman who occupies herself "with the question of who she would have chosen to be if she couldn't have been herself":

> If Jesus had said to her before he made her, "There's only two places available for you. You can either be a nigger or white-trash," what would she have said?…She would have wiggled and squirmed and begged and pleaded but it would have been no use and finally she would have said, "All right, make me a nigger then—but that don't mean a trashy one." And he would have made her a neat clean respectable Negro woman, herself but black."

When Mrs. Turpin gets into a fight with a young white woman from Wellesley while sitting in a doctor's waiting room, her sense of propriety is upset; meaninglessness yawns before her like a great black hole. O'Connor allows us to see what Mrs. Turpin's pride hides from her: how the blacks who work for her condescend to her, how they hide their intelligence so that she won't be tempted to interfere in their lives. One of them asks Mrs. Turpin about the bruise she incurred during the fight and, before she can explain, continues,

"Ain't nothing bad happen to you!" the old woman said. She said it as if they all knew that Mrs. Turpin was protected in some special way by Divine Providence. "You just had you a little fall."

Mrs. Turpin describes the scene in the doctor's office:

"She said…something real ugly," she muttered.

"She sho shouldn't said nothin ugly to you," the old woman said. "You so sweet. You the sweetest lady I know."

"She pretty too," the one with the hat on said.

"And stout," the other one said. "I never knowed no sweeter white lady."

"That's the truth befo' Jesus," the old woman said. "Amen! You des as sweet and pretty as you can be."

Mrs. Turpin knew exactly how much Negro flattery was worth and it added to her rage. "She said," she began again and finished this time with a fierce rush of breath, "that I was an old wart hog from hell."

There was an astounded silence.

"Where she at?" the youngest woman cried in a piercing voice. "Lemme see her. I'll kill her!"

"I'll kill her with you!" the other one cried.

"She b'long in the sylum," the old woman said emphatically. "You the sweetest white lady I know."

"She pretty too," the other two said. "Stout as she can be and sweet. Jesus satisfied with her!"

Jesus is, perhaps, not as satisfied as Mrs. Turpin. No reader can help but be amused and disturbed by this passage, which is representative of O'Connor's subtle observation of a world that was not her own but that informed every inch of the one she inhabited. Blacks may have spent much of their lives on the margins, but she understood the ways in which they entered the circle. The theatrical modesty and duplicity exhibited by these blacks who are an audience for Mrs. Turpin's troubles—despite the fact that she will never be one for theirs—are all just a part of the Southern code of manners.

O'Connor delighted in portraying the forms of domestic terrorism. It is a Catholic tenet that God judges by actions, but virtually all her white woman characters judge by appearances. O'Connor greatly admired Faulkner. "Nobody wants his mule and wagon stalled on the same track the Dixie Limited is roaring down," she remarked of Southern writers' relationship to the Master. But there is no Faulknerian Snopes in O'Connor's fiction. What she describes is far more evil: the nice lady on the bus who calls you "nigger" by offering your child a penny; or the old woman who loves to regale her grandchildren with stories about the "pickaninnies" of her antebellum youth. These are women who wouldn't know grace if it slapped them in the face—which it often does. And why would any black person want to belong to the world that these women and their men have created?

For O'Connor, writing about integration was a way of exposing the dangers of clinging to the fiction of power. But like Faulkner, O'Connor herself had difficulty assimilating the push toward integration that took the region so suddenly and violently in the fifties and sixties. She clung to the provincialism she satirized, and she was sometimes clumsy at conveying real life among blacks beyond her own circles— their class distinctions, their communication with one another apart from whites. The one false note in "The Displaced Person" (1955), for instance, comes when two black workers discussing the woman they work for fall into a kind of rural Amos 'n' Andy routine: "'Big Belly act like she know everything.' 'Never mind...your place too low for anybody to dispute with you for it.'" A curtain falls over O'Connor's insight—and her ear for speech. Luckily, she rarely tried to cover this ground, probably a prudent decision, given the murky and not altogether constructive works of some of the white liberals who did.

O'Connor received her MFA in June of 1947, and Engle arranged for a fellowship that allowed her to stay at Iowa for another year and begin work on her unsettling first novel, *Wise Blood*. Hazel Motes, O'Connor's Evangelical hero, wears a blue shirt and a black hat and has white skin that crackles like pork rind in the hot Southern sun. He may look like a standard preacher, but he's not like any the good citizens of his adopted town, Taulkinham, have ever heard of. An itinerant prophet, he believes only in his own church, "The Church Without Christ...where the blind don't see and the lame don't walk and what's dead stays that way." Motes is a backward innocent, raised a Baptist, who, instead of accepting Christ into his life, decides to be him. By denying Jesus, he turns his back on those who came before him and who no doubt learned much of their discourse from the black preachers whose rhetoric soaks the Southern soil. But Motes has a grudge against Jesus: He equates Him with sin, or more specifically with the sins that he himself has committed and cannot escape—not in the eyes of his relatives, rotten with fake piety, who believe that only the Lord can wash him clean and are no better than niggers who think that the Lord will make them white.

Of *Wise Blood*, the writer and critic Stanley Edgar Hyman said, "Whatever caused Miss O'Connor to choose Protestant Fundamentalism as her metaphor for Catholic vision, it was a brilliant choice... It freed her from the constraints of good taste." O'Connor's humor lay in such paradoxes—in being an alienated Catholic in a world of Bible thumpers, a single girl in a society of matrons. "It becomes more and more difficult in America to make belief believable, but in this the Southern writer has the greatest possible advantage. He lives in the Bible Belt," she wrote, and went on:

The Catholic novelist in the South is forced to follow the spirit into strange places and to recognize it in many forms not totally congenial to him...I think he will feel a good deal more kinship with backwoods prophets and shouting fundamentalists than he will with those politer elements for whom the supernatural is an embarrassment and for whom religion has become a department or sociology or culture of personality development. His interest and sympathy may very well go—as I know my own does—directly to those aspects of Southern life where the religious feeling is most intense and where its outward forms are farthest from the Catholic...The result of these underground religious affinities will be a strange and, to many, perverse fiction, one which...gives us no picture of Catholic life, or the religious experiences that are usual with us, but I believe that it will be Catholic fiction.

In 1948, she was accepted at Yaddo as a writer in residence. There she was championed by several other writers: Alfred Kazin, Robert Lowell, and Lowell's wife-to-be, Elizabeth Hardwick, who once described O'Connor as being "like some quiet, puritanical convent girl from the harsh provinces of Canada." Although Philip Rahv eventually published O'Connor's work in the *Partisan Review*, she first began to attract attention in the *Sewanee Review* and, through the Southern Agrarian John Crowe Ransom, in the *Kenyon Review*. With the exception of Kazin, virtually none of O'Connor's early supporters were Jewish, and O'Connor had little exposure to European immigrants, to intellectual debate as a form of socializing, or to agnosticism. The North was still a black-and-white world, though in a different way than she'd experienced it at home.

The following year, O'Connor secured a contract for *Wise Blood*, with Holt, Rinehart. The association was not a happy one. She wrote to Paul Engle, describing the experience:

I learned indirectly that nobody at Rinehart liked the 108 pages... that the ladies there particularly had thought it unpleasant (which pleased me). I told Selby [O'Connor's editor] that I was willing enough to listen to Rinehart criticism but that if it didn't suit me, I would disregard it...To develope at all as a writer I have to develope in my own way...I will not be hurried or directed by Rinehart. I think they are interested in the conventional and I have had no indication that they are very bright...If they don't feel I am worth giving more money to and leaving alone, then they should let me go...Selby and I came to the conclusion that I was "prematurely arrogant." I supplied him with the phrase.

It is incredible to read, in this age, a letter by a writer whose use of ego serves to protect, not inform, her work. O'Connor was soon released from her contract and, in 1950, signed with Robert Giroux, then at Harcourt, Brace, whom she had met through Robert Lowell. The year before, Lowell had also introduced her to the Catholic poet and translator Robert Fitzgerald and his wife, Sally. The young couple had children and a home in Ridgefield, Connecticut; they needed a boarder to make ends meet, and O'Connor moved in that fall. O'Connor attended Mass daily with the Fitzgeralds. And, as her literary mastery deepened, she became better able to define her faith. She wrote to Elizabeth Hester: "I am a Catholic peculiarly possessed of the modern consciousness, that thing Jung describes as unhistorical, solitary, and guilty. To possess this within the Church is to bear a burden, the necessary burden for the conscious Catholic."

As W.H. Auden put it, "In 1912, it was a real vision to discover that God loves a Pernod and a good fuck, but in 1942 every maiden aunt knows this and it's time to discover something else He loves." Unlike the majority of Catholics the Fitzgeralds had known, O'Connor lived her faith. In a memoir about her, Robert Fitzgerald wrote admiringly of her inability to speak in abstractions: "She could make things fiercely plain, as in her comment, now legendary, on an interesting discussion of the Eucharist Symbol: 'If it were only a symbol, I'd say to hell with it.'"

This most psychologically astute and least "psychological" of writers watched the action unfold in her stories and novels with a kind of amateur glee. As someone whose worldview was in part ecclesiastical, O'Connor also knew that having faith involved hard, often dispassionate work: You did not embrace the leper at the side of the road because you "identified" with him; in fact, "because" wasn't even part of the equation. Seeing his skin drop off in flakes and handing over a fiver to sustain him were actions that called for description, not explanation. O'Connor understood comedy as the flashy side of tragedy. In her work, disaster puts on a red shirt and acts the fool for the Devil's amusement.

In 1950, while typing the first draft of *Wise Blood*, O'Connor began to experience a heaviness in her arms. She was diagnosed with rheumatoid arthritis. But later that year she became seriously ill. She was suffering from lupus, the disease that had killed her father. Lupus put her in and out of hospitals for the rest of her life. It caused her face to swell and her hair to fall out; it required her to give herself injections of cortisone, and, eventually, to walk with aluminum crutches because "the misery," as she termed it, affected her hips.

Except for a few speaking engagements and a visit to Europe with her mother, which included a pilgrimage to Lourdes ("I am going as a pilgrim, not a patient," she wrote. "I will not be taking any bath. I am one of those people who could die for his religion easier than take a bath for it"), O'Connor lived from 1952 until her death, in 1964—at age thirty-nine—near Milledgeville, on Andalusia, a dairy farm that her mother had inherited. There she raised peacocks and ran a theology-and-literature reading group. She also wrote *The Violent Bear It Away*, and the stories that appeared in *A Good Man Is Hard to Find* and *Everything That Rises Must Converge*. These stories glisten with intelligence and with startling antisolipsism: She describes, never preaches.

O'Connor may have found comfort in her religion, which allowed her to enter into a dialogue with God about suffering. But she was surprisingly intolerant of the religious struggle of others, particularly that of women intellectuals. "The life of this remarkable woman… intrigues me while much of what she writes, naturally, is ridiculous to me," O'Connor wrote of Simone Weil, a Jew who immersed herself in Catholicism. "Weil's life is the most comical life I have ever read about…If I were to live long enough and develop as an artist to the proper extent, I would like to write a comic novel about a woman—and what is more comic and terrible than the angular intellectual proud woman approaching God inch by inch with ground teeth?" Was O'Connor instinctively recoiling from her own reflection in the mirror?

O'Connor, in return, was viewed as "homely" by most women of her time. Feminists have long looked up to her for her lack of compromise and her relative isolation, but they rarely factor in the emotional toll both took on her and her work—or the painful rewriting O'Connor has had to endure at the hands of memoirists such as Katherine Anne Porter, who emphasize how attractive she was, as if a woman must balance intelligence with prettiness to be legitimate. What was lacking in O'Connor's life—and in her art—was the spontaneous experience of intimate love, with its attendant joys and tedium and security. In O'Connor's fictional world, carnality, when it comes up at all, is brutal and hilariously symbolic. Mr. Shortly, in "The Displaced Person," for instance, "makes love" to his wife by placing a lit cigarette inside his mouth like the tip of the Devil's tail:

> When he had done his courting, he had not brought a guitar to strum or anything pretty for her to keep, but had sat on her porch steps, not saying a word, imitating a paralyzed man propped up to enjoy a cigarette. When the cigarette got the proper size, he would turn his eyes to her and open his mouth and draw in the butt and then sit there as if he has swallowed it, looking at her with the most loving look anybody could imagine. It nearly drove her wild and every time he did it, she wanted to pull his hat down over his eyes and hug him to death.

Sally Fitzgerald noted in a chronology that accompanies O'Connor's *Collected Works* (1988) that in the early fifties O'Connor had been in love with a visiting Danish textbook editor, but there is scant reference to him in the selected letters, *The Habit of Being* (1979), which was overseen by O'Connor's protective mother. Regina O'Connor's deep-seated respect for the social hierarchy created a gap between her and her daughter, and Flannery wrote amusingly in letters to friends about Regina's efforts to bridge it. In a 1953 letter to the Fitzgeralds:

My mamma and I have interesting literary discussions like the following which took place over some Modern Library books that I had just ordered:

SHE: "Mobby Dick. I've always heard about that."
ME: "Mow-by Dick."
SHE: "Mow-by Dick. The Idiot. You would get something called Idiot. What's it about?"
ME: "An idiot."

Much is left out or elided in the selected correspondence, the rights to which Regina controlled until her death, in 1995. But on the matter of faith the letters are often fierce and beautiful. The most conclusive statement appears in a letter written in the summer of 1955, to Hester:

If you live today you breathe in nihilism. In or out of the Church, it's the gas you breathe. If I hadn't had the Church to fight it with or to tell me the necessity of fighting it, I would be the stinkingest logical positivist you ever saw right now. With such a current to write against, the result almost has to be negative. It does well just to be. Then another thing, what one has as a born Catholic is something given and accepted before it is experienced. I am only slowly coming to experience things that I have all along accepted. I suppose the fullest writing comes from what has been accepted and experienced both and that I have just not got that far yet all the time. Conviction without experience makes for harshness.

And yet she would have little by way of experience for the next nine years. Visitors came through Milledgeville. Admirers wrote letters. But as the years went on, O'Connor's view of what Marianne Moore called "the strange experience of beauty" became the subject of her jokes, not of serious examination. Like many people crippled by illness, O'Connor cleaved to the world as she knew it. In her early work, she had taken an intense interest in hustlers and freaks and "niggers." "Whenever I am asked why Southern writers particularly have this penchant for writing about freaks, I say it is because we are still able to recognize one," she said once. But as her lupus progressed she spent less and less time discussing identity and its political implications, and, when she did, it often felt cavalier. "No I can't see James Baldwin in Georgia," she wrote in 1959 to a friend who had tried to arrange the introduction. "It would cause the greatest trouble and disturbance and disunion. In New York it would be nice to meet him; here it would not. I observe the traditions of the society I feed on—it's only fair. Might as well expect a mule to fly as me to see James Baldwin in Georgia." One feels a sense of loss on reading this, not only because of what such a union might have produced but also because of the limitations of O'Connor's time and place and the inevitable restrictions they placed on her art. Her regionalism was both a strength and a weakness; the emotional distance caused by her physical suffering was the axis on which both her comedy and her cruelty turned.

Had O'Connor and Baldwin met, they could have laughed together about their particular "Christ hauntings": Baldwin was the son of a minister and had preached himself; his experience was not so different from that of the mad, naïve evangelists who populate O'Connor's fiction. And what a discussion they could have had about whiteness! In 1955, after a stay at an all-white Swiss village, Baldwin wrote, "This world is white no longer, and it will never be white again"—meaning that blacks, as artists and men, could no longer be confined to the self-contained enclaves that had produced them. O'Connor's later fiction was, in large part, an acknowledgment of this, and of the fear and fury it produced in her world. That conversation is lost to history. But O'Connor's work is not. One can hear her syntax and thoughts in the stories of Raymond Carver, in Robert Duvall's brilliant movie *The Apostle*, in the Samuel L. Jackson character's final monologue in *Pulp Fiction*. Her work has moved away from the South as she defined and knew it, all the way to Hollywood, where Americans have embraced it, hearing in O'Connor's voice her uneasy and unavoidable union between black and white, the sacred and the profane, the shit and the stars.

GWTW

SO WHAT CAN I tell you about a bunch of unfortunate niggers stupid enough to get caught and hanged in America, or am I supposed to say lynched? I'm assuming this aggressive tone to establish a little distance from these images of the despised and dead, the better to determine the usefulness of this project, which escapes me but doesn't preclude my writing about it. Too often we refuse information, refuse to look or even think about something, simply because it's unpleasant, or poses a problem, or raises "issues"—emotional and intellectual friction that rubs our heavily therapeuticized selves the wrong way. I didn't like looking at these pictures, but once I looked, the events documented in them occurred in my mind over and over again, as did the realization that these pictures are documents of America's obsession with niggers, both black and white. I looked at these pictures and what I saw in them, in addition to the obvious, was the way in which I'm regarded by any number of people: as a nigger. And it is as one that I felt my neck snap and my heart break, while looking at these pictures.

In any case, America's interest in niggers—and people more than willing to treat other people as niggers—is of passing interest since America's propensity to define race and the underclass through hateful language and hateful acts is well-known and much discussed. What isn't discussed is what interests the largely white editors (who constitute what we call Publishing) have in hiring a colored person to describe a nigger's life. For them, a black writer is someone who can simplify what is endemic to him or her as a human being—race—and blow it up to cartoon proportions, thereby making the coon situation "clear" to a white audience. To be fair, no such offensive nonideas were put to me when this present collaboration was suggested, but would my inclusion in this book, as the nearly ahistorical, "lyrical" voice, have been suggested if I were not a Negro? Or am I "lyrical" and ahistorical because I am a Negro? I am not going to adopt a mea culpa tone here, since I agreed to supply what I have always thought of as a soundtrack to these pictures, which, viewed together, make up a sort of blockbuster disaster movie.

But before I can talk about these pictures, such as the picture of the beautiful black guy with the incredibly relaxed shoulders who has been whipped—front and back—and who does not reveal anything to us—certainly not with his eyes—except his obvious pain: his flesh-eating scars, and the many pictures of people with their necks snapped, bowels loosened, feet no longer arched—before I can talk about any of the "feelings" they engender in me, I want to get back to the first question I posed: What is the relationship of the white people in these pictures to the white people who ask me, and sometimes pay me, to be a Negro on the page?

Of course, one big difference between the people documented in these pictures and me is that I am not dead, have not been lynched or scalded or burned or whipped or stoned. But I have been looked at, watched, and seen the harm in people's eyes—fear that can lead to becoming a dead nigger, like those seen here. And it's those photographs that have made me understand, finally, what the word *nigger* means, and why people have used it, and the way I use it here, now: as a metaphorical lynching before the real one. *Nigger* is a slow death. And that's the slow death I feel all the time now, as a colored man.

And according to these pictures, I shouldn't be talking to you right now at all: I'm a little on the nigger side, meant to be seen and not heard, my tongue hanged and, with it, my mind. But before that happens, let me tell you what I see in these photographs: I see a lot of crazy-looking white people, as crazy and empty-looking in the face as some of the white people who stare at me. Who wants to look at these pictures, who are they all? When they look at these pictures, who do they identify with? The maimed, the tortured, the dead, or the white people who maybe told some dumb nigger before they hanged him, You are all wrong, niggerish, outrageous, violent, disruptive, uncooperative, lazy, stinking, loud, difficult, obnoxious, stupid, angry, prejudiced, unreasonable, shiftless, no good, a liar, fucked up—the very words and criticisms a colored writer is apt to come up against if he doesn't do that woe-is-me Negro crap and has the temerity to ask not only why collect these pictures, but why does a colored point of view authenticate them, no matter what that colored person has to say?

In writing this, I have become a cliché, another colored person writing about a nigger's life. So doing, I'm feeding, somewhat, into what the essayist George W.S. Trow has called "white euphoria," which is defined by white people exercising their largesse in my face as they say, Tell me about yourself, meaning, Tell me how you've suffered. Isn't that what you people do? Suffer nobly, even poetically sometimes? Doesn't suffering define you? I hate seeing this, and yet it is what I am meant to write, since I accepted the assignment, am "of the good," and want to know why these pictures, let alone events, have caused me pain. I don't know many people who wouldn't feel like a nigger looking at these pictures, all fucked up and hurt, killed by eyes and hands that can't stand yours. I want to bow out of this nigger feeling. I resent these pictures making me feel anything at all. For a long time, I avoided being the black guy, that is, being black-identified. Back then, I felt that adopting black nationalism would limit my world, my worldview. Now I know from experience that the world has been limited for me by people who see me as a nigger, very much in the way the dead eyes and flashbulb smiles of these photographs say: See what we do to the niggers! They are the fear and hatred in ourselves, murdered! Killed! All of this is painful and American. Language makes it trite, somehow. I will never write from this niggerish point of view again. This is my farewell. I mean to be courtly and grand. No gold watch is necessary as I bow out of the nigger business.

In my life as a city dweller, I have crossed dark nighttime streets so as not to make the white woman walking in front of me feel fear. I have deliberately not come up behind a neighbor opening the door to our apartment building, so as not to make him feel what colored people make him feel: robbed, violated, somehow. I have been arrested on my way to school, accused of truancy. Once, when I was coming out of a restaurant with a friend, four or five cops pinned me to a wall, pointed guns at my head, I looked just like someone else. This is not to be confused with the time I sat with the same friend in his car, chatting, me in the backseat leaning over my friend's shoulder, and suddenly the car was flooded with white lights, police lights, and the lights on the hoods of their cars were turned on, and five or six cops, guns out of their holsters and pointed at me, were ordering me to get out of the car. We thought you were a carjacker, they said, as I stood in that white light which always reminds me of movie premiere lights, you know, where people look like all-dressed-up shadows as those lights hit them, getting out of their cars?

This is what makes me feel niggerish, I'm afraid: being watched. I go to parties with white people. Invariably, one of them will make a comment about my size. They say, We'd know you anywhere, you're so big! I mean, you're so distinctive!, when they mean something else altogether, perhaps this: We have been watching you become what our collective imagination says you are: big and black—niggerish—and so therefore what? Whatever. As long as it can be lynched, eventually.

Once or twice I thought I might actually get killed in my New York of cops and very little safety—a nigger casualty, not unlike the brilliant Negro short-story writer and poet, Henry Dumas, who was shot and killed in a subway station in Harlem, another case of "mistaken iden-tity" in a colored village? He was thirty-three years old when he was killed in 1968, and had written at least one short story that I consider a masterpiece, "Ark of Bones," a story made distinct by the number of lynchings that fill the air without being explicitly referred to. All those colored tragedies, even before you've had a chance to grow up, Dumas seems to say in this tale of two boys who are ignorant of their history, and then not. That is their rite of colored male passage: having to drag all those lynchings around with them, around their necks: those are their ancestors. Too bad when violent deaths define who you are. Here's a little of the narrator, Fish, and his voice, which is all he has: "Headeye, he was followin' me," Fish begins. "I knowed he was followin' me. But I just keep goin', like I wasn't payin' him no mind." What Headeye and Fish eventually see, walking through a wood where maybe a cousin was lynched, maybe not, is an ark floating on a river. The ark is filled with the bones of their black ancestors. The ark carrying those bruised bones is "consecrated" ground, but it is divine ground that can never settle, since its home is a stream. Those bones keep moving, like the dead nigger on these pages. Every time you turn a page, they move.

But back to the idea of being watched—primarily—by white editors and being lynched by eyes. What I mean is that so much care, so much care, is taken not to scare white people simply with my existence, and it's as if they don't want to deal with the care, either. It makes their seeing me as a nigger even more complicated. I know many, many colored people who exercise a similar sensitivity where white people are concerned, anything to avoid being lynched by their tongues or eyes. Certain colored people want to lynch you, too. They are competitive, usually, and stupid people who believe that if they work hard and sell out they can be just like most white people and hate niggers even more than they do since they "know" them. Those colored people are, in some ways, worse than white people, since they imagine that they are the sometimes-lynched class, as opposed to the always lynched. Fact is, if you are even halfway colored and male in America, the dead heads hanging from the trees in these pictures, and the dead eyes or grins surrounding them, it's not too hard to imagine how this is your life, too. You can feel it every time you cross the street to avoid worrying a white woman to death or false accusations of rape, or every time your car breaks down anywhere in America, and you see signs about Jesus, and white people everywhere and your heart begins to race, and your skin becomes clammy, and the perspiration sticks to your flesh, just like Brock Peters in the film version of *To Kill a Mockingbird*, where he's on trial for maybe "interfering" with a white woman; it's her word against his but her word was weight, like the dead weight of a dead lynched body.

Once you're strung up, as they say in *The Ox-Bow Incident*, or maybe the Maureen O'Hara version of *The Hunchback of Notre Dame*, or maybe in *In Cold Blood*, or once they've fixed a pain in the neck for you, as they say in *His Girl Friday* (all these movies have lynchings in them, or make reference to lynchings), once that's happened, what happens to your body? Did the families in these pictures stand at the periphery and wait for it all to be over, when someone, maybe the youngest among them, could climb the tree and cut Cousin or Mother or Father down? It's hard to see if any of the lynched have anything but rope and eyes staring at them in these pictures. When they were lynched their humanity was taken from them, so why not their families? They have no names in these pictures—maybe addresses, I don't know, since I couldn't look past the pictures, really. What difference would it have made to get the facts of any of these lives, colored or white, right? Don't we want this story to go away?

I'm ashamed that I couldn't get into the history of these people. I saw these pictures through a strange light that my mind put up to obscure what I saw when I looked at all these dead niggers, their bodies reshaped by tragedy. I think the white light I saw was the white light those cops put on me. If you look at any number of old newsreel pictures taken at the big Hollywood premieres held at the Pantages, or Grauman's Chinese, in the nineteen thirties, forties, or fifties, some of the guests walking past the movie lights—klieg lights—look like shadowy half people trying to fill their suits or dresses. People as penumbrae. That's the light I saw when I looked at these pictures; it made the people in the pictures look less real. When I thought of that white light, I thought of my introduction to the South, where many of these niggers were killed: it was sitting in a darkened movie theater with my mother and little brother, watching the revival of *Gone With the Wind*, which some people called *GWTW*. We ignored the pitiful colored people in the film because we wanted to enjoy ourselves, and in Margaret Mitchell's revisionist tale of the South, Vivien Leigh was so pretty. We couldn't think of those dumb niggers hanging from the trees in some field or another in Atlanta, or outside of it, even though we knew about that by then, I'm sure we did, though I don't think I'd heard Billie Holiday sing "Strange Fruit," about all those black bodies swinging in the Southern trees. At any rate, I didn't like Billie Holiday for a long time: her voice didn't make sense to me, nor did those black bodies, nothing so terrible was ever going to happen to me in Brooklyn, where I was considered cute and knew I would live forever. The world was going to love me forever. Whites and blacks. I could make them love me, just as Vivien Leigh made so many men fall in love with her before the fall of Atlanta, in a movie that came out around the time Billie Holiday was singing "Strange Fruit," and perhaps that's an interesting thing to try now, watching GWTW to the sound of Billie Holiday singing "Strange Fruit." See her black bodies and weariness smeared all over Vivien Leigh's beautiful face, and Hattie McDaniel's—at times—calculated, inflexible one.

Sitting in the movie theater, watching GWTW for the first time, I was in love with Vivien Leigh and not all those niggers, the most hateful among them being a brown-faced, oily-skinned carpetbagger who looks at our Vivien Leigh with some kind of lust and disgust. I hated him then because he intruded on the beautiful pink world. Leigh's girlishness could have smothered me; I would have made her forget that I was colored and that she could lynch me if she wanted to because I knew I could make her love me. But how do you get people to ignore their history? I never thought of those things when I had love on my mind.

In the middle of the movie, Vivien Leigh as Scarlett suffers, and says she will never suffer again, and I loved her so much I didn't want her to suffer. As I grew up, I retained that feeling toward women who looked like my first movie star love: I didn't want them to suffer, even though they, like Vivien Leigh as Scarlett, could lynch a nigger to pay for all their hardship: God didn't make people of her class and wealth and race to suffer. For sure, Scarlett, in real life, might have lynched a nigger in order to make that person pay for all the inexplicable pain she had gone through and eventually come out the other side of, a much better person. After that, her world might have looked different.

PHILOSOPHER OR DOG?

I SHOULD LIKE SO much to begin with an idea, would you mind? This idea—it concerns the definition of one or two words. Some words— they are defined by the exigencies of time, right? And generally words defined by their epoch become very stupid words. The words currently defining our epoch are *otherness* and *difference*. Appropriate definitions of these words are "beside the point" and "never mind." Those defini-tions—they must stick. And why? Because writers of a color who find their expression—so called—in their "otherness" and "difference" do so in a manner comfortable to the legions who buy their work not to read it, oh no, but because these writers confirm the nonideas stupid people assume about otherness and difference—two words that define privilege in the epoch of some.

If pressed by the thumb of thought, where does the idea of this otherness and difference come from? It is an acquired habit really. One learns it in infancy, sitting on the knee of someone—perhaps Mom—who may not be unlike oneself in a respect: her appearance.

Appearances speak not of themselves but of preceding generations and the haunting of each subsequent one with: Because I appear not unlike you, we are each other. What folly! The belief that the dimensions of some mother's mask, say, fitting—becoming—one's physiognomy is oneself. What manipulation! To appropriate her mask of a different sex—if you are a boy—a different generation—if you are a child—so experientially different—if you are a person—because experience is an awful thing. Truly, who "loves" it? In order not to have it—experience—we do a number of things, chief among them speaking to stupid people who cannot possibly understand us. How slimily we creep toward them—on our bellies, masks intact, the better to make our way toward the inconvenient places their ignorant experience hides—in their armpit, in their speech, in their sex, the last being, for many, experience in toto.

The cowardly experience described previously—applying that mother's mask, say, to protect oneself. How easily this is done! How easily this is done! We apply her mask to get us through a world we do not understand wherein we embrace the experience of people who cannot understand us. We accomplish this brand of retarded experience by nursing her words through the tit of her experience. Are we less lonely because of it? In X situation, Mother does exactly as I would have done. Mother says. And I am so much like her, et cetera. What if all this was simply untrue? What if one were to remove oneself from the lap of comfort—the comfort of identification with Mom? It is never done. One fears the isolation of one's own language so much one upholsters Mom and others like her in the blind fabric of others-like-myself.

These others like myself. What does their mask of piety yield? For those who write but do not care to dissect the mask—let alone its expression of piety—it yields a career. This career is celebrated by very stupid people who define an epoch with one or two words. Their entire world comprises one or two words—in it they support writers of a color who do not challenge their privilege by writing against it. These writers are limited to becoming those one or two words—*other* and *different*. What can this mean? It does not mean writing. These writers are killed by stupid people and their acceptance. Their acceptance is a form of control, as it has always been, and for generations.

When these writers of a color are embraced—it is wrong. The world is too quick to celebrate their wearing of the mask of piety, behind which they sit, writing nothing. These writers of a color often center on the figure of Mom, say, as a symbol of piety—she of an oppressed race, depressed sex, and the bad men who didn't love her and how meek and self-sacrificing she was and what shape her mask of piety took and just how big her lap was—which the child, the writer, knew the measure of because of crapping in it. Once Mom is crapped upon, she is never wondered about or cared for again because she's beside the point, she's Mom and a symbol of all one would like to get away from in this common world. Which is one reason a career as an author, and authorship, is crazily struggled for in the first place: to get away from all the true and infinitely more horrible stories Mom could tell about how she came to wear the mask of piety in the first place. The mask of piety—it is the one thing standing between her children and death. Yes sir, yes ma'am, she says from behind the mask. And, with eyes lowered, Please, sir, do not kill my children. And with breasts exposed, We will not take too much. And in the bile of a tearful farewell: Children, please do not reach toward the world that despises you because it despises me.

Regardless of what Mother says, everyone reaches toward the world, everyone, and when it burns the only thing standing between you and this burning death is the idea of others like myself—a wall that protects. Writers of a color write stupidly on this wall of race for the approval of very stupid people who, in granting their approval, may decide not to kill you. If these stupid people decide not to kill you, something must be compromised, given up. Generally, what is compromised is one's voice. That voice—it is all a writer has. Stupid people do not ask to claim this voice outright—one way in which they are not stupid. They acquire it slowly: at drinking parties and over the telephone to discuss the drinking party of the night before and at dinner and the walk following dinner under the glare of gossip dinner chat generates, and in the feigned intimacy of shared experience. That experience—it is found in the armpit and has been described at length before. It is so dreary, the scenario people of a color follow as they live an experience they believe to be intimate. This experience generally amounts to: Let me wear the mask of my mother, the mask of piety, generosity, and forbearance, for you. The "you" to whom all this is addressed—it is almost never to another person of a color. That would be too much. If the mask of piety were understood, one would be forced to speak from behind it, and the fake piety, generosity, and forbearance one has used to get what one needs: feigned intimacy, the armpit not of a color.

Perhaps Mom knows all of this. What Mom knows: in reaching

toward the world, her child of a color will eventually have to wear the mask of piety, too. What Mom knows: very stupid people look upon this mask with affection, especially as it stutters: Yes, sir, Yes, ma'am. This bowing down—it is so familiar and colored one kills oneself in it, speaking to people who cannot understand us, hoping they are not colored beneath all that ignorance.

Does Mom protect and nurture this child so that the child remains "open" to experience? Or to a career? Or to fill her lap? In the end, no one can say, but I should like to so much anyway: What Mom wants is for her child's life not to be loveless and to have some fortitude and be capable of calling a thing stupid if it is so, not behind a mask, oh no, and without fear of death.

But I digress.

Past the ostensible subject, Mrs. Louise Little.

In writing "Mrs. Louise Little," I digress even further. For in writing her name do you not see my intention? To become a writer of a color complicit with another—Malcolm X—who will compromise any understanding of her for a career. This career—it is a handful of dust in the end. One may fixate on it as if it were not. Presumably this career safeguards one from having to regard one's face and the mask behind it, which reveals, truly, what is in the mind and the quality of what is in the mind. When this mask cracks—underneath it, that is writing. How rarely does that happen? Is *The Autobiography of Malcolm X* on Mrs. Little writing? "My mother, who was born in Grenada, in the British West Indies, looked like a white woman. Her father was white. She had straight black hair, and her accent did not sound like a Negro's." What beauty in the sentence "She had straight black hair, and her accent did not sound like a Negro's"! Enough beauty undoubtedly to provoke nonthought in the mind of very stupid people: no complexity whatsoever, just Mom as the symbol of her son's career-to-be: reverence of people not of a color.

Could any critical analysis of Mrs. Little substantiated by biographical fact bear up to "My mother...looked like a white woman"? No, it could not. Unless one's sense of competition as a writer of a color in relation to another—Malcolm X—were very keen on representing Mrs. Little as something other than a nearly colorless vision. Since practically any audience will make me a writer of a color solely and, as such, I am meant to suffer, I will gladly undertake the gargantuan task of remaking Mrs. Little. But how? And according to whose specifications? Shall I begin with the hatred and self-hatred Malcolm projected onto his mother's face—"My mother...looked like a white woman...I looked like my mother"—while remembering—at times—my own passion for Mother? How shall I "capture" Mrs. Little? As an abhorrent phantom eventually driven mad by her ghostly, noncolored half? What if one were to write of her not as a mother at all, but as Louise, adrift in Grenada, in the then-British West Indies—as part of this common world my own female forebearers understood well enough to escape? To write of Louise in the crêpe de chine dress—her only one—limping as she eventually made her way to America—are these facts? Did she see her future in the stars—the murder of her husband by men not of a color; the murder of her son by men perhaps of a color; her not-gradual slide into madness following her husband's death and the removal of her children to one foster home or another? Why could she not save them? Didn't she know obeah? She was so alone. Was her life more horrible than Malcolm's? And if so, why did she not make the world pay for it, like Malcolm? Was she lonelier than Malcolm, living in this common world? Was she not lonelier than Malcolm, living in this common world? Malcolm lived less for other people than he did for power. His mother had no choice but to live for other people, being first a woman and then a mother. She was not alone long enough to know herself, emigrating, as she did, from Grenada, in the then-British West Indies, to Canada, where she met Earl Little, "an itinerant minister," whom she married and settled with, finally, in Lansing, Michigan, in western America. No one knew just how young she was before she met Earl Little. In Canada, what did Earl Little preach as an "itinerant" minister? Was Louise Little charmed by his speech? Was it as mad as Malcolm's? Was Earl Little charmed by Louise Little's crêpe de chine dress—her only one—as he limped through the provinces, preaching what? Did Louise Little have more language? No one knew what her presence would mean to the United States, its future. Her emigrating to the States—it is never explained let alone described in the *Autobiography*. She exists in the *Autobiography* to give birth to Malcolm, go mad, and look nearly colorless. What did Louise feel, growing up in Grenada? What did Louise feel in America? She came from Grenada, in the West Indies, and its green limes, subbitter people, the blue sea, and sense, garnered from her family, that the yellowness of her skin raised her above having to don the mask of piety. Being yellow in the West Indies—what does it mean? It is a kind of elevated status, based in delusions and folly. This folly began in the minds of those who contributed to the creation of this yellow skin. It began: Those smart-mouthed coloreds who want to come into this house where they will learn to hate darkness and the dark ones who remain in the sun, please come in. The stupid people—no, the Masters—who offered this up: They created another race within the colored race when they separated the dark ones from the Yellows. The meaning of the Yellows to people in the West Indies is this: Their external self calls up hatred, self-hatred, and contempt in the dark; pity and fascination in the whites.

People not of a color who "loved" the *Autobiography*: in the main they are not different from the noncolored people Louise Little was born to. Since we know so little about these people, we have to assume what Bruce Perry's biography says about one pivotal person is true: Louise "had never seen her Scottish father." Had Louise Little's father read his grandson's book, I am certain he would have loved it. I am certain of this because for someone neither Earl nor Malcolm knew, Mrs. Little's Scottish father commanded so much attention. The success of a thing is best measured by the attention men pay it. The noncolored ghost that is Louise Little's father hovers happily in the *Autobiography*. That is because he commands the attention of the living ghosts who read this book and love it, not knowing why. They love it, for starters, because of Grandfather. He is what Malcolm's noncolored readers identify with—a power. Earl and Malcolm speak of no one else with such passion. Earl Little is reported to have said to his parents, on the occasion of Malcolm's birth: "It's a boy...But he's white, just like mama!" Malcolm is reported to have said to his collaborator, Alex Haley: "Of this white father of hers I know nothing except her shame about it." What is Louise reported to have said about her own father? And of Louise's "shame." Did she ever describe it as that? And to a child? Malcolm said: "I remember hearing her say she was glad that she had never seen him. It was, of course, because of him that I…was the lightest child in our family." Was Louise Little glad not to have seen her father for reasons other than his skin not of a color? Was she glad not to have seen him so as to imagine him dead as her unfortunate mother who died "giving birth to the last of her three illegitimate children?" Was Louise Little glad not to have seen him because she was frightened by Malcolm's more than physical resemblance to her father's side of the family? Did Malcolm want to be noncolored too? He had so much ambition—was it genetic? And his need for love on his own terms. From whom did he learn the need not to ask for it? Grandfather? Grandfather did not wear the mask of piety. In order not to, one must believe in oneself to the exclusion of other people. Malcolm believed in the reality of his experience to the exclusion of all other realities except one: Grandfather, who was a ghost.

Earl and Malcolm attached themselves to Louise's male, noncolored half. Louise did not have to meet her father. Earl and Malcolm loved him by competing with his ghost at every turn. Is that why Earl loved Louise? Because she looked like the memory of someone he might have loved before her? Had Earl known noncolored people he thought beautiful at one time or another? As a preacher who "[roamed] about spreading the word of Marcus Garvey" in Omaha or one place and another, did Earl spot someone with Louise Little's father's red hair, blue eyes, and, long before knowing Louise, think that person beautiful? Was that person with red hair and blue eyes kind to Earl

Little? Did she feed him a cool drink of water with her own hands by the side of some road time has forgotten? When he met Louise, did he find her to be the living embodiment of a memory, which is to say was Louise Little that cool drink of water in that noncolored hand that did not lie to Earl Little? Admittedly, this cool water slipping through a noncolored hand past Earl Little's lips and onto the side of a side road—it would have been a remarkable thing to see outdoors in Omaha, Nebraska, in the late nineteen twenties. It would not have been a remarkable thing to have happened secretly, in America, ever. Did Earl really want Louise's father? Malcolm holds Louise Little's father responsible for his mangled consciousness: "I was among the millions of Negroes who were insane enough to feel that it was some kind of status symbol to be light-complexioned...But...later, I learned to hate every drop of that white rapist's blood that is in me." I am sure Malcolm did not mean that literally. How do we know that Louise Little's mother—who is not mentioned in the *Autobiography* at all—did not love Louise's father? In my mind's eye I see Louise Little's parents meeting on the side of a road in Grenada. Mrs. Little's mother—she is on foot. Mrs. Little's father—he is not. What he is: red in the red sun and on a horse. There's the sound of crickets, and a mongoose's stuttering run. As they pause to look at one another, the man and woman don't pause to consider the eventual outcome of their meeting: Louise Little, Louise Little in America, Louise Little in America with Malcolm.

Does history believe in itself even as it happens? Malcolm wrote, "I feel definitely that just as my father favored me for being lighter... my mother gave me more hell for the same reason. She was very light herself…I am sure that she treated me this way partly because of how she came to be light herself." Which was? "Her father." The judgmental air emanating from the above! The judgmental air that comes with knowing nothing! If Malcolm were in the least his mother's son, he would know that in the West Indies a father is an immaterial thing—a scrap of man born as torment. Louise Little knew that. Perhaps Louise Little's lack of interest in her father was cultural. Malcolm knew nothing of his mother's culture. Instead, Malcolm preferred to indulge in the fantasy of Grandfather, his "rape." That is all Malcolm cared to know of his mother's past or all that was useful to him about his mother's past. It is clear Malcolm indulged in this potential fantasy of Grandfather as rapist because it endowed Grandfather with the power Malcolm needed to emulate in order to learn how to take and take in this common world.

Mrs. Little, as I call her, was "smarter" than Mr. Little. How much did Malcolm hate knowing that? He hated the fact of his mother's smartness because he admired it. He admired his mother's mind in the way he admired most things—with loathing and fear, if he couldn't control it. What Mrs. Little is in the *Autobiography*: representative of Malcolm's fear that because he and Mom shared a face, he and Mom shared intelligence. Was Louise Little's smartness the precursor of her madness?

Malcolm felt envy for Mrs. Little's "smartness." Was his expression of this envy only for himself, or for his father too? "My father and mother…seemed to be nearly always at odds. Sometimes my father would beat her. It might have had something to do with the fact that my mother had a pretty good education." Malcolm said, "An educated woman, I suppose, can't resist the temptation to correct an uneducated man. Every now and then, when she [my mother] put those smooth words on him [my father], he would grab her." Is this not mad? Being smart—it made Mrs. Little feel so different. It made my mother silent so as not to feel different. Did Mrs. Little ask, by speaking, to be punished? Is that how she lost her mind, really? The famous photograph of Malcolm standing at a window in his house with a gun looking out the window—I believe he is on the lookout for his mother. What did he see, looking out that window? Did he see his mother's quite appropriate anger? Based on the fact that in the *Autobiography* he refers to her as Louise and in *Malcolm: The Life of a Man Who Changed Black America*, Bruce Perry refers to her as Louisa? What was her name? Her date of birth? What parish was she born in in Grenada? When Malcolm looked out that window, did he see his mother holding a diary? What was written in it? Mrs. Little (as I call her) did not write: He did not know my name. He could not bear my presence. What did Mrs. Little write? I had a son named Malcolm? Mrs. Little did not write anything. I am writing her anger for her and therefore myself since I hate the nonwriting I have done about my own mother. The fact is, my nonwriting couldn't contain my mother's presence. The fact is, Malcolm knew his nonwriting couldn't support Mrs. Little. My mother's presence showed my nonwriting up. I am writing the idea of Mrs. Little with, I hope, some authenticity, in the hope that every fake word, idea, gesture, lie I ever told about my mother and others like her will vanish.

Therein lies the paradox of trying to create an autobiography Mrs. Little can inhabit. Since I am not capable of writing about my mother, how can I honor Mrs. Little? I did not know her. How did I not know my mother? What I know: Malcolm's interest in his mother is evident in his avoidance. In one of his typically Johnsonian sentences, Malcolm writes of the effect his father's death had on her, but only as it affected him: "We began to go swiftly downhill. The physical downhill wasn't as quick as the psychological. My mother was, above everything else, a proud woman, and it took its toll on her that she was accepting charity. And her feelings were communicated to us." I cannot break Mrs. Little's heart by not at least trying to imagine what the emotional truth of the following might have meant to her. "I remember waking up to the sound of my Mother's screaming again…My father's skull, on one side, was crushed in, I was told later…Negroes in Lansing [the town they lived in then] have always whispered that he was attacked, and then laid across some tracks for a streetcar to run over him. His body was cut almost in half."

Mrs. Little was in her early thirties when her husband was murdered for "political" reasons. Earl Little was a Garveyite. Marcus Garvey was a native of Jamaica. Mrs. Little was a native of Grenada. I do not know what Mrs. Little's political beliefs were. Were they the same as Earl Little's? Earl Little's being a Garveyite—was this the result of Mrs. Little's political influence? Her being West Indian? This is just one more thing that Malcolm did not speak of: Mrs. Little's politics.

Mrs. Little lost her mind for political reasons, in a sense. When Mrs. Little lost her mind, she was not quite ready not to believe in love, the bed empty of her mortal enemy—according to Malcolm— whom she loved—according to Malcolm—and with whom she lived first in Canada and then in Omaha and then in Michigan. And I am also sure Mrs. Little was not quite ready for a space in her mind to be filled with unconquerable grief and madness. I am sure Mrs. Little did not want to see her children parceled off to one foster home or another. A young woman in her early thirties, her husband dead, with no means of support for herself and with eight children. What did Malcolm make of that? What do I make of that? I cannot bear to imagine unraveling my mother, her hair, her retribution. There is my mother—what to make of her? What to make of Mrs. Little? What to make of these questions? Will they always be at the fore of my consciousness? Is Mom all one will ever have to say who one is or care what one will become? It is difficult to forgive Mom for having to shoulder this responsibility alone as precious few pay attention to her language. It is difficult to forgive the world for not being a place conducive to this complexity. It is not difficult to produce nonwriting that rejects Mom as too great a reality.

American people of a color who "loved" the *Autobiography*. The *Autobiography* plays out the violence of their feelings toward the colored immigrant. Once Malcolm has identified his mother as an immigrant in his book, it is impossible not to see her at a remove. That is the true nature of difference: something stupidly defined so as to be controlled. When American people of a color look at this photograph of Malcolm, gun in hand, and cheer, it is because they believe he is looking for his mother, too—in a sense. People like Mrs. Little expose the myth of the dishonesty of their fellow feeling Americans. Mrs. Little's appearance is not a comfort; her story is not a comfort; her place of birth is not a comfort: she is a woman of a color, but different. Malcolm represented an intolerance of this difference, and for a very long time. Malcolm says his mother was different at every turn: "She would go into Lansing and find different jobs—in housework, or sewing—for white people. They didn't realize, usually, that she was a Negro...Once when one of us...had to go for something to where she was working, and the people saw us, and realized she was actually a Negro, she was fired on the spot, and she came home crying, this time not hiding it." And "Louise Little, my mother, who was born in Grenada, in the British West Indies, looked like a white woman."

In the countries they emigrate from, West Indians of a color are in the majority. They project the arrogance and despair that comes with this sense of being central but small onto everything and everyone else in the world. Everyone else in the world counters this arrogance by defining it as that—especially American people of a color. They do so because they are Americans first and prefer to exclude the complexity inherent in imagining what despair means to someone else and how that despair may shape arrogance. Arrogance is a theatrical device, and self-protective. The West Indians I grew up with employed this arrogance to mask their feelings less than most things and seeing this less feeling everywhere. This feeling does not exclude one's relationship to people of a color.

For example: most West Indians regard most American people not of a color as ghosts. A ghost is a part of one's consciousness at times but is not a constant. West Indians are generally not ambivalent about the relationship one must establish with these ghosts: West Indians believe in ghosts. One takes from these ghosts what one must: warnings given in dreams and one's waking life, so as to live as profitably in the real world as possible. For American people of a color, these ghosts are real because they rent other people's blood—the blood, specifically, of American people of a color. This blood—it feeds their "double-consciousness," as Du Bois termed it. This double-consciousness is not so much the "two souls, two thoughts, two unreconciled strivings; two warring ideals in one dark body" Du Bois wrote of but, rather, hatred of people not of a color and their reverence for this hatred.

My grandmother, a native of Barbados, was a Royalist. She did not grow up in a "free" Barbados but in a Barbados not so different from the Grenada Louise Little emigrated from. Both islands were part of the British commonwealth, which meant both islands were the province of Royals who sold their subjects the sense that wearing the mask of piety was identity.

My grandmother refused to accept that description of herself by believing she was not of any color. She was as wrong in this as she was in her belief that the world attempted to ignore the fact she was a woman. To forget herself and the hideousness of her reality, she attempted to ignore her children who were women, and their children, who were dark. Not unlike Louise Little, my grandmother was Yellow. In my mind's eye I can see my grandmother now. She is wearing her crêpe de chine dress—her only one—and sits, as she often did, with her legs spread, smelling not of limes but of something equally bitter. Because I am not Yellow, my grandmother encouraged me not to play in the sun; often she said I had the look of someone who had been covered in germs. My color—it was an illness to her. Was Malcolm's color an illness to his mother? "I feel definitely that just as my father favored me for being lighter…my mother gave me more hell for the same reason." My grandmother emulated so many

Royalist tendencies. She had so little to rule, though. There were no mountains, colonies, or large groups of smart-mouthed coloreds to whom she could say shut up. There was just my little self who hated her for this so much I wrote this hatred down so as not to forget it. Like Malcolm. My version of an *Autobiography* would be just as mad as his, but more so, since it is difficult for me to speak this madness. Like my mother. Like Louise Little.

Did Louise Little beg Mr. Little to work harder than was possible to attain property that might protect her children against the ghosts who eventually murdered him for his Garveyite preachings? Could Earl Little not attain this dream of protection? Theirs was a mixed marriage, in every sense. There was such a difference in their cultures. There is no photograph of that difference. There is just Malcolm's memory of it, which he hated—a hatred which became his career. Did Mr. Little wear a mask of piety familiar to Mrs. Little given her ghostly noncolored half? Did she pull rank with her yellow skin, which Malcolm hated as much as he hated his own? Mrs. Little is one long sentence that is a question.

For not writing any of that outright but sneaking in bits about his hatred of Mom just the same; for transferring his hatred of Mom's light skin onto a race of people he deemed mad because their skin was lighter than Mom's and, therefore, madder still, Malcolm was rewarded. He was rewarded by very stupid people who labeled his ideologically twisted tongue "marvelous."

Stupid Americans define their epoch and defend their privilege through one or two words. These words generally connote the sublime in order to bear the truth of what is being said. Americans distrust knowledge if it is presented as empirical—a fear of the "European." Since the root function of language is to control the world through describing it and most Americans are embarrassed by their will to do so, language is made palpable by being nice. Americans defend this niceness by declaring it makes language more social. Language, no matter how stupid, always leaves someone out. That is because an idea belongs first to an individual and not a public.

The word *marvelous* was popular in the nineteen thirties through the early seventies, not least because of Diana Vreeland and Delmore Schwartz, and not least because Diana Vreeland and Delmore Schwartz were connected to two powerful industries that propagated the idea of the marvelous and "genius"—the fashion industry and the university. For Schwartz, an author who delineated manners in a book—say Proust—was marvelous, or one should marvel at the author's ability to represent manners, regardless of class, as a way of describing a moral code in either decline or ascendance. For Vreeland the thought was the same but as it was expressed on the body, its look. Since Malcolm was lauded in *Vogue* for telling people not of a color that their faces and bodies were ugly, and since Malcolm was a treasured speaker at universities where he said he and others like himself would one day blow privilege out from between their student ears, he was taken by the marvelous, just as those people in fashion and at universities were taken by Malcolm's not tolerating their difference. They applauded and supported his "rage" because it reinforced their privilege.

As Malcolm became more famous, Mrs. Little was diminished by the loving glare of his publicity. That publicity—did it love him more than any mother could? In the *Autobiography*, he describes this love in great detail and more fervor than he ever describes Mrs. Little:

> *Life, Look, Newsweek* and *Time* reported us [the Nation of Islam]. Some
> newspaper chains began to run not one story but a series of three,
> four, or five "exposures" of the Nation of Islam. *The Reader's Digest,*
> with its worldwide circulation of twenty-four million copies in thir-
> teen languages, carries an article titled "Mr. Muhammad Speaks,"...
> and that led off other major monthly magazines' coverage of us.

Us against them. The *them* to whom Malcolm refers—that was
Mrs. Little. She exists not at all during this period. Malcolm visited
her from "time to time" in the state mental hospital at Kalamazoo,
where she was committed—by whom?—for twenty-six years. She
existed there, Malcolm says, in "a pitiful state" as her son became
more and more famous. What was her bed like in that institution?
What did Malcolm speak of to this woman? Did other inmates call
her Madame X or Mrs. Little? When he saw her face did he see his
own? Did she slap him? "She didn't recognize me at all...Her mind,
when I tried to talk, to reach her, was somewhere else...She sat,
staring, 'All the people have gone.'" Gone where? Malcolm did not
ask. Did he attempt to convert her? Was it too late? Had she become
a Jehovah's Witness? She could not speak. Did anyone place a sheet of
paper before her? A pencil? She did not write the book we need. This
book—it is already forgotten. Mrs. Little survived her son—insane, by
all accounts, but she survived him. Did she read his book? Did she find
herself missing? Did she consider writing her own? Presumably, writers
of a color have one story—the mask of piety, Mom, and what have

you. Did Mrs. Little believe her son's book could not be surpassed? Did she ever possess the confidence to believe she could smash that piety by writing it down? She was a mother, and therefore responsible for the life of her children, one of whom did write her life down but for himself, not her, and in scraps, and incorrectly.

The *Autobiography* has everything very stupid people embrace— the mother driven mad by her husband's murder, the dust of patriarchy, religious conversion into the sublime—and yet it has nothing. The *Autobiography*—how can it be rewritten? This question—it must not be mistaken as a deconstructionist ploy, oh no. We mean to create an autobiography rich in emotional fiber, with a love of God and children and Mrs. Little and so forth.

As a model, the *Autobiography* can be used. Mrs. Little's autobiography has some potential for success if we use her son's book as a model. Think of *Manchild in the Promised Land*. That is the *Autobiography* of the streets, but without the religious conversion. If *The Autobiography of Malcolm X* were written by Mrs. Little, it is certain it would not be the same book; Louise Little would not be capable of writing nothing. She was a mother. Consider Louise Little's story inside the model of the *Autobiography*, the book we need. In her son's book, the beginning is written this way:

Chapter One: Nightmare
When my mother was pregnant with me, she told me later, a party of hooded Ku Klux Klan riders galloped up one night. Surrounding the house, brandishing their shotguns and rifles, they shouted for my father to come out. My mother went to the front door and opened

it. Standing where they could see her pregnant condition, she told them that she was alone with her three small children, and that my father was away…

If Louise were to speak this, how would it be written? Must one remember one's own mother to reconstruct Louise Little's Chapter One: Nightmare, point by point? Would Louise Little write: Can you see me from a description? Was I fat? When I opened the door to those men, did it appear to them that I ate empty food? In a fat body—did I appear self-sufficient to some, a mountain of solace to my husband and children as they took and took? Did I require nothing? Will I go mad requiring nothing still?

To construct Mrs. Little point by point—would an "honest" approach be to transplant my mother's emotional history in her story? Speak for herself—that is what I mean Mrs. Little to do. Speaking for myself—that is what I can do. And in doing so, say: I am writing of Mrs. Little. What will this make of me? A boy who speaks—badly—for silent women—a too-familiar story? There is Mrs. Little in the British West Indies. There she is in the hot sun. There she is before she became a mother driven partially mad with love for her children. There she is as a young girl with broad feet curled in gray or yellow sand. There she is in America with feet curled in bad shoes too small for her broad feet. There she is dead, lying upon the verbal catafalques created by her son Malcolm and me. There are Mrs. Little's sons, including me, with their experience, wearing masks of piety as they sit in their mother's death, resembling every inch of her face, speaking loudly, hating everything, writing nothing.

WHITE NOISE

IT'S OUTRAGEOUS, THIS white boy not a white boy, this nasal sounding harridan hurling words at Church and State backed by a 4/4 beat. "Fuck you Ms. Cheney, / fuck you Tipper Gore. / Fuck you with the freest speech this Divided States of Embarrassment will allow me to have," declares the recording artist and producer Eminem in "White America," one of the nineteen tracks on his 2002 release, *The Eminem Show*. What can be done with this trickster whose phallus is made limp by a nation whose standards of beauty—"Britney's garbage. / What's this bitch, retarded? / Gimme back my sixteen dollars"—are as ridiculous to him as the popular custodians of his country's musical culture, those paragons of respectability who cast a wary eye on his mouth, his mind, his body?

There's a certain redundancy of tone to many, if not most, of the public discussions Marshall Mathers III has engendered in his by-now seventeen-year career. On one side stand Mathers's apologists—rock critics, academics, "wiggers" and the like—who cite the rapper as an officer in the war against at least one political fiction: "liberty and justice for all, now and forever." As a way of explaining his "rage," Mathers's supporters turn to his biography. They describe him as a lower-class id joyfully eviscerating Mom, faggots, Vicodin, and everything else he can wrap his bitter, white-trash tongue around, everything else Americans hold dear—or love to hate—but America could never hold him or anyone like him dearly: he will not be categorized. "I ain't Back Street and Ricky Martin," he opines on "Marshall Mathers," one of eighteen tracks making up his 2000 release, *The Marshall Mathers LP*. "With instincts to kill N'Sync, don't get me started."

Mathers was born in St. Joseph, Missouri, in 1973. His mother, Debbie Mathers-Briggs, described giving birth to her eldest child as a "living hell." Certainly the mother gave birth to the son when it came to the drama of his language as well. Mrs. Mathers-Briggs—a second marriage would end in divorce, too—was barely out of her teens when she separated from Mathers's father. Thus unencumbered, she hit the road with her young son in tow, staying first with relatives in various parts of the Midwest—North Dakota, Missouri—before making a provisional home for herself and her boy in Warren, Michigan.

Warren: a blue-collar suburb of Detroit populated by white laborers from the South who so longed for the "old country" and the old ways that they referred to their small community as "Warrentucky." Confederate flags in the windows, beer for breakfast, and watery hominy grits ladled onto chipped enamel plates by women whose time was split between being a waitress and Mom, if there is a distinction to be made.

In any case, as Marshall was growing up, the ghosts and artifacts of the "old country" were everywhere, especially its language, "the enduring speech of ain'ts and hain'ts and hit's down yonder, elevated by friendly philologists to an honorable heritage from old England or Scotland," as the Lexington, Kentucky native Elizabeth Hardwick tells us in an essay about the famous racehorse Seabiscuit. England, Scotland, or no, the "ain'ts" and "hain'ts" of Hardwick's generation were carried over into that of Mrs. Mathers-Briggs. In her son's head, the sounds of the hills commingled with their urban equivalent—the "Yo's" and "What what whats" punctuating urban Negro speech, which, though speeded up, carried the same possibility for expression as "hit's down yonder."

Every poet begins with the word. But every epic poet begins with the word as it shapes and reflects his or her world and thus the world. At home, or homes—when Mathers was nine years old, Mrs. Mathers-Briggs and her son moved to Roseville, another "white trash" dumping ground surrounded by Detroit's black underclass—there was a certain insistence on Mathers's mother's self, her "I," and her drama queen fantasies about her physical and mental abuse as she wiped her hangover vomit off the Formica countertop in the efficiency, and her son developed his imagination.

Mrs. Mathers-Briggs's identification with Marshall was, from the first, complete, and, as they say, "inappropriate." This is not an uncommon phenomenon if one has given birth to a child while still a child. For women like Mrs. Mathers-Briggs, parenting doesn't begin or end with providing food, shelter, the odd scrap of affection or worry, as you send your child into the world. For the male child of a single mother, Mother quickly becomes synonymous with Wife, and the child is thought of as Husband. Or, at least, the kind of husband she can identify with, since he is small and defenseless and feminized by the tyranny of poverty and Daddy need, too. Just like Mommy.

But the relationship shifts. The child, the tiny husband, may grow up and speak out about the drama of his upbringing, his marriage, to this wife that was his by birth, not choice. And in language not too far, in tone at least, from Mrs. Mom's. "Put yourself in my position," Mathers raps on "Cleaning Out My Closet," one of the strongest tracks on *The Eminem Show*. "Just try to envision witnessin' / your mama poppin' prescription pills in the kitchen, bitchin' that / someone's always goin' / through her purse and shit's missin'. / Going through public housing systems, / victim of Munchausen's syndrome, my whole life I was made to believe I was sick when I wasn't."

As autobiography, this is interesting. Mathers's "I" doesn't declare itself until the fifth verse. By that time, we've seen the pills, the kitchen, the public housing system; we've understood the symbolism of Munchausen's syndrome. And we've gleaned Mathers's sorrow and anger over feeling practically nonexistent amidst his mother's (at times) overwhelming demands and addictions. These narrative steps and the kind of emotional leaps and connections they allow the listener to make are typical of Mathers's work and account for the force and universality of his poetry.

Had Mathers merely relegated himself to the small, secular world he and his mom shared, he would be yet another poet of domestic calamity talking about "viciousness in the kitchen!," as Sylvia Plath wrote once. To widen the scope of his work and give it a novelistic sweep that has generally been the province of folk music, not rap, Mathers had to marry something other than his mom, as it were. He had to connect the petty grievances that crowded his small kitchen at home to other, bigger grievances—namely those of whites against blacks in Detroit, Michigan, where he still lives.

During World War II, nearly thirty years before Mathers's birth, Detroit was known as the "arsenal of democracy." Instruments of war such as guns and jeeps were produced there at a higher rate than anywhere else in the U.S., which meant that factory manpower was always in demand. Southern blacks made their way north in search of better jobs; they assumed that by moving to cities like Detroit, Chicago, and New York, they would be escaping the lash of racism. And there was the hope that in the North blacks would be able to foster and keep close what had always been threatened in the South: the black family.

But by 1943, Detroit's 200,000 black residents had been crammed into sixty square blocks in the city's East End. There, they lived in deplorable filth. The black scourge threatened to spill over into the city's white, moneyed community. White politicians, hoping to keep them out, used dubious legal means to protect "their" community. They developed new city ordinances. They developed arbitrary county lines. They also built, along Eight Mile Road, where blacks lived in close proximity to whites, a wall six feet high and one foot thick. Civil liberties at a dead end.

To insist that the black underclass lives in the urban equivalent of slave quarters implied a return to the old order: slaves over there, masters over here. Among blacks, this attitude generated rage and a need for destruction. The race riots in the summer of 1943 were an outgrowth of a number of these long-festering indignities. By the summer of 1943, "Liberty and justice for all" had become, for black Detroit, something of a joke. Liberty for whom? Justice from what? By the nineteen fifties, 23 percent of the city's white citizens had moved to the suburbs. The industries that sprang up during World War II no longer needed as many workers because production had slowed since the end of World War II. Automobiles were being manufactured, but there was an excess of manpower.

In 1967, rioting again broke out in the city. By then, urban planners had added "progress" to their list of affronts against blacks. Paradise Valley, a black community also known as "Black Bottom," had been razed prior to the riots to make way for Interstate 75, another road out of the city for those, white or black, who could manage it.

In the meantime, there was violence and dancing in the streets. Bricks were thrown through shop windows, arrests were made, blood was shed, and young black men were stopped by cops who, if they didn't like their looks or what their looks projected—fear, resentment, disgust—rearranged their young faces with billy clubs, and maybe a little stinging spittle on the lips and eyelids.

While Mrs. Mathers-Briggs was subjecting her husband by birth to her various psychological illnesses and heartbreaks, Mathers was reading the dictionary with the TV on, looking for words to describe his world, where blacks and whites had nowhere to go but their respective trailers, and nothing to imagine but their segregated poverty. How had things come to this? Did blacks and whites not have the same aspirations when the war presented all the able-bodied poor with new economic possibilities? Perhaps the dream was not the same after all. Perhaps, on the road north, white workers who had also come up from the South dreamt of no longer being part of the permanent underclass, and therefore not so closely identified with niggers. Perhaps, on the road north, black workers dreamed that city life would be the great equalizer, and that skin color would no longer matter.

As it turned out, upper- and middle-class whites—that is, white-collar workers—didn't much identify with blacks or poor whites. By the nineteen fifties, it had become clear that white manual laborers could only hold on to the dream of whiteness by living among their own kind. In "If I Had," one of the fifteen tracks on his 1999 album, *The Slim Shady LP*, Mathers writes from the perspective of the dude with the Confederate flag tied around his head, dreaming of restitution. "I'm tired of being white trash, broke and always poor," Marshall says. "Tired of taking pop bottles back to the party store. / I'm tired of not having a phone, / tired of not having a home to have one in if I did have it on. / Tired of not driving a BM, / tired of not working at GM."

Mathers's elders could not keep blackness away from their children, who had to attend the city's public schools, which were predominantly black. There, Marshall found his voice—in black music. He also ran up against race hatred.

When he was nine years old, a black classmate attacked Mathers a number of times—at recess, in the school bathroom. Once, the same bully knocked his skinny white victim down with a heavy snowball; Mathers sustained severe head injuries. Subsequently, Mathers's mother filed a claim against the school, saying the attacks had also caused her son to have debilitating headaches, intermittent loss of vision and hearing, nightmares, nausea, and a tendency toward anti-social behavior. The lawsuit was dismissed in 1983, when a Macon County judge in Michigan declared that public schools were immune when it came to such lawsuits.

Mrs. Mathers-Briggs's failed litigation must have felt like a failure of language. Unlike her son, she never learned to control it. How could she not bend the law to her will? Her hysteria, telling tales about her victimhood, had worked on Marshall, making other kinds of knots in his head. Why should the courts be any different? (Her tendency to treat the wrongs that had been inflicted on her son and thus herself as an occasion for a public airing was not restricted to Mathers's defense. Indeed, after her son's second album came out, his mother sued him for defamation of character.)

Mrs. Mathers-Briggs had a penchant for showing off the knocks and bruises incurred by living. Just like an American. Mathers's inheritance was the Mrs. Mathers-Briggs show. He brought it with him when he left her to marry his audience. But he refined her hysteria, controlled it, gave it a linguistic form. By becoming an artist, he served and separated from Mother. He served her divorce papers by making records where he talked about their marriage. And then he married her again by talking about her again. But a mom that is your Mrs. can never forgive you for believing you are someone different, and not herself. That separateness belies her existence.

That the slings and arrows of Mathers's outrageous misfortune in and out of school, in the outside of Detroit's black world, did not deter him from falling increasingly in love with black music is a testament to his interest in and commitment to exploring difference—his and theirs. Unlike many of the whites he grew up with, Mathers never claimed whiteness and its privileges as his birthright because he didn't feel white and privileged. Being emotionally beaten up at home, having his ass kicked at school, slinging hash in a number of fast-food joints after he quit school in the ninth grade, all contributed to Mathers's sense that he was about as welcome in the world as any black man. And rap's dissonant sound was the soundtrack to all that. The music's form—with its barrage of words and double entendres, shouting and silence, conversation and singing—was as familiar and natural to the burgeoning artist as the short story form was to Flannery O'Connor.

That Mathers should be open to a musical culture not his own is interesting. For some artists—white as well as black—there is the sense that delving into "otherness" allows them to articulate their own feelings of difference more readily. One thinks of the white, French-born photographer and art director Jean-Paul Goude and his 1981 masterwork, *Jungle Fever*. The book is a visual diary of Goude's fascination with and exploration of the world of colored women—black American, Puerto Rican, Tunisian—and their erotic pull on Goude's imagination. *Jungle Fever* is as emotionally explicit as Mathers's lyrics. The sound of blackness—rap, soul, funk—freed Mathers to feel articulate and alive to his white pain: black music allowed him to be present as an artist, and to tell the world who he was since he was a translator in a lexicon he could never make his own: he was white. And that was his freedom.

To say, as many critics have, that whites steal from blacks who originate important work in music or fashion is beside the point.

Black American style has had a prevailing influence on the way Americans dress and create music for decades now, long before Black Panther wives were covered in *Vogue*. What makes Mathers particularly annoying to his detractors is his brave acknowledgment of how whiteness sells blackness in America, not just as a style, but as a feeling, which Mathers—along with most black artists—knows is not divisible. In "White America," which appears on *The Eminem Show*, Mathers says:

> Look at these eyes, baby blue, baby just like yourself, if they were brown, Shady lose, Shade sits on the shelf, but Shady's cute, Shady knew, Shady's dimples would help, make ladies swoon baby, ooh baby, look at my sales, let's do the math, if I was black, I would've sold half.

Of course, part of Mathers's genius lies in his ability to market his story to the white counterculture. He knew he wasn't the only wigger out there. From the beginning, he wrote for the white counterculture as much as he produced music that blacks could identify with. This bears some resemblance to Sly Stone's marketing technique in the early nineteen seventies. Sly produced funk, but his lyrics were all about love, peace, and understanding. He made black dance music for white hippies.

Nowhere in his music does Mathers ever claim he wants to be black, like some sad, inner-city Elvis. Critics who assume he does are missing the point, along with so much else. In the superficial writing that has grown up around his white hair and white T-shirt, the pathos at the heart of his lyrics is gilded over if not missed altogether. His "rage" is that of the disillusioned romantic. Mathers can't quite believe the world is the world. Nor can he believe there's not enough love in it—especially for him. He writes with the hyperrealistic vividness of the romantic who can recall every slight, real or imagined. On "Kim," a song about his estranged wife that appears on *The Marshall Mathers LP*, Mathers sends this letter from home:

> How could you?
> Just leave me and love him out of the blue
> Oh, what's the matter, Kim?
> Am I too loud for you?
> Too bad, bitch, you're gonna finally hear me out this time
> At first, I'm like all right
> You wanna throw me out? That's fine!
> But not for him to take my place, are you out of your mind?
> This couch, this TV, this whole house is mine!
> How could you let him sleep in our bed?
> Look at Kim
> Look at your husband now!

The operative word here is "look." Given Mathers's background, where all eyes were turned on Mom as she made scenes, could Mathers feel he was real? That he existed? Moms and bullies sucked all the air out of the room. In order to be heard, he did what born writers do: he learned to listen—to himself, and to others, to stories. And like most born performers, he longed for his work to be seen. As a teen-ager in Detroit, he began rapping on the underground music scene, where he made a name for himself. He released an album, but it didn't do much. He was given a second chance at fame when the music producer and rapper Dr. Dre got a hold of the disc, liked the lyrics, and commissioned Mathers to record something else. He was given the money and time to fine-tune his sense of difference through the hard work of making words carry meaning in a country where intel-lection is viewed with suspicion. Yet instead of looking at Mathers's words—the core of his art—which would generate analysis, discourse, a complicated response, his gang looks at his public persona, which is relatively simple. He's the rude American boy with a class chip on his shoulder. But what does that boy see, feel, think? Why the anger over how humanity has fucked up the Garden of Eden, a place that is nothing if not a metaphor for love? Love of man for woman, black for white, all the things Mathers feels he has seen too little of?

Instead he looks for love in the music. As one of the producers behind the popular black rapper 50 Cent, Mathers gets to mentor blackness. A movie could be made of all this. Sam Peckinpah, the master of blood and grit and male vanity, could direct this flick. We open on Mathers as a boy; he looks up, adoringly, at his mother, as she looks intently but blindly at herself. He's sitting near her feet as he sings a song—not one of his own, he's too little to imagine writing one. Perhaps a song from Lee Breuer's brilliant stage play *Gospel at Colonus*, where five blind black men sang Mathers's autobiography first: "Who is this man? What is his name? Where does he come from? What is his race?"

MICHAEL

1.

THE FEMALE ELDERS tell us what to look out for. Staring straight
ahead, they usher us past the Starlite Lounge, in the Bedford-
Stuyvesant section of Brooklyn, and whisk us across the street as soon
as they see "one of them faggots" emerge from the neon-lit bar. This
one—he's brown-skinned, like nearly everyone else in that neighborhood, and skinny—has a female friend in tow, for appearances must
be kept up. And as the couple runs off in search of another pack of
cigarettes, the bar's door closes slowly behind them, but not before we
children hear, above the martini-fed laughter, a single voice, high and
plaintive: Michael Jackson's.

It's 1972, and "Ben," the fourteen-year-old star's first solo hit, is
everywhere. The title song for a film about a bullied boy and his love
for a rat named Ben (together they train a legion of other rodents
to kill the boy's tormentors; eventually Ben helps kill his human
companion), the mournful ballad quickly became Jackson's early

signature song—certainly among the queens at the Starlite, who ignore its Gothic context and play it over and over again as a kind of anthem of queer longing. For it was evident by then that Michael Jackson was no mere child with a gift. Or, to put it more accurately, he was all child—an Ariel of the ghetto—whose appeal, certainly to the habitués of places like the Starlite, lay partly in his ability to find metaphors to speak about his difference, and theirs.

2.

The Jackson 5 were America's first internationally recognized black adolescent boy band. They were as smooth as the Ink Spots, but there was a hint of wildness and pathos in Michael Jackson's rough-boy soprano, which, with its Jackie Wilson– and James Brown–influenced yelps, managed to remain just this side of threatening. He never changed that potent formula, not even after he went solo, more or less permanently, in 1978 at the age of twenty. Early on he recognized the power mainstream stardom held—a chance to defend himself and his mother from the violent ministrations of his father, Joe Jackson (who famously has justified his tough parenting, his whippings, as a catalyst for his children's success), and to wrest from the world what most performers seek: a nonfractured mirroring.

After "Ben," the metaphors Michael Jackson used to express his difference from his family became ever more elaborate and haunting: there was his brilliant turn as an especially insecure, effete, and, at times, masochistic scarecrow in Sidney Lumet's 1978 film version of the Broadway hit *The Wiz*. There was his appropriation of Garland's later style—the sparkly black Judy-in-concert jacket—during the 1984 *Victory* tour, his last performances with his brothers, whose costuming made them look like intergalactic superheroes. And there were the songs he wrote for women—early idols like Diana Ross or his older sister, Rebbie—songs that expressed what he could never say about his own desire. "She said she wants a guy / to keep her satisfied. / But that's all right for her, / but it ain't enough for me," Jackson wrote in the 1981 Diana Ross hit "Muscles." The song continues: "Still, I don't care if he's young or old, / (just make him beautiful)…I want muscles / all over his body." The following year, Jackson wrote "Centipede," which became Rebbie Jackson's signature song. It begins: "Your love / is like a ragin' fire, oh. / You're a snake that's on the loose, / the strike is your desire." In bars like the Starlite and, later, in primarily black and Latin gay dance clubs like the Paradise Garage on Manhattan's Lower West Side, the meaning was clear: Michael Jackson was most himself when he was someone other than himself.

Ross was more than an early idol; she served as a kind of beard during a pivotal period of Jackson's self-creation. During the late nineteen seventies and early nineteen eighties, as he moved away from being a Jackson but was not willing to forgo his adorable-child-star status, Jackson "dated" a number of white starlets—Tatum O'Neal, Brooke Shields—but once those girls were exhibited at public events two or three times, they were never seen with him again. Ross, on the other hand, was a constant. Gay fans labeled her as the ultimate fag hag, or sister, who used her energetic feline charm to help sexualize Jackson. But intentionally or not, the old friends perverted this notion in the 1981 television special *Diana*. In it, the two singers wear matching costumes: slacks, shirt, and tie. The clip was shown over and over again in the clubs: Jackson dances next to Ross, adding polish to her appealingly jerky moves; he does Ross better than Ross.

The anxiety of influence is most palpable on the spoken-word introduction to his 1979 album *Off the Wall,* the first of his three collaborations with the producer Quincy Jones. Here, Jackson can be heard struggling against his own imitation of Ross's breathy voice (a voice canonized in *Diana,* her brilliant Bernard Edwards– and Nile Rodgers–produced 1980 album featuring the militaristic hit "I'm Coming Out," which has subsequently become a gay anthem of sorts). It was during this period that a number of black gay men began to refer to Jackson as "she" and, eventually, "a white woman"—one of the slurs they feared most, for what could be worse than being called that which you were not, could never be? As his physical transformations began to overshadow his life as a musician, Jackson's now-famous mask of white skin and red lips (a mask that distanced him from blackness just as his sexuality distanced him from blacks) would come to be read as the most arresting change in the man who said no to life but yes to pop.

3.

The chokehold of black conservatism on black gay men has been chronicled by a handful of artists—Harlem Renaissance poet Bruce Nugent, playwright and filmmaker Bill Gunn, James Baldwin, and AIDS activist and spoken-word artist Marlon Riggs among them—but these figures are rare and known mostly to white audiences. In black urban centers across the U.S., where Jesus is still God, men who cannot conform to the culture's edicts—adopting a recognizably heterosexual lifestyle, along with a specious contempt for the spoils of white folk—are ostracized or worse; being "out" is a privilege many black gay men still cannot afford. Bias-related crimes aside (black gay men are more likely to be bashed by members of their own race than by nonblacks), there's the bizarre fact that queerness reads, even to some black gay men themselves, as a kind of whiteness. In a black, Christian-informed culture, where relatively few men head households anymore, whiteness is equated with perversity, a pollutant further eroding the already decimated black family. So in their wretchedness, and their guilt, the black gay men who cannot marry women, and those who should not but do, meet on the "down low" for closeted gay sex and, less often, love and fraternity.

During Jackson's childhood in Gary, Indiana, black conservatism would have reigned. Among U.S. cities with a population of 100,000 or more, Gary—a steel town twenty-five miles southeast of downtown Chicago—has the highest percentage of black residents, mostly Southern transplants, mostly Christian, and steadfastly heterosexual. Both of Jackson's parents' roots were in the South. His mother, Katherine, was a devout Jehovah's Witness. She suffered Joe's various infidelities and cruelties to their nine children with the forbearance of one whose reward will come not in this world but the next. (Joe Jackson has never adopted his wife's faith.) In her 2006 study, *On Michael Jackson*, the critic Margo Jefferson discusses this split in parenting, the fractured mirroring in the home:

> Katherine Jackson's pursuit of her faith was analogous to what she had been doing all along: housekeeping. Dirt and disorder were the

enduring enemy in the household. Germ-free spiritual cleanliness was the goal in her religion. The Witnesses say you are not pure in heart unless you are pure in body. You must follow scriptural condemnation of fornicators, idolators, masturbators, adulterers and homosexuals…So while Katherine works to lead their souls to God, Joseph works to bend their minds, bodies and voices to his will for success. Not that Katherine objects: she has her own suppressed ambitions. The boys become singing and dancing machines. And little Michael becomes a diligent Witness.

For her children ever to have raised the issue of Katherine Jackson's complicity with her husband's drive for his sons' stardom (and thus his own), and with his various cruelties—Jefferson writes, "He put on ghoulish masks and scared his children awake, tapping on their bedroom window, pretending to break in and standing over their beds, waiting for them to wake up screaming"—would have meant the total loss of family: she was the only emotional sustenance they knew. And who would object to the riches Joe Jackson's management eventually yielded, despite his hard-line style? Two years after his fifth son, Michael, began to sing lead in the family band in 1966, they were signed to Motown Records, where they would remain for more than a decade. And despite their uneven career paths, none of the Jackson children would ever lack for financial security again.

4.

In his 1985 essay "Freaks and the American Ideal of Manhood," Baldwin wrote of Michael Jackson:

> The Michael Jackson cacophony is fascinating in that it is not about Jackson at all. I hope he has the good sense to know it and the good fortune to snatch his life out of the jaws of a carnivorous success. He will not swiftly be forgiven for having turned so many tables, for he damn sure grabbed the brass ring, and the man who broke the bank at Monte Carlo has nothing on Michael.

Baldwin goes on to claim that "freaks are called freaks and are treated as they are treated—in the main, abominably—because they are human beings who cause to echo, deep within us, our most profound terrors and desires." But Jackson was not quite that articulate or vocal about his difference, if he even saw it as such after a while. Certainly his early interest in subtext—expressed primarily by wordplay and choice of metaphor—receded after he released his synthesizer-heavy 1991 album, *Dangerous*. That album gave us "In the Closet," where an uncredited Princess Stéphanie of Monaco pleads, at the beginning of the song, for the singer not to ignore their love, "woman to man." (It's another link in the chain of influence; she sounds like Jackson doing Diana Ross.) In a later part of the song, Michael pleads: "Just promise me / whatever we say / or whatever we do / to each other, / for now we'll make a vow / to just keep it in the closet."

But this would be his last engagement of this kind. Unlike Prince, his only rival in the black pop sweepstakes, Jackson couldn't keep mining himself for material for fear of what it would require of him—a turning inward, which, though arguably not the job of a pop musician, is the job of the artist. After *Dangerous*, Jackson became a corporation, concerned less with creative innovation than with looking backward to re-create the success he had achieved almost ten years before with *Thriller*. In contrast, over a career spanning roughly the time of Jackson's own, Prince has released more than thirty albums, not all of them great, but each reflective of the current permutation of his musical mind, with its focus on sex and religion as twin transformative experiences. When not content to sing as himself, Prince has created an alter ego, Camille, to explore his feminine side and thus help promote his stock in trade: androgyny (which is Prince's freakishness, along with his interest in bending racial boundaries without resculpting his face). For Jackson to have admitted to his own freakishness might have meant, ultimately, being less canny about his image and more knowledgeable about his self—his body, which was not as impervious as his reputation.

James Baldwin did not live long enough to see Jackson self-destruct. And the most interesting aspect of his essay in light of Jackson's death is Baldwin's identification with Michael Jackson, another black boy who saw fame as power, and both did and did not get out of the ghetto he had been born into, or away from the father who became his greatest subject. But the differences are telling. While Baldwin died in exile, he did not presumably die in exile from his body, and while Baldwin died an artist, Jackson did not. After 1991, Jackson's focus was his career—which is work, too, but not the work he could have done. And his tremendous gifts as a singer and arranger, and as a synthesizer of world music in a pop context, became calcified. He forgot how to speak, even behind the jeweled mask of metaphor.

In the end, the chief elements of his early childhood—his father, his blackness, the church, his mother's silence—won, and the prize was his self-martyrdom: the ninety-pound frame; the facial operations; the dermatologist as the replacement family; the disastrous finances; the young boys loved and then paid off. Michael Jackson died a long time ago; it's just taken years for anyone to notice.

THE ONLY ONE

ONE NIGHT IN the spring of 1993, the fashion editor André Leon
Talley attended an all-male nude revue at the Gaiety Theatre, on
West Forty-sixth Street. He was dressed in a red waist-length military jacket with gold epaulets and black cuffs, black military trousers
with a gold stripe down each leg, black patent-leather pumps with
grosgrain bows, gray silk socks with black ribbing, white gloves, and a
faux-fur muff. Accompanying him, rather like another accessory, was
the young English designer John Galliano.

As the driver opened the car door in front of the theater, Talley,
characteristically, issued a directive followed by a question: "I shall
expect you here upon my return at once! Lord, child, how am I gonna
get out of this car in all this drag?" He did not pause for an answer. He
stretched out his long left leg, placed his foot on the sidewalk, and,
grabbing the back of the driver's seat, hoisted himself up and out—a
maneuver whose inelegance he countered by adjusting his muff with
a flourish.

Appearances are significant to André Leon Talley, who seeks always to live up to the grand amalgamation of his three names. He has sienna-brown skin and slightly graying close-cropped hair. He is six foot seven and has large hands and large feet and a barrel chest. He has been described as "a big girl." He is gap-toothed and full-mouthed. His speech combines an old-school Negro syntax, French words (for sardonic emphasis), and a posh British accent. Though a wide audience may know him from his periodic television appearances on CNN and VH1, it is in the world of magazines that he has made his name. Currently the creative director of *Vogue*, formerly the creative director of *HG*, and a writer, stylist, and photographer for *Women's Wear Daily*, *Interview*, and the *New York Times Magazine*, André Leon Talley is, at forty-six, fashion's most voluble arbiter, custodian, and promoter of glamour.

Inside the Gaiety—a small, dark space with a stage, a movie screen, and two tiers of seats—some men sat in various states of undress and arousal while others dozed quietly. Talley and Galliano stood in the middle of the aisle to the left of the stage and waited for the dancers to appear. Talley was hoping for a "moment." He finds moments in other people's impulses ("I can tell you were about to have a moment"), work ("What Mr. Lagerfeld and I were after in those photographs was a moment"), architecture ("This room could use a certain…moment"), social gatherings ("These people are having a moment"). When the dancers entered, one by one, Talley said, "This is a major moment, child." Swaying to loud disco music and against a backdrop of gold lamé, the young men, who were either nude or partly so, offered the men in the front row a thigh to be touched, a bicep to be rubbed.

"Ooh!" Talley exclaimed. "It's *nostalgie de la boue!* It's *Déjeuner sur l'Herbe*, no? Manet. The flesh. The young men. The languorous fall and gall of the flesh to dare itself to fall on the herbe." André Leon Talley came down hard on the word *herbe* as he caught sight of a lavishly tanned young man onstage who was naked except for cowboy boots and, as his smile revealed, a retainer. "What can one do?" Talley moaned. "What can one do with such piquant insouciance? How can one live without the vitality of the cowboy boots and teeth and retainers and so forth?"

Before the end of the performance, Talley led Galliano into a room on one side of the theater, where several other men were waiting for the dancers. Upon identifying André Leon Talley as "that fashion man off the TV," a black drag queen, who wore jeans, a cream-colored halter top, and an upswept hairdo and sat on the lap of a bespectacled older white man, said, "That's what I want you to make me feel like, baby, a white woman. A white woman who's getting out of your Mercedes-Benz and going into Gucci to buy me some new drawers because you wrecked them. Just fabulous."

"This is charming," Talley said, calling attention to a makeshift bar with bowls of pretzels and potato chips and fruit punch. "For the guests who have come to pay homage to the breathtaking ability of the personnel." His muff grazed the top of the potato chips.

The room contained framed photographs from Madonna's book *Sex*, which depicted scenes of louche S&M violence (Madonna, in an evening dress, being abused; nude dancers, with collars, being ridden by Daniel de la Falaise in a dinner jacket). The scenes had been enacted and photographed at the Gaiety. "Miss Ciccone," Talley said, with disdain, barely looking at the photographs. "My dear, we do not discuss the vulgar."

In inspecting and appraising his surroundings, André Leon Talley was working—the creative director in pursuit of inspiration. It is the same sort of work he does in the more conventional environs of his working day. At *Vogue*, Talley is many things—art director, stylist, fashion writer, and producer. As a producer, Talley suggests unlikely combinations, hoping for interesting results. Recently, he arranged to have Camilla Nickerson, a young fashion editor at *Vogue* and a proponent of the glamour-misshapen-by-irony look, design a photo spread on Geoffrey Beene, a designer committed to glamour not misshapen by anything. As an art director, Talley from time to time oversees cover shoots, especially those involving celebrities. He tries to ensure that the photographer will produce an image that makes both the clothes and the celebrity look appealing and provides enough clear space in the frame for the magazine's art director to strip in cover lines. At the same time, Talley encourages the celebrity to project the kind of attitude that *Vogue* seeks to promote on its covers: relaxed and elegant but accessible. He does so by acting as both therapist and stylist. He soothes his subjects' anxieties about the cover shoot by exclaiming, as he dresses them, that this or that garment has never looked better.

It is in the production of stories he conceives on his own that Talley employs all his talents simultaneously. Before a season's new designer collections are shown to the press, Talley visits various houses to look for recurring motifs, in order to build a story around them. During a recent season, he discerned that two or three collections featured lace. *Vogue* then devised a story based on the mystery of lace, and had Helmut Newton photograph lace gloves, lace boots, and lace bodices in a way that enhanced the mystery. Talley chose which details of the clothes should be photographed. In conjunction with Newton, he also chose the models, the hair-and-makeup people, and the locations.

Talley will sometimes write the text to accompany the fashion spread he has conceived. At other times, he will act simply as a cultural reporter, writing pieces on new designers and choosing the best examples of their work to be photographed. Talley has written on interiors, too, directing the photographer to capture images that complement his text. "My dear, an editor must, must be there to fluff the pillows!" he says, explaining his presence at these photo shoots.

André Leon Talley's office at *Vogue* in Paris, where he is based, is a high-ceilinged space, painted white, with large windows facing the Boulevard Saint-Germain; it is surprisingly bare, except for two desks and many photographs on the walls, including a large one in color by Karl Lagerfeld of Talley carrying a big fur muff. There Talley will some-times perform a kind of boss-man theater—throw papers about, slam telephones down, noisily expel the incompetent. "This is too much. What story do we need to be working on, children? What story? Let's get cracking, darlings, on fur. Fuh, fuh, fuh. One must set the mood around the fuh and the heels, the hair, the skin, the nipples under the fuh, the hair around the nipples, the fuh clinging to the nipples, sweat, oysters, champagne, régence!" He conveys not only dissatisfaction but also the promise that, once he is satisfied, his reflexive endearments ("darling," "child," and so forth) will be heartfelt.

André Leon Talley, in a blue pinstriped suit, walked into his office one day making several demands that could not be met, since his assistant was not there to meet them. That Talley had, hours before, dismissed his assistant for the day was a fact he chose to ignore. He sat at his desk and began upsetting papers on it—papers that had clearly been left in some order. He then complained about the lack of order. He complained about the lack of a witness to the lack of order. He summoned by intercom a young woman named Georgie Newbery, an assistant in the fashion department, to be such a witness.

"Georgie!" Talley exclaimed as she quietly entered the room. Her eyes were focused on Talley, who, as a result of the attention, seemed to grow larger. "I told Sam never, nevah to leave my desk in this state of…disorder! I can't find my papers."

"What papers, André?" Newbery asked.

"The papers, darling! The papers! I need a telephone number on the…papers! Can you believe this, child?" Talley asked of no one in particular. "I need the number of the soirée, darling," he said, slumping in a caricature of weariness. He covered his face with his hands and moaned. Newbery picked a piece of paper off his assistant's desk and handed it to him. Talley looked at the paper: on it was the telephone number. There was a silence; Talley seemed dissatisfied at having the phone number, the problem solved, the event over. He paused, as if to consider the next event he would create. Looking up at Newbery, Talley said, "Georgie, I need three thousand francs! At once!"

André Leon Talley has been the creative director of *Vogue* for six years. During that time, he has seen many looks come and go—the grunge look, the schoolgirl look, the sex-kitten look, the New Romantic look, the reconstituted-hippie look, the athletic-wear-meets-the-street look. In the years I have known him, though, Talley's own look has consistently been one of rigorous excess. In his way, he has become the last editorial custodian of unfettered glamour, and the only fashion editor who figures at all in the popular imagination. He is the fashion editor who, seemingly sparing no expense for models, clothes, props, photographers, and airplane tickets to far-flung locations—a farm in Wales, a burlesque house on West Forty-sixth Street—pursues that which the public will perceive, without naming it, as allure.

This pursuit begins in Talley's Paris apartment, which is situated near the Invalides, where Napoleon is entombed. The apartment is small but rich in talismans of allure: scented candles, flower-patterned draperies that puddle on the floor, a large flower-patterned screen, a Regency bed, books artfully arranged on a table in the vestibule. The walls are covered in beige rice paper. There is a small dark room off the vestibule with a VCR attached to an oversized television; on the walls are a number of drawings by Karl Lagerfeld and a poster-size, black-and-white photograph of a black man's torso by Annie Leibovitz.

Talley begins telephoning in the morning, often as early as six o'clock, to suss out what might be "the next thing." When Talley telephones a designer, he may ask, "Darling, have you had a moment?" In an industry notoriously suspicious of language, Talley's grandiloquence transports the designer into the role of artist. It does so by placing the designer's work in the realm of the historic: "This collection is more divine than the last, Monsieur Ferrè, in that it is a high moment of Grecian simplicity, of fluted skirts in the material of a high rustling mega-moment, from room to room, à la the essence of King Louis XV, à la the true spirit of couture!"

On the other hand, Talley does not see the work without the frame of commerce around it; in this sense, he is like an art dealer, whose survival is based on an evaluation of the market and of how the work at hand will shape the market, or be shaped by it, in future months. When Chanel, Dior, de la Renta, and other couture and ready-to-wear houses advertise in *Vogue*, they signal the affinity between their aesthetic and the world that André Leon Talley has created. Designers trust him, the moneyed women he brings to the designers trust him, and the women's husbands trust him with their wives. Drawing on this fund of trust, Talley presents, in the pages of *Vogue*, the work of European designers in an atmosphere of guilt-free exuberance that an American audience, standing in line at the supermarket reading *Vogue*, can trust.

"Magazines are not a Diderot moment of œuvreness," Talley says. "They are monthly ventures that should amuse and earn money by showing how kind money can be." In the stories that Talley has produced for *Vogue* in recent years—"The Armani Edge," "Feets of Brilliance," "Which Way Couture?," and "The Couture Journals," among others—everything is seduction. Talley's delicate orchestration and manipulation of the designers and buyers and photographers and editorial staff contributing to his vision are never seen, of course. What matters most to André Leon Talley is the image in his head of a woman looking at the page and imagining herself on it, unaware of all that André Leon Talley has contributed to her imagination.

André Leon Talley says he owes his desire to uphold what he calls "the world of opulence! opulence! opulence! maintenance! maintenance! maintenance!" to the late Diana Vreeland, who was the fashion editor for twenty-five years at *Harper's Bazaar*, the editor-in-chief of *Vogue* for eight years, and thereafter a special consultant to the Metropolitan Museum's Costume Institute, where she mounted audacious shows on Balenciaga, the eighteenth-century woman, equestrian fashion, and Yves Saint Laurent. It was during Vreeland's planning and installation of one such show—*Romantic and Glamorous Hollywood Design*, in 1974—that Talley and Vreeland first met, through the parents of one of his college classmates. He later came to work for her as an unpaid assistant.

Vreeland was the most recognizable person in the fashion industry— indeed, the very image of the fashion editor—with her heavily rouged cheeks and lips, red fingernails, and sleek black hair; her red environments; her pronouncements (blue jeans "are the most beautiful things since the gondola"; Brigitte Bardot's "lips made Mick Jagger's lips possible"); her credos ("Of course, you understand I'm looking for the most far-fetched perfection"; "There's nothing more boring than narcissism—the tragedy of being totally… me"); her standards (having her paper money ironed, the soles of her shoes buffed with rhinoceros horn); and her extravagance of vision (photographic emphasis on nudity, drugs, and jewels).

By the time they met, Talley had gradually constructed a self that was recognizably a precursor of the André Leon Talley of today. And its most influential component was the formidable chic of his maternal grandmother. Talley was born in Washington, D.C., and when he was two months old he was sent by his parents to live with his grandmother Bennie Frances Davis, in Durham, North Carolina. "An extraordinary woman with blue hair, like Elsie de Wolfe," is how he describes her. "You know what one fundamental difference between whites and blacks is? If there's trouble at home for white people, they send the child to a psychiatrist. Black folks just send you to live with Grandma."

As a teenager, Talley made regular trips to the white section of Durham to buy *Vogue*, and these forays were another significant influence on his development. "My uncles cried 'Scandal! Scandal!' when I said I wanted to grow up to be a fashion editor," he says. "I discovered so early that the world was cruel. My mother didn't like my clothes. Those white people in Durham were so awful. And there I was, just this lone jigaboo…creature. And fashion in *Vogue* seemed so kind. So opulently kind. A perfect image of things. I began to think like an editor when I began to imagine presenting the women I knew in the pages of *Vogue*: my grandmother's style of perfection in the clothes she made; her version of couture."

In a snapshot of Talley from his college days, he is sitting with two female friends. What makes him recognizable is not just his physical appearance—the long, thin body; the large, vulnerable mouth jutting out from the long, thin face—but also his clothes. Unlike the other students, who are dressed in T-shirts and jeans, Talley wears a blue sweater with short sleeves over a white shirt with long sleeves, a brooch in the shape of a crescent moon, large aviator glasses with yellow lenses, and a blue knit hat. He looks delighted to be wearing these clothes. He looks delighted to be with these women.

Talley earned a BA in French literature at North Carolina Central University in 1970. His interest in the world of allure outside his grandmother's closet, away from Durham, coincided with his interest in French. He says of his discovery that couture was a part of French culture, and that his grandmother practiced her version of it, "You could have knocked me over with a feather! And it was stretching all the way back to the Ancien Régime, darling! Introduced to me by my first French instructor, Miss Cynthia P. Smith, in the fields of Durham, North Carolina! The entire French œuvre of oldness and awfulness flipping one out into the Belle Époque bodice of the music hall, Toulouse-Lautrec, an atmosphere of decadence, leading us to Josephine Baker and... me!"

Talley's immersion in French gave him a model to identify with: Baudelaire, on whose work he wrote his master's thesis, at Brown University in the early seventies. And it was while he was at Brown, liberated by the Baudelairean image of the flaneur, that Talley began to exercise fully his penchant for extravagant personal dress. He was known for draping himself in a number of cashmere sweaters. He was known for buying, on his teaching-assistant stipend, Louis Vuitton luggage.

"Obviously, he was not going to teach French," Dr. Yvonne Cormier, a schoolmate of Talley's at Brown, says. "André thought it was just good manners to look wonderful. It was a moral issue. And his language reflected that. André could never just go to his room and study. He had to exclaim, 'They've sent me to this prison! Now I have to go to my chambers and have a moment.'"

After Talley left Brown and completed his stint as a volunteer with Diana Vreeland at the Met, he became known in New York fashion circles for these things: insisting, at his local post office, on the most beautiful current stamps and holding up the line until they materialized; serving as a personal shopper for Miles Davis at the request of Davis's companion, Cicely Tyson; answering the telephone at Andy Warhol's *Interview*, in his capacity as a receptionist, with a jaunty "Bonjour!" and taking down messages in purple ink (for bad news) and gold (good news); wearing a pith helmet and kneesocks in the summer; being referred to by the envious as Queen Kong; becoming friends with the heiress Doris Duke and attending, at her invitation, many of her appearances as a singer with a black gospel choir; overspending on clothes and furnishings and running up personal debts in his habitual effort to live up to the grand amalgamation of his three names.

André Leon Talley came into his own in the late seventies, when designers like Yves Saint Laurent and Halston produced the clothes that he covered at the beginning of his career as a fashion editor at *WWD*, clothes often described as glamorous. It is the period referred to in the clothes being produced now by designers like Marc Jacobs and Anna Sui. "It was a time when I could take Mrs. Vreeland and Lee Radziwill to a LaBelle concert at the Beacon and it wouldn't look like I was about to mug them," Talley says.

Daniela Morera, a correspondent for Italian *Vogue*, has a different recollection. "André was privileged because he was a close friend of Mrs. Vreeland's," she says. "Black people were as segregated in the industry then as they are now. They've always been the don't-get-too-close-darling exotic. André enjoyed a lot of attention from whites because he was ambitious and amusing. He says it wasn't bad, because he didn't know how bad it was for other blacks in the business. He was successful because he wasn't a threat. He'll never be an editor-in-chief. How could America have that dictating what the women of America will wear? Or representing them? No matter that André's been the greatest crossover act in the industry for quite some time. Like forever."

Talley's fascination stems, in part, from his being the only one. In the media or the arts, the only one is usually male, always somewhat "colored," and almost always gay. His career is based, in varying degrees, on talent, race, nonsexual charisma, and an association with people in power. To all appearances, the only one is a person with power, but is not the power. He is not just defined but controlled by a professional title, because he believes in the importance of his title and of the power with which it associates him. If he is black, he is a symbol of white anxiety about his presence in the larger world and the guilt such anxiety provokes. Other anxieties preoccupy him: anxieties about salary and prestige and someone else's opinion ultimately being more highly valued than his. He elicits many emotions from his colleagues, friendship and loyalty rarely being among them, since he does not believe in friendship that is innocent of an interest in what his title can do.

Talley is positioned, uniquely, at the intersection of fashion, magazine publishing, television, and high society. He regards his position as a privilege, and he flaunts it. "A large part of his life is *Vogue*," Candy Pratts Price, the magazine's fashion director, says about him. "Which explains the vulnerable, intense moods he goes through when he thinks someone here is against him. We've all been there with those moods of his, and they are pretty intense."

Talley's emotional involvement with women rises in part from nostalgia. He seems to project his grandmother's intentions and concerns for him, and Cynthia P. Smith's and Diana Vreeland's as well, onto his female colleagues at *Vogue*, and he seems to feel spurned when they exercise the independence inherent in a modern-day professional relationship. Often, the results are disastrous. When Talley is in favor, his colleagues adopt him as a totem of editorial success; when he is not, they regard him as a glittering but superfluous accessory.

His interest in romance is nostalgic, too. For him, romance is not about ending his loneliness; rather, it flows from the idea, expounded by Baudelaire, that love is never truly attained, only yearned for. (Talley's contemporary version of this: "No man, child," he might say, telephoning from his apartment in Paris. "No man. Just another video evening alone for the child of culture.") Talley's romantic yearnings are melancholic: he is susceptible to the prolonged, unrequited "crush" but is immune to involvement. He avoids engaging men he is attracted to. Generally, he is attracted to men who avoid him. He avoids the potential rejection and hurt that are invariable aspects of romantic love. Going to a gay bar with Talley, then, is an odd experience. In gay bars, as a rule, all bets are off: everyone is the same as everyone else because everyone is after the same thing. In a sense, the common pursuit divests everyone present of his title. Talley rarely speaks to anyone in this sort of environment. Mostly, he glowers at men he finds appealing and lays the blame for their lack of immediate interest in him on racism, or on the sexually paranoid environment that AIDS has fostered everywhere. Perhaps he just prefers the imagery of love made familiar by fashion magazines: images of the subject exhausted by "feeling," undone by a crush, recuperating in an atmosphere of glamour and allure.

Once, in New York, I had dinner with Talley and his friend the comedian Sandra Bernhard. She asked me how long I had known André. I said, "I fell in love with him in Paris." There was a silence—a silence that André did not fill with being pleased at or made shy by my comment. He grew large in his seat. He grew very dark and angry. And then he exclaimed, with great force, "You did not fall in love with me! You were in love with Paris! It was all the fabulous things I showed you in Paris! Lagerfeld's house! Dior! It wasn't me! It wasn't! It was Paris!"

When I first met Talley, I did not tell him that my interest in him was based in part on what other blacks in the fashion industry had said about him, on the way they had pointed him out as the only one. Blacks in the fashion industry have spoken of Talley with varying degrees of reverence, envy, and mistrust (which is how nonblacks in the fashion industry have spoken of him as well). One black American designer has called André Leon Talley "a fool. He'll only help those kids—designers like Galliano—if they've got social juice, if they're liked by socialites, the women who tell André what to do." Talley complains about people who underestimate the difficulty of his position. "It's exhausting to be the only one with the access, the influence, to prevent the children from looking like jigaboos in the magazine—when they do appear in the magazine. It's lonely."

Talley gave a luncheon in Paris a few years ago to celebrate the couture season's start. The people he welcomed to the luncheon—held in the

Café de Flore's private dining room, on the second floor—included Kenneth Jay Lane, a jewelry designer; Inès de la Fressange, a former Chanel model and spokesperson; Joe Eula, a fashion illustrator; Roxanne Lowitt, a photographer; and Maxime de la Falaise, a fashion doyenne, and her daughter, LouLou, the Yves Saint Laurent muse.

Following shirred eggs and many bottles of wine, Roxanne Lowit, her black hair and black Chinese jacket a blur of organization, invited the guests to assemble in order to be photographed. LouLou de la Falaise removed an ancient huge round compact from her purse and began to powder her nose as her mother sat in readiness. Joe Eula ignored Lowit and continued drinking. Talley got up from his seat to sit near Maxime de la Falaise, who had admired a large turquoise ring he wore.

"Look, LouLou!" Talley shouted. "The color of this ring is divine, no? Just like the stone you gave me!"

"What?" LouLou de la Falaise asked, barely disguising her boredom.

"This ring, child. Just like the stone you gave me, no?"

LouLou de la Falaise did not respond. She nodded toward Roxanne Lowit, and Lowit instructed her to stand behind Maxime de la Falaise and Talley. LouLou de la Falaise said, "I will stand there only if André tries not to look like such a nigger dandy."

Several people laughed, loudly. None laughed louder than André Leon Talley. But it seemed to me that a couple of things happened before he started laughing: he shuttered his eyes, his grin grew larger, and his back went rigid, as he saw his belief in the durability of glamour and allure shatter before him in a million glistening bits. Talley attempted to pick those pieces up. He sighed, then stood and said, "Come on, children. Let's see something. Let's visit the House of Galliano."

I AM THE HAPPINESS
OF THIS WORLD

I AM LOUISE BROOKS, whom no man will ever possess. Photographed in profile, or three-quarter profile, or full front, photographed and filmed for as long as I can remember (before and after I was forgotten); slandered and revered for as long as I can remember—I remain Louise Brooks, whom no man will ever possess. There is my hair, as black as all that, and the crest of my eyebrows, as black as all that, too, but they do not meet in the center of my forehead but nearly meet at the edge of my bangs, the enameled black of my bangs attached to the rest of it, my hair, which I wore less as a helmet than as a shroud. There is my face and there are my eyes, implanted in that absolutely alabaster exterior known as my face, seen time and again in profile and three-quarter profile and full front, which did not convey the vitality of youth so much as it conveyed the dissatisfaction one might have with one's youth upon realizing one's youth is there to be ruined, capsized, and sometimes one simply wants to get on with it. In my face you did not see death at work but death at play, hence my film "character," the same one again and again, living in the mortuary of this world and knowing that Death, as an entity, has no regard for whether or not one takes one lover or sixteen, or seeks the ravages of gin to ravage and/or revenge one's beauty, to accelerate hate or disappoint love—in the end, we are all assassinated. My "character"—in everything from *Love 'Em and Leave 'Em* to *Pandora's Box* to *Prix de Beauté* to *Diary of a Lost Girl*—thinks of nothing beyond this moment, the moment of assassination ("It is Christmas Eve and she [Lulu] is about to receive the gift that has been her dream since childhood: death by a sexual maniac," I wrote once, elsewhere). No Christian ethic to speak of for "her." And yet I myself died a devout Catholic. I am Louise Brooks, whom no man will ever possess.

I am Louise Brooks, whom no man will ever possess—not the biographer, chronicler, or fan. We are all the product of someone else's dream. This I have known since childhood. It was then that a man, a neighborhood friend, did things to me that hurt and hurt. There was no Jesus for me then, just him, this man. And the things he did—my beauty was a conduit for violence against me. And yet I became "her," desired to be seen time and again.

There is nothing unusual in that. There was nothing, ever, to recommend myself to myself except the alabaster skin, the hair I wore as a shroud, the combined effect of which was to make men want to disappear in it. Again and again, I wanted them to absent themselves in the perfection of a beauty I never owned. Believe me in this: my distance from it was so great that I viewed my face as one would a misremembered dream featuring a face and a story I would never come to know, that of Louise Brooks, whom no man will ever possess.

And yet these men did seek to possess me, again and again, and primarily as authors of a text—biography, film criticism, memoirs—that features my name and descriptions of myself—or herself, the "star"—and sometimes photographs as well. But they did it for themselves. They did it by becoming authors of a text in which they are in control of me or herself, that thing that moves them to want to define and fix me through language that is not my own.

The least an object can do is shut up. Speech is impertinent. And yet, although it was, primarily, as a silent film actress that I was known, the complexity and ultimate failure of language was what I conveyed. As one critic wrote upon the 1929 release of *Pandora's Box*: "Miss Brooks is attractive and she moves her head and eyes at the proper moment, but whether she is endeavoring to express joy, woe, anger, or satisfaction it is often difficult to decide." What we have here is language that is prohibitive; words fail the author in this case because the language I conveyed was not prescriptive. In which instance, as in life, is it not? There are those words—joy, woe, anger—and there is my expression of them: in the face that appears under my hair, in my neck that seems to be carved out of any and all the space surrounding it, through my body, which was a complete style unto itself.

Again, I wrote once, elsewhere: "That I was a dancer and Pabst essentially a choreographer in his direction came as a wonderful surprise to both of us…As I was leaving the set, he caught me in his arms, shaking me and laughing as if I had played a joke on him. 'But you are a professional dancer!' It was the moment when he realized that his choice of me for Lulu was instinctively right. He felt as if he had created me. I was his Lulu."

But in creating movement that matters, there is no need to invent a "character"—it is the self that we strive to express. In that early self, that early Louise Brooks, neither Pabst nor anyone else "created" me in a role—I was there myself, in it.

"Louise Brooks cannot act. She does not suffer. She does nothing," wrote yet another critic of one of my early performances. In this review, the language is more to the point, although it, too, conveyed little of what I actually did: it does not analyze why I chose not to "act" but, rather, to be, and was among the first of my kind to do so.

One of the essential rules of screen acting is not to "do" anything at all. This happens when, and only when, one is free or absent enough from one's self to believe we have nothing to lose. Which I did not: before I had lived, my life was lost to me at the hands of a man who did things to me that hurt and hurt. And about my "life" as it was lived: the biographer, Mr. Barry Paris, describes the events constituting it with such caution and at such a remove that my life, in the reading, becomes yet another experience of nonreading; I am less written about in his book than chronicled. There is nothing to suggest "How I Became Louise Brooks," yet another thing I should have written.

Several biographical details for the more documentary-minded among you: I was born in Cherryvale, Kansas, in 1906, and raised in Wichita, Kansas; from my father I inherited my eyebrows and love of scholarship; from my mother I inherited everything that was inattentive, moody, critical. I became interested in dance at an early age; I danced and danced; I left home to dance with Ruth St. Denis and Ted Shawn and their troupe, Denishawn, another member of which was Martha Graham; I left Denishawn at the insistence of Miss St.

Denis (I was too critical of others, she said, and too lax with myself).
I was asked to perform with the Ziegfeld Follies; I was the most hated
Follies girl, ever (too well-read, too much attitude); I was loved then
and only then by several lesbians of intellectual distinction and many
fairy boys who drank and wrote; I left the Ziegfeld Follies to make films.
I slept with Chaplin, Garbo, Pepi Lederer (Marion Davies's niece),
William S. Paley, G.W. Pabst—in no particular order. I married twice
but, by my own admission, loved only one man, George Marshall, who
never restricted himself to the role of fan. I made a number of films,
here and in Europe—twenty-four in all; was roundly hated for doing
as I pleased and was regarded by many as a child to be cast out, especially in Hollywood—the studio system as fucked family. Many years
of drinking; years of writing or not writing. Several people along the
way fell in love with me for what I once had been: that image played
in their minds as my self, old, stooped, a recluse, talked some to some
and little or nothing to others.

There is something to be said for dropping out, saying no, the gin
in bed, and books, reading those writers who probably didn't give a
damn about their bodies and tried to write them away. Writers' bodies
don't make sense in a place like Hollywood: soft and white, defenseless in a town where everyone's defended, right up to their celluloid
tits. Maybe that's why I drank so much and did so little during at
least part of the second part of my life: Did I lose my dancer's body
and slowly acquire a writer's in preparation for writing? I could only
be what I played, and for years before I started writing, I played the
dropout. I saw little of my old friends and gradually withdrew my
swinish behavior from the so-called pearls who wanted to convince

me the world wasn't a sty after all, like Lillian Gish. Or Garbo, who saw me from her automobile once—I was living in another hole then, reading and drinking; I was maybe forty, through with being looked at, or so I thought. Me and Garbo shared a moment back in the day; what the hell, we both squandered her beauty. When she saw me from the car window, the sun was so sad; it slanted through the Third Avenue El train tracks; it was winter, I was growing older. I had on a black coat. I was carrying a bottle in a brown paper bag. I think she saw me before I saw her, but I knew it was her the minute I saw her car, and then I saw her face, that face, in a passenger seat, I saw her eyes, she wanted to offer me a ride, but just looking at me she could also see that I wasn't up for a reunion, or even her help, and so she drove right by, what grace.

Here's the thing: if you drop out you're not so much bottoming out but rising: above the mundane, above being anyone's wife. The pots and pans, kids, it's your call, honey, someone else's needs—they are beyond you. You float in your own thin air, your time is your own. Admittedly, I wouldn't have made it out of my little flat in New York, where I supported myself in my early forties as a kind of call girl sometimes, or (more disastrously) as a counter girl in a department store, who cares, I drank most of my earnings away, but I wouldn't have made it on those scullery-maid wages anyway were it not for the largesse of former lovers like William S. Paley, the CBS head, who gave me a monthly stipend that kept a roof over my head and in gin and books until I died. Sometimes I wonder when he wrote the check what he smelled like when he looked down the ledger of his life and saw my name. My pink skin, his hand imprinted on my neck, my black bangs?

It takes great courage to do nothing. You wear the world's tolerance down with your passivity and mind for nothingness. You have no season like spring in you to be reborn, because nothing has been planted. People leave you alone, because you are the face of that which they fear most: failing, not caring, doing nothing. In that freedom you have time, then, to face what most performers never face, and that I could face, with all that time on my hands: how little I wanted to be seen even as I longed to be seen. Back in Cherryvale, the same old story: the elderly man who finds me, a little girl, charming, and then his cunty fingers in my mouth; don't tell the folks; it's your fault; I have to lick myself off his fingers; this pleases him; I gag, but I do it because, after all, what's a body for? What does beauty mean? And I smile as I do it, and gag; and, after all, how different is that smile from smiling in toe shoes, standing on a b   lock of wood, en pointe, smiling under the Ziegfeld brand or taking a movie light on the chin, the light like a fist assaulting the mug that launched a disappointment? Once you give up on trying to change any of that, which is to say, reversing your story so it jibes with the American way of health—I will be a beautiful and free and prosperous white woman, I know I am, you must work to deserve me—you can relax and sink into being as dull and monstrous as the mirrors you once plagued looking for someone called I am Louise Brooks, whom no man will ever possess.

*   *   *

What the mirror shows: your looks looking at you as you change. Your beauty becoming a memory. I am a woman and feast on memory, having had no children to feast on. I kept a scrupulously clean hovel as I worked my way down, always. Meanwhile, my heart beat for that which I couldn't help but respond to: a director. Whenever one showed up in the guise of a lover, I responded with all my being. I wanted nothing, and a director. Obliteration, and someone to tell me where to hit my mark.

James Card was the next to last man who gave me direction. In 1955 I received a letter from him; some people never give up. His letter said he was the director of the Eastman House in Rochester, New York; it housed one of the great film libraries, a place that contained, he told me, examples of my work, ha, if you want to call it that. Well, he did. In his first letter, he described how, on a recent visit to Paris, he sat with Henri Langlois, the venerable founder of the Cinémathèque Française, when Langlois screened *Pandora's Box* and *Diary of a Lost Girl*. Langlois was apparently knocked out by what he saw, he had no idea, and was moved to put my picture up, along with Falconetti's, at the entranceway to his exhibition, *60 Ans de Cinéma*. When people asked why me over Garbo or Dietrich, Langlois is reported to have said, "There is no Garbo! There is no Dietrich! There is only Louise Brooks!"

In response to Card's letter and attention, I wrote this:

The mystery of life…that you should, after almost thirty years, bring me the first joy I ever tasted from my movie career. It's like throwing away a mask. All these years making fun of myself with everyone overjoyed to agree…away all false humility forever!

You see, they had to hog-tie me to get me into pictures. They didn't know what to do with me, I did not fit into any of it. After the day I went into the projection room with Walter Wanger and the director to my second picture, and they laughed and kidded me about my acting, I vowed that I would never see another picture that I was in—and I never have, not even my pictures made in Europe.

Save me from my past. I was living in grimy shade near the Queensboro Bridge when Card came running to me the first time. He was married, what did I care, it was impossible, I could care, he would never leave his wife for me, I could care less. The point was to hate him for what he did and did not give me: himself. The truth is, I wasn't interested in any man being there, not completely, and the minute I felt they wanted to be there, I accused them of being unavailable, which scared them off, of course: no one likes being told they don't exist. But the fact is, most of the men I was with were never smart enough to get the fact that when I accused them of not being available, I was talking about myself.

I moved to Rochester in '56, something like that, and Card got me writing about cinema by looking at films and thus memories. I looked at movies starring "her"—myself—and bitterly despised the vomit that lodged in my throat: my sentimental streak. Whatever dream I had about her—myself—was stripped away by my writer's eyes. I couldn't pity her! And that's when I knew I could write about her for real, and give as good on the page as she gave me on the screen, which is to say no pity at all.

Card and I were through by '63. After him, I wrote and drank for sixteen years in that little room in Rochester. Loneliness is what every writer deserves for all their ruthless betrayals—telling other people's stories their way—and what every actress deserves for all the intimacies they're offered because of their beauty, and seductiveness, which the actress does or does not believe in. Either way, she'll treat you like shit for having fallen for any of it. It's true because I know it.

I thought I was on my own until the last director or translator or whatever showed up. That would be Kenneth Tynan. But that didn't last long. Once his *New Yorker* piece about me came out, and I saw what it was—fan-based, he couldn't be as critical of "her," as I learned to be; he couldn't discipline his ardor, but I could; I had to be the best, so vain, it's true—I jettisoned him from my life, forever. Again and again my dismissal of these men. What can it mean to any of you that that dynamic—the quivering male heart bent in gratitude at the unfeeling heel of my shoe—meant and can mean everything and nothing to someone like me, and that that ambivalence can consume a life? Or that that is all one's life sometimes becomes—what Proust called "reciprocal torture," or what Virginia Woolf called her "looking-glass shame." Perhaps they did what I sought to do: to become the living embodiment of everything being nothing at all, this Death we live, this life the living never fully comprehend, or claim.

BUDDY EBSEN

IT'S THE QUEERS who made me. Who sat with me in the automobile
in the dead of night and measured the content of my character without even looking at my face. Who—in the same car—asked me to
apply a little strawberry lip balm to my lips before the anxious kiss that
was fraught because would it be for an eternity, benday dots making up
the hearts and flowers? Who sat on the toilet seat, panties around her
ankles, talking and talking, girl talk burrowing through the partially
closed bathroom door and, boy, was it something. Who listened to
opera. Who imitated Jessye Norman's locutions on and off the stage.
Who made love in a Queens apartment and who wanted me to watch
them making love while at least one of those so joined watched me,
dressed, per that person's instructions, in my now dead aunt's little-girl
nightie. Who wore shoes with no socks in the dead of winter, intrepid,
and then, before you knew it, was incapable of wiping his own ass—
"gay cancer." Who died in a fire in an apartment in Paris. Who gave
me a Raymond Radiguet novel when I was barely older than Radiguet

was when he died, at twenty, of typhoid. Who sat with me in his automobile and talked to me about faith—he sat in the front seat, I in the back—and I was looking at the folds in his scalp when cops surrounded the car with flashlights and guns: They said we looked suspicious, we were aware that we looked and felt like no one else.

It's the queers who made me. Who didn't get married and who said to one woman, "I don't hang with that many other women," even though or perhaps because she herself was a woman. Who walked with me along the West Side piers in nineteen eighties Manhattan one summer afternoon and said, apropos the black kids vogueing, talking, getting dressed up around us, "I got it; it's a whole style." Who bought me a pair of saddle shoes and polished them while sitting at my desk, not looking up as I watched his hands work the leather. Who knew that the actor who played the Ghost of Christmas Past in the George C. Scott version of *A Christmas Carol* was an erotic draw for me as a child—or maybe it was the character's big beneficence. Who watched me watching Buddy Ebsen dancing with little Shirley Temple in a thirties movie called *Captain January* while singing "At the Codfish Ball," Buddy Ebsen in a black jumper, moving his hands like a Negro dancer, arabesques informed by thought, his ass in the air, all on a wharf—and I have loved wharfs and docks, without ever wearing black jumpers, ever since.

It's the queers who made me. Who talked to me about Joe Brainard's *I Remember* even though I keep forgetting to read it. Who keep after me to read *I Remember* even though perhaps my reluctance has to do with Brainard's association with Frank O'Hara, who was one queer who didn't make me, so interested was he in being a status quo pet, the kind of desire that leads a fag to project his own self-loathing onto any other queer who gets into the room—How dare you. What are you doing here? But the late great poet-editor Barbara Epstein—who loved many queers and who could always love more—was friendly with Brainard and O'Hara and perhaps the Barbara who still lives in my mind will eventually change my thinking about all that, because she always could.

It's the queers who made me. Who introduced me to Edwin Denby's writings, and George Balanchine's "Serenade," and got me writing for *Ballet Review*. Who wore red suspenders and a Trotsky button; I had never met anyone before who dressed so stylishly who wasn't black or Jewish. Who, even though I was "alone," watched me as I danced to Cindy Wilson singing "Give Me Back My Man" in the basement of a house that my mother shared with her sister in Atlanta. Who took me to Paris. Who let me share his bed in Paris. Who told my mother that I would be okay, and I hope she believed him. Who was delighted to include one of my sisters in a night out—she wore a pink prom dress and did the Electric Slide, surrounded by gay boys and fuck knows if she cared or saw the difference between herself and them—and he stood by my side as I watched my sister dance in her pink prom dress, and then he asked what I was thinking about, and I said, "I'm just remembering why I'm gay." It's the queers who made me. Who laughed with me in the pool in Lipari. Who kicked me under the table when I had allotted too much care for someone who would never experience love as such. Who sat with me in the cinema at Barnard College as *Black Orpheus* played, his bespectacled eyes glued to the screen as I weighed his whiteness against the characters' blackness and then my own. Who squatted down in the bathtub and scrubbed my legs and then my back and then the rest of my body the evening of the day we would start to know each other for the rest of our lives. Who lay with me in the bed in Los Angeles, white sheets over our young legs sprinkled with barely-there hair. Who coaxed me back to life at the farmers' market later the same day, and I have the pictures to prove it. Who laughed when I said, "What's J. Lo doing in the hospital?" as he stood near his bed dying of AIDS, his beautiful Panamanian hair—a mixture of African, Spanish and Indian textures—no longer held back by the white bandanna I loved. Who gave me Michael Warner's *The Trouble with Normal* and let me find much in it that was familiar and emotionally accurate, including the author's use of the word *moralism* to describe the people who divide the world into "us" and "them," and who brutalize the queer in themselves and others to gain a foothold on a moralist perch.

It's the queers who made me. Who introduced me to a number of straight girls who, at first, thought that being queer was synonymous with being bitchy, and who, after meeting me and becoming friends kept waiting and waiting for me to be a bitchy queen, largely because they wanted me to put down their female friends and to hate other women as they themselves hated other women, not to mention themselves, despite their feminist agitprop; after all, I was a queen, and that's what queens did, right, along with getting sodomized, just like them, right—queens were the handmaidens to all that female self-hatred, right? And who then realized that I didn't hate women and so began to join forces with other women to level criticism at me.

It's the queers who made me. Who said: Women and queers get in the way of your feminism and gay rights. Who listened as I sat, hurt and confused, describing the postfeminist or postqueer monologue that had been addressed to me by some of the above women and queers, who not only attacked my queer body directly—you're too fat, you're too black, the horror, the horror!—but delighted in hearing about queers flinging the same kind of pimp slime on one another, not to mention joining forces with their girlfriends of both sexes to establish within their marginalized groups the kind of hierarchy straight white men presumably judge them by, but not always, not really. Who asked, "Why do you spend so much time thinking about women and queers?" And who didn't hear me when I said, "But aren't we born of her? Didn't we queer her body being born?" It's the queers who made me. Who introduced me to the performer Justin Bond, whose various characters, sometimes cracked by insecurity, eaglets in a society of buzzards, are defined by their indomitability in an invulnerable world. Who told me about the twelve-year-old girl who had been raised with love and acceptance of queerness in adults, in a landscape where she could play without imprisoning herself in self-contempt, and who could talk to her mother about what female bodies meant to her (everything), which was a way of further loving her mother, the greatest romance she had ever known, and who gave me, indirectly, my full queer self, the desire to say "I" once again.

It's my queerness that made me. And, in it, there is a memory of Jackie Curtis. She's walking up Bank Street, away from the river, a low orange sun behind her like the ultimate stage set.

It's my queer self that goes up to Jackie Curtis—whom I have seen only in pictures and films; I am in my twenties—and it is he who says, "Oh, Miss Curtis, you're amazing," and she says, in front of the setting sun, completely stoned but attentive, a performer to her queer bones, snapping to in the light of attention and love, "Oh, you must come to my show!" as she digs into her big hippie bag to dig out a flyer, excited by the possibility of people seeing her for who she is, even in makeup.

A PRYOR LOVE

SKIN FLICK

WINTER 1973. LATE afternoon: the entr'acte between dusk and darkness, when the people who conduct their business in the street—numbers runners in gray chesterfields, out-of-work barmaids playing the dozens, adolescents cultivating their cigarette jones and lust, small-time hustlers selling "authentic" gold wristwatches that are platinum bright—look for a place to roost and to drink in the day's sin. Young black guy, looks like the comedian Richard Pryor, walks into one of his hangouts, Opal's Silver Spoon Café. A greasy dive with an R&B jukebox, it could be in Detroit or in New York, could be anywhere. Opal's has a proprietor—Opal, a young and wise black woman who looks like the comedian Lily Tomlin—and a little bell over the door that goes tink-a-link, announcing all the handouts and gimmes who come to sit at Opal's counter and talk about how needy their respective asses are.

Black guy sits at the counter, and Opal offers him some potato soup—"something nourishing," she says. Black guy has moist, on-the-verge-of-lying-or-crying eyes and a raggedy Afro. He wears a green fatigue jacket, the kind of jacket brothers brought home from 'Nam, which guys like this guy continue to wear long after they've returned home, too shell-shocked or stoned to care much about their haberdashery. Juke—that's the black guy's name—is Opal's baby, flopping about in all them narcotics he's trying to get off of by taking that methadone, which Juke and Opal pronounce "methadon"—the way two old-timey Southerners would, the way Juke and Opal's elders might have, if they knew what that shit was, or was for.

Juke and Opal express their feelings for each other, their shared view of the world, in a lyrical language, a colored people's language, which tries to atomize their anger and their depression. Sometimes their anger is wry: Opal is tired of hearing about Juke's efforts to get a job, and tells him so. "Hand me that jive about job training," she says. "You trained, all right. You highly skilled at not working." But that's not entirely true. Juke has submitted himself to the rigors of "rehabilitation." "I was down there for about three weeks, at that place, working," Juke says. "Had on a suit, tie. Shaving. Acting crazy. Looked just like a fool in the circus." Pause. "And I'm fed up with it." Pause. "Now I know how to do a job that don't know how to be done no more." Opal's face fills with sadness. Looking at her face can fill your mind with sadness. She says, "For real?" It's a rhetorical question that black people have always asked each other or themselves when they're handed more hopelessness: Is this for real?

Night is beginning to spread all over Juke and Opal's street; it is the color of a thousand secrets combined. The bell rings, and a delivery man comes in, carting pies. Juke decides that everyone should chill out—he'll play the jukebox, they'll all get down. Al Green singing "Let's Stay Together" makes the pie man and Juke do a little finger-snapping, a little jive. Opal hesitates, says, "Naw," but then dances anyway, and her shyness is just part of the fabric of the day, as uneventful as the delivery man leaving to finish up his rounds, or Opal and Juke standing alone in this little restaurant, a society unto themselves.

The doorbell's tiny peal. Two white people—a man and a woman—enter Opal's. Youngish, trenchcoated. And the minute the white people enter, something terrible happens, from an aesthetic point of view. They alienate everything. They fracture our suspended disbelief. They interrupt our identification with the protagonists of the TV show we've been watching, which becomes TV only when those white people, who are social workers, start hassling our Juke, our Opal, equal halves of the same resilient black body. When we see those white people, we start thinking about things like credits, and remember that this is a television play, after all, written by the brilliant Jane Wagner, and played with astonishing alacrity and compassion by Richard Pryor and Lily Tomlin on *Lily*, Tomlin's second variety special, which aired on CBS in 1973, and which remains, around forty years later, the most profound meditation on race and class that I have ever seen on a major network.

"We're doing some community research and we'd like to ask you a few questions," the white woman social worker declares as soon as she enters Opal's. Juke and Opal are more than familiar with this line of inquiry, which presumes that people like them are always available for questioning—servants of the liberal cause. "I wonder if you can tell me, have you ever been addicted to drugs?" the woman asks Juke.

Pryor-as-Juke responds instantly. "Yeah, I been addicted," he says. "I'm addicted right now—don't write it down, man, be cool, it's not for the public. I mean, what I go through is private." He is incapable of making "Fuck you" his first response—or even his first thought. Being black has taught him how to allow white people their innocence. For black people, being around white people is sometimes like taking care of babies you don't like, babies who throw up on you again and again, but whom you cannot punish, because they're babies. Eventually, you direct that anger at yourself—it has nowhere else to go.

Juke tries to turn the questioning around a little, through humor, which is part of his pathos. "I have some questions," he tells the community researchers, then tries to approximate their straight, white tone: "Who's Pigmeat Markham's mama?" he asks. "Wilt Chamberlain the tallest colored chap you ever saw?"

When the white people have left and Juke is about to leave, wrapped in his thin jacket, he turns to Opal and says, "You sweet. You a sweet woman…I'll think aboutcha." His eyes are wide with love and need, and maybe fear or madness. "Be glad when it's spring," he says to Opal. Pause. "Flower!"

Lily was never shown again on network television, which is not surprising, given that part of its radicalism is based on the fact that it features a white female star who tries to embody a black woman while communicating with a black man about substantive emotional matters, and who never wears anything as theatrically simple as blackface to do it; Tomlin plays Opal in whiteface, as it were. Nevertheless, "Juke and Opal," which lasts all of nine minutes and twenty-five seconds, and which aired in the same season in which *Hawaii Five-O*, *The Waltons*, and *Ironside* were among television's top-rated shows, remains historically significant for reasons other than the skin game.

As Juke, Richard Pryor gave one of his relatively few great performances in a project that he had not written or directed. He made use of the poignancy that marks all of his great comedic and dramatic performances, and of the vulnerability—the pathos cradling his sharp wit—that had seduced people into loving him in the first place. Tomlin kept Pryor on the show over objections from certain of the network's executives, and it may have been her belief in him as a performer, combined with the high standards she set for herself and others, that spurred on the competitive-minded Pryor. His language in this scene feels improvised, confessional, and so internalized that it's practically nonverbal, not unlike the best of Pryor's own writing—the stories he tells when he talks shit into a microphone, doing stand-up. And as he sits at Opal's counter we can see him falling in love with Tomlin's passion for her work, recognizing it as the passion he feels when he peoples the stage with characters who might love him as much as Tomlin-as-Opal seems to now.

Although Richard Pryor was more or less forced to retire in 1994, eight years after he discovered that he had multiple sclerosis ("It's the stuff God hits your ass with when he doesn't want to kill ya—just slow ya down," he told *Entertainment Weekly* in 1993), his work as a comedian, a writer, an actor, and a director amounts to a significant chapter not only in late-twentieth-century American comedy but in American entertainment in general. Pryor is best known now for his work in the lackadaisical Gene Wilder buddy movies or for abominations like *The Toy*. But far more important was the prescient commentary on the issues of race and sex in America that he presented through stand-up and sketches like "Juke and Opal"—the heartfelt and acute social observation, the comedy that littered the stage with the trash of the quotidian as it was sifted through his harsh and poetic imagination, and that changed the very definition of the word "entertainment," particularly for a black entertainer.

The subject of blackness has taken a strange and unsatisfying journey through American thought: first, because blackness has almost always had to explain itself to a largely white audience in order to be heard, and, second, because it has generally been assumed to have only one story to tell—a story of oppression that plays on liberal guilt. The writers behind the collective modern ur-text of blackness—James Baldwin, Richard Wright, and Ralph Ellison—all performed some variation on the theme. Angry but distanced, their rage blanketed by charm, they lived and wrote to be liked. Ultimately, whether they wanted to or not, they in some way embodied the readers who appreciated them most—white liberals.

Richard Pryor was the first black American spoken-word artist to avoid this. Although he reprised the history of black American comedy—picking what he wanted from the work of great story-tellers like Bert Williams, Redd Foxx, Moms Mabley, Nipsey Russell, LaWanda Page, and Flip Wilson—he also pushed everything one step further. Instead of adapting to the white perspective, he forced white audiences to follow him into his own experience. Pryor didn't manipulate his audiences' white guilt or their black moral outrage. If he played the race card, it was only to show how funny he looked when he tried to shuffle the deck. And as he made blackness an acknowledged part of the American atmosphere he also brought the issue of interracial love into the country's discourse. In a culture whose successful male Negro authors wrote about interracial sex with a combination of reverence and disgust, Pryor's gleeful "fuck it" attitude had an effect on the general population that Wright's *Native Son* or Baldwin's *Another Country* had not had. His best work showed us that black men like him and the white women they loved were united in their disenfranchisement; in his life and onstage, he performed the great, largely unspoken story of America.

"I love Lily," Pryor said in a *Rolling Stone* interview with David Felton, in 1974, after "Juke and Opal" had aired and he and Tomlin had moved on to other things. "I have a thing about her, a little crush...I get in awe of her. I'd seen her on *Laugh-In* and shit, and something about her is very sensual, isn't it?"

Sensuality implies a certain physical abandonment, and an acknowledgment of the emotional mess that we try to keep from our public self. The work of the brilliant performer is to make a habit of disjunction. (One of Tomlin's early audition techniques was to tap-dance with taps taped to the soles of her bare feet.) It is difficult to find that human untidiness—what Pryor called "the madness" of everyday life—in the formulaic work now being done by the performers who ostensibly work in the same vein as Pryor and Tomlin. Compare the rawness of the four episodes of a television show that Pryor cowrote and starred in for NBC in 1977 with Tracey Ullman's last HBO show (in which she needed blackface to play a black woman): the first Pryor special opens with a close-up of his face as he announces that he has not had to compromise himself to appear on a network-sponsored show. The camera then pulls back to reveal Pryor seemingly nude but with his genitalia missing.

Pryor's art defies the very definition of the word *order*. He based his style on digressions and riffs—the monologue as jam session. He reinvented stand-up, which until he developed his signature style, in 1971, had consisted largely of borscht-belt-style male comedians telling tales in the Jewish vernacular, regardless of their own religion or background. Pryor managed to make blacks interesting to audiences that were used to responding to a liberal Jewish sensibility—and, unlike some of his colored colleagues, he did so without "becoming" Jewish himself. (Dick Gregory, for example, was a political comedian in the tradition of Mort Sahl; Bill Cosby was a droll Jack Benny.) At the height of his career, Pryor never spoke purely in the complaint mode. He was often baffled by life's complexities, but he rarely told my-wife-made-me-sleep-on-the-sofa jokes or did "bits" whose sole purpose was to "kill" an audience with a boffo punch line. Instead, he talked about characters—black street people, mostly. Because the life rhythm of a black junkie, say, implies a certain drift, Pryor's stories did not have badda-bing conclusions. Instead, they were encapsulated in a physical attitude: each character was represented in Pryor's walk, in his gestures—which always contained a kind of vicarious wonder at the lives he was enacting. Take, for instance, his sketch of a wino in Peoria, Illinois—Pryor's hometown and the land of his imagination—as he encounters Dracula. In the voice of a Southern black man, down on his luck:

Hey man, say, nigger—you with the cape...What's your name, boy? Dracula? What kind of name is that for a nigger? Where you from, fool? Transylvania? I know where it is, nigger! You ain't the smartest mother-fucker in the world, you know, even though you is the ugliest. Oh yeah, you a ugly motherfucker. Why you don't get your teeth fixed, nigger? That shit hanging all out your mouth. Why you don't get you an ortho-dontist?...This is 1975, boy. Get your shit together. What's wrong with your natural? Got that dirt all in the back of your neck. You's a filthy little motherfucker, too. You got to be home 'fore the sun come up? You ain't lyin', motherfucker. See your ass during the day, you liable to get arrested. You want to suck what? Suck some blood? Nigger, you, you some kind of freak, boy?...You ain't suckin' nothing here, junior.

Pryor's two best comedy albums, both of which were recorded during the mid- to late seventies—*Bicentennial Nigger* and *That Nigger's Crazy*—are not available on CD, but his two concert films, *Richard Pryor Live in Concert* and *Richard Pryor Live on the Sunset Strip*, which were released in 1979 and 1982, respectively, are out on video. The concert films are excellent examples of what the *Village Voice* critic Carrie Rickey once described as Pryor's ability to "scare us into laughing at his demons—our demons—exorcising them through mass hyper-ventilation." "Pryor doesn't tell jokes," she wrote, "he tells all, in the correct belief that without punch lines, humor has more punch. And pungency." Taken together, the concert films show the full panorama of Pryor's moods: brilliant, boring, insecure, demanding, misogynist, racist, playful, and utterly empathetic.

Before Richard Pryor, there were only three aspects of black maleness to be found on TV or in the movies: the suave, pimp-style blandness of Billy Dee Williams; the big-dicked, quiet machismo of the football hero Jim Brown; and the cable-knit homilies of Bill Cosby. Pryor was the first image we'd ever had of black male fear. Not the kind of Stepin Fetchit noggin-bumpin'-into-walls fear that turned Buckwheat white when he saw a ghost in the *Our Gang* comedies popular in the twenties, thirties, and forties—a character that Eddie Murphy resuscitated in a presumably ironic way in the eighties on *Saturday Night Live*. Pryor was filled with dread and panic—an existential fear, based on real things, like racism and lost love. (In a skit on *In Living Color*, the actor Damon Wayans played Pryor sitting in his kitchen and looking terrified, while a voiceover said, "Richard Pryor is scared for no reason.")

"Hi. I'm Richard Pryor." Pause. "Hope I'm funny." That was how he introduced himself to audiences for years, but he never sounded entirely convinced that he cared about being funny. Instead, Pryor embodied the voice of injured humanity. A satirist of his own experience, he revealed what could be considered family secrets—secrets about his past, and about blacks in general, and about his relationship to the black and white worlds he did and did not belong to. In the black community, correctness, political or otherwise, remains part of the mortar that holds lives together. Pryor's comedy was a high-wire act: how to stay funny to a black audience while satirizing the moral strictures that make black American life like no other.

The standard approach, in magazine articles about Pryor, has been to comment on his anger—in an imitation-colloquial language meant to approximate Pryor's voice. "Richard Pryor said it first: That Nigger's Crazy," begins a 1978 article in *People* magazine. And Pryor had fun with the uneasiness that the word *nigger* provoked in others. (Unlike Lenny Bruce, he didn't believe that if you said a word over and over again it would lose its meaning.) Take his great "Supernigger" routine: "Look up in the sky, it's a crow, it's a bat. No, it's Supernigger! Yes, friends, Supernigger, with X-ray vision that enables him to see through everything except Whitey."

In 1980, in the second of three interviews that Barbara Walters conducted with Richard Pryor, this exchange took place:

Walters: When you're onstage ... see, it's hard for me to say. I was
   going to say, you talk about niggers. I can't... you can say it.
   I can't say it.
Pryor: You just said it.
Walters: Yeah, but I feel so ...
Pryor: You said it very good.
Walters: ... uncomfortable.
Pryor: Well, good. You said it pretty good.
Walters: Okay.
Pryor: That's not the first time you said it. (*Laughter.*)

Pryor's anger, though, is actually not as interesting as his self-loathing. Given how much he did to make black pride part of American popular culture, it is arresting to see how at times his blackness seemed to feel like an ill-fitting suit. One gets the sense that he called himself a "nigger" as a kind of preëmptive strike, because he never knew when the term would be thrown at him by whites, by other blacks, or by the women he loved. Because he didn't match any of the prevailing stereotypes of "cool" black maleness, he carved out an identity for himself that was not only "nigger" but "sub-nigger." In *Live on the Sunset Strip* he wears a maraschino-red suit with silk lapels, a black shirt, and a bow tie. He says, "Billy Dee Williams could hang out in this suit and look cool." He struts. "And me?" His posture changes from cocky to pitiful.

Pryor believed that there was something called unconditional love, which he alone had not experienced. But to whom could he, a "sub-nigger," turn for that kind of love? The working-class blacks who made him feel guilty for leaving them behind? His relatives, who acted as if it was their right to hit him up for cash because he'd used their stories to make it? The white people who felt safe with him because he was neurotic—a quality they equated with intelligence? The women who married him for money or status? The children he rarely saw? He was alienated from nearly everyone and everything except his need. This drama was what made Pryor's edge so sharp. He acted out against his fantasy about love by testing it with rude, brilliant commentary. A perfect role for Pryor might have been Dostoyevsky's antihero, Alexei, in *The Gambler*, whose bemused nihilism affects every relationship he attempts. (Pryor once told Walters that he saw people "as the nucleus of a great idea that hasn't come to be yet.") That antiheroic anger prevents him from just telling a joke. He tells it through clenched teeth. He tells it to stave off bad times. He tells it to look for love.

HIS LIFE, AS A BIT

Black guy named Richard Pryor, famous, maybe a little high, appears on the eleventh Barbara Walters special, broadcast on May 29, 1979, and says this about his childhood, a sad house of cards he has glued together with wit:

> Pryor: It was hell, because I had nobody to talk to. I was a child, right, and I grew up seeing my mother…and my aunties going to rooms with men, you understand…
>
> Walters: Your grandmother ran a house of prostitution or a whorehouse.
>
> Pryor: Three houses. Three.
>
> Walters: Three houses of prostitution. She was the chief madam.
>
> Pryor: …There were no others.
>
> Walters: Okay…Who believed in you? Who cared about you?
>
> Pryor: Richard Franklin Lennox Thomas Pryor the Third.

The isolation that Richard Pryor feels is elaborated on from time to time, like a bit he can't stop reworking. The sad bit, he could call it, if he did bits anymore, his skinny frame twisting around the words to a story that goes something like this: born in Peoria, on December 1, 1940. "They called Peoria the model city. That meant they had the niggers under control." Grew up in one of the whorehouses on North Washington Street, which was the house of his paternal grandmother, Marie Carter Pryor Bryant. "She reminded me of a large sunflower— big, strong, bright, appealing," Pryor wrote in his 1995 memoir, *Pryor*

Convictions, and Other Life Sentences. "But Mama, as I also called her, was also a mean, tough, controlling bitch."

Pryor called his father's mother Mama, despite the fact that he had a mother, Gertrude. When Richard's father, Buck Carter, met Gertrude, she was already involved in Peoria's nefarious underworld, and she soon began working in Marie's whorehouse. Everything in Richard Pryor's world, as he grew up, centered on Marie, and he never quite recovered from that influence. "I come from criminal people," he told one radio interviewer. At the age of six, he was sexually abused by a young man in the neighborhood (who, after Richard Pryor became Richard Pryor, came to his trailer on a film set and asked for his autograph). And Pryor never got over the division he saw in his mother: the way she could separate her emotional self from her battered body and yet was emotionally damaged anyway.

"At least, Gertrude didn't flush me down the toilet, as some did," Pryor wrote in his memoir. "The only person scarier than God was my mother...One time Buck hit Gertrude, and she turned blue with anger and said 'Okay, motherfucker, don't hit me no more...Don't stand in front of me with fucking undershorts on and hit me, motherfucker.' Quick as lightning, she reached out with her finger claws and swiped at my father's dick. Ripped his nutsack off. I was just a kid when I saw this." Pryor records the drama as a born storyteller would—in the details. And the detail that filters through his memory most clearly is the rhythm of Gertrude's speech, its combination of profanity and rhetoric. Not unlike a routine by Richard Pryor.

Pryor soon discovered humor—the only form of manipulation he had in his community of con artists, hookers, and pimps. "I wasn't much taller than my daddy's shin when I found that I could make my family laugh," Pryor wrote.

> I sat on a railing of bricks and found that when I fell off on purpose everyone laughed, including my grandmother, who made it her job to scare the shit out of people…After a few more minutes of falling, a little dog wandered by and poo-pooed in our yard. I got up, ran to my grandmother, and slipped in the dog poop. It made Mama and the rest laugh again. Shit, I was really onto something then. So I did it a second time. "Look at that boy! He's crazy!" That was my first joke. All in shit.

When Pryor was ten years old, his mother left his father and went to stay with relatives in Springfield, Illinois, but Pryor stayed with his grandmother. In a biography by John and Dennis Williams, Pryor's teacher Marguerite Yingst Parker remembered him as "perpetually exhausted, sometimes lonely, always likable…He was a poor black kid in what was then a predominantly white school, who didn't mingle with his classmates on the playground." Pryor often got through the tedium of school by entertaining his classmates. Eventually, Parker struck a deal with him: if he got to school on time, she would give him a few minutes each week to do a routine in front of the class. Not long afterward, Pryor met Juliette Whittaker, an instructor at the Carver Community Center. "He was about eleven, but looked younger because he was such a skinny little boy. And very bright," she recalled in the Williams book. "We were rehearsing Rumpelstiltskin and he was watching. He asked if he could be in the play. I told him we only had one part left, and he said, 'I don't care. I'll take anything. I just want to be in the play.'...He took the script home and, unbeknownst to anybody, he memorized the entire thing."

When Pryor was in the eighth grade, a teacher who was fed up with his classroom routines asked him to leave school. He slowly became absorbed into the mundane working-class life that Peoria had to offer, taking a job at a packing plant, running errands. When he was seventeen, he discovered that the black woman he was seeing had also been sleeping with his father. Then, in an attempt to escape, Pryor enlisted in the army, in 1958. He was stationed in Germany, where he was involved in a racial incident: a young white soldier laughed too hard about the painful black parts in the Douglas Sirk film *Imitation of Life*, and Pryor and a number of other black inductees beat and stabbed him. Pryor went to jail, and when he was discharged, in 1960, he returned to his grandmother's twilight world of street life and women for hire.

Pryor had some idea of what he wanted to be: a comedian like the ones he had seen on TV, particularly the black comedians Dick Gregory and Redd Foxx. He began performing at small venues in Peoria, telling topical jokes in the cadence of the time: "You know how to give Mao Tse-tung artificial respiration? No. Good!" The humor then "was kind of rooted in the fifties," the comedian and actor Steve Martin told me. "Very straight jokes, you know. The dominant theme on television and in the public's eye was something Catskills. Jokes. Punch lines." And it was within that form that Pryor began to make a name for himself in the local clubs.

But Pryor was ambitious, and his ambition carried him away from

Peoria. In 1961, he left behind his first wife and their child, "because I could," and began working the nightclub circuit in places like East St. Louis, Buffalo, and Youngstown, Ohio. In 1963, he made his way to New York. "I opened *Newsweek* and read about Bill Cosby," Pryor told Donnie Simpson. "That fucked me up. I said, 'God damn it, this nigger's doin' what I'm fixin' to do. I want to be the only nigger. Ain't no room for two niggers.'" In New York, Pryor began appearing regularly at Café Wha?. By 1966, he had begun to make it nationally. He appeared on a show hosted by Rudy Vallee called *On Broadway Tonight*. Then on Ed Sullivan, Merv Griffin, and Johnny Carson—appearing each time with marcelled hair and wearing a black suit and tie that made him look like an undertaker. But his jokes were like placards that read "Joke": "When I was young I used to think my people didn't like me because they used to send me to the store for bread and then they'd move." Or "I heard a knock on the door. I said to my wife, 'There's a knock on the door.' My wife said, 'That's peculyar, we ain't got no door.'"

He was feted as the new Bill Cosby by such show-business luminaries as Bobby Darin and Sid Caesar, and other comedians and writers counseled him to keep it that way: "Don't mention the fact that you're a nigger. Don't go into such bad taste," Pryor remembers being told by a white writer called Murray Roman. "They were gonna try to help me be nothin' as best they could," he said in the *Rolling Stone* interview. "The life I was leading, it wasn't me. I was a robot. Beep. Good evening, ladies and gentlemen, welcome to the Sands Hotel. Maids are funny. Beep…I didn't feel good. I didn't feel I could tell anybody to kiss my ass, 'cause I didn't have no ass, you dig?"

A drug habit kicked in. Then, in 1967, while Pryor was doing a show in Las Vegas, he broke down. "I looked out at the audience," Pryor wrote. "The first person I saw was Dean Martin, seated at one of the front tables. He was staring right back at me…I checked out the rest of the audience. They were staring at me as intently as Dean, waiting for that first laugh…I asked myself, Who're they looking at, Rich?…And in that flash of introspection when I was unable to find an answer, I crashed…I finally spoke to the sold-out crowd: 'What the fuck am I doing here?' Then I turned and walked off the stage."

He was through with what he'd been doing: "I was a Negro for twenty-three years. I gave that shit up. No room for advancement."

In the following years—1968 through 1971—Pryor worked on material that became more or less what we know today as the Richard Pryor experience. A close friend, the comedian and writer Paul Mooney, took him to the looser, more politicized environs of Berkeley, and Pryor holed up there and wrote.

The black folklorist and novelist Zora Neale Hurston once wrote that, although she had "landed in the crib of negroism" at birth, it hadn't occurred to her until she left her hometown that her identity merited a legitimate form of intellectual inquiry. It was only after Pryor had left Peoria and wrested a certain level of success from the world that he was able to see his own negroism, and what made it unique. As Mel Watkins writes, in his book *On the Real Side: Laughing, Lying, and Signifying*, after Pryor moved to Berkeley and met the writers Cecil Brown and Ishmael Reed he discovered that "accredited intellectuals" could share "his affection and enthusiasm for the humor and lifestyles of common black folks." Pryor also discovered Malcolm

X's speeches and Marvin Gaye's album *What's Going On.* Both taught him how to treat himself as just another character in a story being told. He distanced himself from the more confessional Lenny Bruce—whose work had already influenced him to adopt a hipper approach to language—and "Richard Pryor" became no more important than the winos or junkies he talked about.

Pryor began to reconstruct himself first through the use of sound—imagining the sound of Frankenstein taking LSD, for example, or a baby "being birthed." His routines from this time regularly involved gurgles, air blown through pursed lips, beeps. He also began playing with individual words. He would stand in front of an audience and say "Goddamn" in every way he could think to say it. Or he'd say, "I feel," in a variety of ways that indicated the many different ways he could feel. And as he began to understand how he felt he began to see himself, to create his body before his audience. He talked about the way his breath and his farts smelled, what he wanted from love, where he had been, and what America thought he was.

In those years, Pryor began to create characters that were based on his own experience; he explored the territory and language of his family and his childhood—that fertile and unyielding ground that most artists visit again and again. The producer George Schlatter, who watched Pryor's transformation at a number of clubs in the late sixties and the early seventies, told me, "Richard grew up in a whorehouse. The language he used, he was entitled to it. Now the kids coming up, they use the word *fuck* and that becomes the joke. Richard used the word *fuck* on the way to the joke. It was part of his vocabulary. It was part of his life experience." As Pryor began to recall his relatives' voices, he became able to see them from the outside, not without a certain degree of fondness. "My aunt Maxine could suck a neckbone, it was a work of art," he'd say. Or:

> My father was one of them eleven o'clock niggers. [*Voice becoming more high-pitched*] Say, say, where you going, Richard? Say, huh? Well, nigger, you ain't ask nobody if you could go no place. What the fuck, you a man now, nigger? Get a job, that's what—yeah! I don't give a fuck where you go, be home by eleven. You understand eleven, don't you, nigger? You can tell time, can't you?...Eleven o'clock, bring your ass here. I don't mean down the street singing with them niggers, either. I ain't getting your ass out of jail no more, mother-fucker. That's right. [*Pause*] And bring me back a paper.

Pryor's routines became richer in depth, in imagination—rather like the characters Edgar Lee Masters created for his brilliant, problematic *Spoon River Anthology*. But the most popular and best-known of Pryor's characters—Mudbone, an old black man from Tupelo, Mississippi, whom Pryor created in 1975—also shows how a Pryor character can be too well drawn, too much of a crossover tool. Mudbone spoke with a strong Southern dialect and his tales were directly descended from the slave narratives that told (as the critic Darryl Pinckney described them) "of spirits riding people at night, of elixirs dearly bought from conjure men, chicken bones rubbed on those from whom love was wanted." From "Mudbone Goes to Hollywood":

Old Negro Man's Voice: There was an old man. His name was Mudbone…And he used to sit right here in front of the barbecue shop and he'd dip snuff…and he'd spit…He'd been in a great love affair. That right. He had a woman—he loved her very much—he had to hurt her, though, 'cause she fucked around on him. He said he knew she was fucking around 'cause I'd leave home and go to work and come back home, toilet seat be up…So I set a little old trap for her there. Went to work early, you know, always did get up early, 'cause I like to hear the birds and shit…So this particular morning, went on to work. Set my trap for this girl. She was pretty, too. Loved her. Sweet as she could be. Breast milk like Carnation milk. So I nailed the toilet seat down and doubled back and I caught that nigger trying to lift it up. So, say, Well, nigger, send your soul to heaven, 'cause your ass is mine up in here.

Mudbone was the character that Pryor's audiences requested again and again. But, as Pauline Kael noted in her review of *Live on the Sunset Strip*, Pryor became tired of him: "Voices, ostensibly from the audience, can be heard. One of them calls, 'Do the Mudbone routine,' and, rather wearily, saying that it will be for the last time, Pryor sits on a stool and does the ancient storyteller [who] was considered one of his great creations. And the movie goes thud…Pryor looks defeated."

And he should: Mudbone was the trick he turned and got tired of turning—a safe woolly-headed Negro, a comic version of Katherine Anne Porter's old Uncle Jimbilly. Compare Mudbone, for example, to the innovative and threatening *Bicentennial Nigger* character: "Some nigger two hundred years old in blackface. With stars and stripes on his forehead, lips just a-shining." "Battle Hymn" theme music, and Pryor's voice becomes Stepin Fetchit–like. "But he's happy. He happy, 'cause he been here two hundred years…Over here in America. 'I'm so glad y'all took me out of Dahomey.'" Shuckin' and jivin' laugh. "'I used to could live to be a hundred and fifty, now I dies of the high blood pressure by the time I'm fifty-two.'"

By 1973, Richard Pryor had become a force in the entertainment industry. He now appeared regularly in such diverse venues as Redd Foxx's comedy club in Central L.A., where the clientele was mostly black, and the Improv, on Sunset Strip, which was frequented by white show-business hipsters. And he behaved as badly as he wanted to wherever he wanted to—whether with women, with alcohol, or with drugs. "I got plenty of money but I'm still a nigger," he told a radio interviewer. He had become Richard Pryor, the self-described "black greasy motherfucker," whose new style of entertainment was just one of many innovations of the decade—in music (Sly and the Family Stone and the Average White Band), in acting (Lily Tomlin and Ronee Blakley), and in directing (Martin Scorsese and Hal Ashby). Cultural rebellion and political activism defined hip in Hollywood then—an era that is all too difficult to recall now.

"The idea of a black guy going out and saying he fucked a white woman was outrageous…but funny," Schlatter told me. "White women dug Richard because he was a naughty little boy, and they wanted some of that. He was talking about real things. Nobody was talking below the waist. Richard went right for the lap, man."

Pryor had directed a film called *Bon Appétit* a few years before—the footage is now lost. "The picture opened with a black maid having her pussy eaten at the breakfast table by the wealthy white man who owned the house where she worked," he recalled in *Pryor Convictions*. "Then, a gang of Black Panther types burst into the house and took him prisoner. As he was led away, the maid fixed her dress and called, 'Bon appétit, baby!'"

Each time someone asked why "that nigger was crazy," Pryor upped the ante by posing a more profound question. On a trip to a gun shop with David Felton in the early seventies, for example, Pryor asked the salesman, "How come all the targets are black?" The salesman smiled, embarrassed. "Uh, I don't know, Richard," he said, shaking his head. "I just—" "No, I mean I always wondered about that, you know?" Pryor said.

Pryor's edginess caught the attention of Mel Brooks, who was already an established Hollywood figure, and in 1972 Brooks hired him to work on a script called *Black Bart*, the story of a smooth, Gucci-wearing black sheriff in the eighteen-seventies American West. This was to be Pryor's real crossover gig, not only as a writer but as an actor, but the leading role eventually went to Cleavon Little. Whatever the reason for not casting Pryor (some people who were involved with the movie told me that no one could deal with his drinking and his drug use), there are several scenes in the film (renamed *Blazing Saddles*) that couldn't have been written by anyone else. One scene didn't make it in. It shows a German saloon singer, Lili Von Schtupp, in her darkened dressing room with Bart, whom she is trying to seduce.

Lili: Let me sit next to you. Tell me, schatzi, is it true vat zey say

about the way you people are gifted?...Oh, it's twue, it's twue,
it's twue, it's twue.

Bart: Excuse me, you're sucking my arm.

Pryor's best performances (in films he didn't write himself) date from these years. There is his poignant and striking appearance in Sidney J. Furie's 1972 film *Lady Sings the Blues*. As the Piano Man to Diana Ross's Billie Holiday, Pryor gives a performance that is as emotional and as surprising as his work in "Juke and Opal." And then there is his brilliant comic turn as Sharp Eye Washington, the disreputable private detective in Sidney Poitier's 1974 film, *Uptown Saturday Night*—a character that makes use of Pryor's ability to convey paranoia with his body: throughout the movie, he looks like a giant exclamation point. And as Zeke Brown, in *Blue Collar*, Paul Schrader's 1978 film about an automobile plant in Detroit, Pryor gives his greatest sustained— if fraught—film performance. In an interview with the writer Kevin Jackson, Schrader recalls his directorial début:

> There were...problems. Part of it was to do with Richard's style of acting. Being primarily versed in stand-up comedy he had a creative life of between three and four takes. The first one would be good, the second would be real good, the third would be terrific, and the fourth would probably start to fall off...The other thing Richard would do when he felt his performance going flat was to improvise and change the dialogue just like he would have done in front of a live audience, and he would never tell me or anyone what he was going to do.

Generally, though, Pryor had a laissez-faire attitude toward acting. One always feels, when looking at the work that he did in bad movies ranging from *You've Got to Walk It Like You Talk It* or *You'll Lose That Beat*, in 1971, to *Superman III*, released twelve years and twenty-four films later, that Pryor had a kind of contempt for these mediocre projects—and for his part in them. Perhaps no character was as interesting to Richard Pryor as Richard Pryor. He certainly didn't work hard to make us believe that he was anyone other than himself as he walked through shameful duds like *Adiós Amigo*. On the other hand, his fans paid all the love and all the money in the world to see him be himself: they fed his vanity, and his vanity kept him from being a great actor.

In September, 1977, Lily Tomlin asked Pryor to be part of a benefit at the Hollywood Bowl to oppose Proposition Six, a Californian antigay initiative. Onstage, Pryor started doing a routine about the first time he'd sucked dick. The primarily gay members of the audience hooted at first—but they didn't respond well to Pryor's frequent use of the word *faggot*. Pryor's rhythm was thrown off. "Shit...this is really weird," he exploded. "This is an evening about human rights. And I am a human being...I just wanted to test you to your motherfucking soul. I'm doing this shit for nuthin'...When the niggers were burnin' down Watts, you motherfuckers was doin' what you wanted to do on Hollywood Boulevard...didn't give a shit about the riot." And as he walked offstage: "You Hollywood faggots can kiss my happy, rich black ass."

Pryor liked to tell the truth, but he couldn't always face it himself. Although he spent years searching for an idealized form of love, his relationships were explosive and short-lived. From 1969 to 1978, he had three serious relationships or marriages—two with white women, one with a black woman—and two children. There were also affairs with film stars such as Pam Grier and Margot Kidder, and one with a drag queen. He was repeatedly in trouble for beating up women and hotel clerks. His sometimes maudlin self-involvement when a woman left him rarely involved any kind of development or growth. It merely encouraged the self-pity that informed much of his emotional life.

By the late seventies, Pryor was freebasing so heavily that he left his bedroom only to go to work and even then only if he could smoke some more on the set. He was even more paranoid than he'd always been and showed very little interest in the world. The endless cycle of dependence—from the drinking to the coke to the other drugs he needed to come down from the coke—began to destroy his health. Then, in 1980, he tried to break the cycle by killing himself. He wrote his own account of the episode in *Pryor Convictions*:

> After free-basing without interruption for several days in a row, I wasn't able to discern one day from the next…"I know what I have to do," I mumbled. "I've brought shame to my family…I've destroyed my career. I know what I have to do."…I reached for the cognac bottle on the table in front of me and poured it all over me. Real natural, methodical. As the liquid soiled my body and clothing, I wasn't scared…I was in a place called There…I picked up my Bic lighter…WHOOSH! I was engulfed in flame…Sprinting down the driveway, I went out the gates and ran down the street…Two cops tried to help me…My hands and face were already swollen. My clothes burnt in tatters. And my smoldering chest smelled like a

burned piece of meat…"Is there?" I asked. "Is there what?" someone asked. "Oh Lord, there is no help for a poor widow's son, is there?"

Pryor was in critical condition at the Sherman Oaks Community Hospital for six weeks. When Jennifer Lee—a white woman, whom he married a year later—went to visit him, he described himself as a "forty-year-old burned-up nigger." And, in a sense, Pryor never recovered from his suicide attempt. *Live on the Sunset Strip*, which came out three years later, is less a pulled-together performance than the performance of a man trying to pull himself together. He could no longer tell the truth. He couldn't even take the truth. And, besides, people didn't want the truth (a forty-year-old burned-up nigger). They wanted Richard Pryor—"sick," but not ill.

WHITE HONKY BITCH

Jennifer Lee was born and grew up in Cropseyville, New York, one of three daughters of a wealthy lawyer. In her twenties, she moved to L.A. to become an actress, had affairs with Warren Beatty and Roman Polanski, and appeared in several B movies. She met Pryor in 1977, when she was hired to help redecorate his house. "We sat on an oversized brass bed in Richard's house," she wrote in an article for *Spin* magazine. "He was blue—heartsick over a woman who was 'running game' on him. He was putting a major dent in a big bottle of vodka.

You could feel the tears and smell the gardenias, even with hip, white-walled nasal passages." Since that day, she told me, laughing, she has always been "the head bitch."

As Jennifer talked with me that afternoon, dressed in black leather pants and a black blazer, her white skin made even whiter by her maroon lipstick, I thought of the photographs I had seen of her with Pryor, some of which were reproduced in her 1991 memoir, *Tarnished Angel: Surviving in the Dark Curve of Drugs, Violence, Sex and Fame: A Memoir.* These images were replaced by others: the white actress Shirley Knight berating Al Freeman Jr., in the film version of Amiri Baraka's powerful play, *Dutchman,* and Diane Arbus's haunting photograph of a pregnant white woman and her black husband sitting on a bench in Washington Square Park in the sixties. Then I thought of Pryor's routines on inter-racial sex. From "Black Man/White Woman":

Don't ever marry a white woman in California. A lot of you sisters probably saying "Don't marry a white woman anyway, nigger." [*Pause*] Shit…Sisters look at you like you killed yo' mama when you out with a white woman. You can't laugh that shit off, either. [*High-pitched, fake-jovial voice*] "Ha-ha, she's not with me."

From a routine entitled "Black & White Women":

There really is a difference between white women and black women. I've dated both. Yes, I have…Black women, you be suckin' on their pussy and they be like, "Wait, nigger, shit. A little more to the left, motherfucker. You gonna suck the motherfucker, get down." You can fuck white women and if they don't come they say, "It's all right, I'll just lay here and use a vibrator."

Pryor was not only an integrationist but an integrationist of white women and black men, one of the most taboo adult relationships. The judgments that surround any interracial couple: White girls who are into black dudes are sluts. White dudes aren't enough for them; only a big-dicked black guy can satisfy them. Black dudes who are into white girls don't like their kind. And, well, you know how they treat their women: they abuse them; any white girl who goes out with one is a masochist. The air in America is thick with these misconceptions, and in the seventies it was thicker still. Plays and films like *A Taste of Honey*, *A Patch of Blue*, *Deep Are the Roots*, *All God's Chillun Got Wings*, and *The Great White Hope* gave a view of the black man as both destroyer and nursemaid to a galaxy of white women who were sure to bring him down. But no real relationships exist in these works. The black male protagonists are more illustration than character. (Though they make excellent theatrical agitprop: what a surplus of symbols dangles from their mythic oversized penises!) In his work, Pryor was one of the first black artists to unknot the narrative of that desire and to expose it. In life he had to live through it as painfully as anyone else.

When Jennifer Lee first slept with Pryor, she told me, she touched his hair and he recoiled: its texture was all the difference in the world between them. That difference is part of the attraction for both members of interracial couples. "Ain't no such thing as an ugly white woman," says a character in Eldridge Cleaver's 1968 polemic, *Soul on Ice*. In some ways Pryor found it easier to be involved with white women than with black women: he could blame their misunderstandings on race, and he could take advantage of the guilt they felt for what he suffered as a black man.

Yet, while Pryor may have felt both attracted by and ashamed of his difference from Lee, he also pursued her through all his drug blindness and self-absorption because he saw something of himself in her. "What no one gets," Lee told me, "is that one of the ways Richard became popular was through women falling in love with him—they saw themselves in him, in his not fitting in, the solitude of it all, and his willingness to be vulnerable as women are. And disenfranchised, of course, as women are." That black men and white women were drawn to each other through their oppression by white men was a concept I had first seen expressed in the feminist Shulamith Firestone's book *The Dialectic of Sex: A Case for Feminist Revolution*. There is a bond in oppression, certainly, but also a rift because of it—a contempt for the other who marks you as different—which explains why interracial romance is so often informed by violence. Cleaver claimed that he raped white women because that was the only kind of empowerment he could find in his brutal world. At times, Pryor directed a similar rage at Jennifer Lee, and she, at times, returned it.

Life in the eighties: Pryor gets up. Does drugs. Drives over to the Comedy Store to work out a routine. Has an argument with Jennifer after a party. Maybe they fly to Hawaii. Come back in a week or so. Some days, Pryor is relaxed in his vulnerability. Other days, he tries to throw her out of the car. Richard's Uncle Dickie says about Jennifer, who is from an Irish family, "Irish are niggers turned inside out." Richard says about Jennifer, "The tragedy was that Jennifer could keep up with me." And she did. They married in 1981. They divorced in 1982.

With Lee, Pryor took the same trajectory that he had followed with many women before her. He began with a nearly maudlin reverence for her beauty and ended with paranoia and violence. In *Tarnished Angel*, Lee describes Pryor photographing her as she was being sexually attacked by a drug dealer he hung out with—a lowlife in the tradition of the people he had grown up with. Pryor could be brutally dissociative and sadistic, especially with people he cared about: he did not separate their degradation from his own. He was also pleased when Lee was jealous of the other women he invariably became involved with. And when she left him, she claims, he stalked her.

Pryor got married again in 1986, to Flynn BeLaine, two years after she'd given birth to his son Steven. Lee moved back to New York, where she wrote a challenging review of Pryor's film *Jo Jo Dancer, Your Life Is Calling*, for *People*:

Well, Richard, you blew it. I went to see *Jo Jo Dancer*...I went looking for the truth, the real skinny. Well, guess what? It wasn't there...How sad. After all, it was you who was obsessed by the truth, be it onstage or in your private life...You had no sacred cows. That's why I fell in love with you, why I hung in through the wonder and madness...Listen to your white honky bitch, Richard: Ya gotta walk it like you talk it or you'll lose that beat.

But later the same year, when Lee interviewed Pryor for *Spin*, they had reached a kind of détente:

Lee: What about the rage, the demons?
Pryor: They don't rage much anymore.
Lee: Like a tired old monster?
Pryor: Very tired. He hath consumed me.
Lee: Has this lack of rage quieted your need to do stand-up?
Pryor: Something has. I'm glad it happened after I made money.

Pryor had gone sober in 1983 and he soon recognized that, along with alcohol, he needed to relinquish some of the ruthless internal navigations that had given his comedy its power. He performed live less and less. There were flashes of the old brilliance: on *Johnny Carson*, for example, when he responded to false rumors that he had AIDS. And when his public raised its fickle refrain—"He's sick, he's washed up"—he often rallied, but in the last eight years of his performing life he became a more conventional presence.

Pryor divorced Flynn in 1991, and in 1994 he placed a call to Jennifer. He was suffering from degenerative multiple sclerosis, he told her, and wouldn't be able to work much longer. "He said, 'My life's a mess. Will you help me out?'" she recalls. "I thought long and hard about it...I wasn't sure it would last, because Richard loves to manipulate people and see them dance. But, see, he can't do that anymore, because he finally bottomed. That's the only reason Richard is allowing his life to be in any kind of order right now."

Lee came back to Pryor in July of that year. "When I got there, he was in this ridiculous rental for, like, six thousand dollars a month," she told me. "Five bedrooms, seven bathrooms. Honey, it was classic. You couldn't write it better." Lee helped him to find a smaller house in Encino, and she has cared for him since then. He had two care-givers and was bathed and dressed in a collaborative effort that had shades of Fellini. He spent his final days in a custom-made wheelchair while others read to him or gave him physical or speech therapy. Every Friday, he went to the movies. According to Lee, he could speak well when he wanted to, but he didn't often want to. "Sometimes he'll say, 'Leave me the fuck alone, Jenny,'" she told me, laughing. "Just the other day, Richard was sitting, staring out the window, and his care-giver said, 'Mr. Richard, what are you thinking about?' He said, 'I'm thinking about how much money I pay all you motherfuckers.'" He didn't see his children much, or his other ex-wives, or the people he knew when he still said things like "I dig show business. I do…I wake up every morning and I kiss it. Show business, you fine bitch."

BLUE MOVIE

"Was that corny?" Lily Tomlin once said to me when I told her I'd heard that certain CBS executives hadn't wanted her to kiss Pryor good-night at the close of *Lily*, back in 1973. After all, Pryor was then a disreputable black comic with an infamous foul mouth, and Lily Tomlin had just come from *Laugh-In*, where she had attracted nationwide attention. Tomlin kissed him anyway, and it was, I think, the first time I had ever seen a white woman kiss a black man—I was twelve—and it was almost certainly the first time I had ever seen Richard Pryor.

Tomlin and I were sitting with Jane Wagner, her partner and writer for thirty years, in a Cuban restaurant—one of their favorite places in Los Angeles. Tomlin and Wagner were the only white people there.

"We just loved Richard," Tomlin told me. "He was the only one who could move you to tears. No one was funnier, dearer, darker, heavier, stronger, more radical. He was everything. And his humanity was just glorious."

"What a miracle "Juke and Opal" got on," Wagner said. "The network treated us as if we were total political radicals. I guess we were. And they hated Richard. They were so threatened by him."

CBS had insisted that Tomlin and Wagner move "Juke and Opal" to the end of the show, so that people wouldn't switch channels in the middle, bringing down the ratings. "It threw the whole shape of the show off," Tomlin recalled in a 1974 interview. "It made "Juke and Opal" seem like some sort of Big Message, which is not what I intended...I wasn't out to make any, uh, heavy statements, any real judgments."

"Everybody kept saying it wasn't funny, but we wanted to do little poems. I mean, when you think of doing a drug addict in prime time!" Wagner told me. And what they did is a poem of sorts. It was one of the all too few opportunities that Tomlin had to show-case, on national television, the kind of performance she and Pryor pioneered.

"Lily and Richard were a revolution, because they based what they did on real life, its possibilities," Lorne Michaels, the producer of *Saturday Night Live*, told me. "You couldn't do that kind of work now on network television, because no one would understand it…Lily and Richard were the exemplars of a kind of craft. They told us there was a revolution coming in the field of entertainment, and we kept looking to the left, and it didn't come."

It is odd to think that Richard Pryor's period of pronounced popularity and power lasted for only a decade, really—from 1970 to 1980. But comedy is rock and roll, and Pryor had his share of hits. The enormous territory he carved out for himself remains more or less his own. Not that it hasn't been scavenged by other comedians: Eddie Murphy takes on Pryor's belligerent side, Martin Lawrence his fearful side, Chris Rock his hysteria, Eddie Griffin his ghoulish goofiness. But none of these comedians approaches Pryor's fundamental strangeness, vulnerability, or political intensity. Still, their work demonstrates the power of his influence: none of them would exist at all were it not for Richard Pryor. The actor Richard Belzer described him to me as "the ultimate artistic beacon." "It was like he was the sun and we were planets," Belzer said. "He was the ultimate. He took socially complex situations and made you think about them, and yet you laughed. He's so brilliantly funny, it was revelatory. He's one of those rare people who define a medium."

According to Lee, Pryor had been approached by a number of artists who saw something of themselves in him. Damon Wayans and Chris Rock wanted to star in a film version of Pryor's life. The Hughes brothers expressed interest in making a documentary. In

1998, the Kennedy Center gave Pryor its first Mark Twain Prize, and Chevy Chase, Whoopi Goldberg, Robin Williams, and others gathered to pay tribute to him. Pryor's written acceptance of the award, however, shows a somewhat reluctant acknowledgment of his status as an icon: "It is nice to be regarded on par with a great white man— now that's funny!" he wrote. "Seriously, though, two things people throughout history have had in common are hatred and humor. I am proud that, like Mark Twain, I have been able to use humor to lessen people's hatred!"

In some ways, Pryor probably realized that his legendary status has weakened the subversive impact of his work. People are quick to make monuments of anything they live long enough to control. It's not difficult to see how historians will view him in the future. An edgy comedian. A Mudbone. But will they take into account the rest of his story: that essentially American life, full of contradictions; the life of a comedian who had an excess of both empathy and disdain for his audience, who exhausted himself in his search for love, who was a confusion of female and male, colored and white, and who acted out this internal drama onstage for our entertainment.

YOU AND WHOSE ARMY?

SOME FAMOUS PEOPLE get cancer. That's a look. Other famous peo-ple—my brother, for one—get MS, and that's a look, too. But the attitude I can't take is the one that says you better sympathize. Like when a famous acting bitch gets pregnant. Bitch plays her condition up like it's Mother Superior time. You've seen it on *Access Hollywood*, on the TV: Bitch pushes that baby out and Hollywood acts like she ain't ever laid down with dogs, gotten up with fleas, and bitten their heads off. In the press, she's pressed, correct, done, 'cause she's living the right way: Mrs. Morality.

Acting has come to this: engaging less in make-believe than in making a bad carbon copy of reality. All an actress needs to do to get a little juice these days is give up on being an actress and take on the real-life role of wife. Or mother. I never got to that. I always preferred playing myself.

Famous Bitch says in an interview (*simpering voice*): "Well, even though I done sucked off every piece of trade from Hollywood to wherever to get what I wanted, I'm pure now—I have a child." I say, is this a woman? She goes on: "Oh, no, I could never do that now"—be it drugs, going down on a girl producer, whatever—ever since she's given birth to innocence. Breasts leaking, she could feed a nation. I say, is this a woman?

Uh-huh, especially when she's a so-called actress. For them, the world is a photo op too great to give up once it's been gotten. There she is, working the phone lines on TV telethons, raising funds for the surviving family members of this or that whatever. Fuck *Medea*. Fuck doing rep. Tell today's acting bitch where America's axis of sentiment is turning, and she'll turn that way as well.

I won't live long enough to learn how to play that part. I'm sixty-four. And look what I got. A half-assed career. Laughter. Many faggots on my phone: That's hysterical.

Aren't the queens fabulous? They don't want much: an orgasm and a cocktail. And all they want from an always-looking-for-a-job acting bitch like me is that I be fierce, go to premieres, be. And I love it. Love their demands. Helps keep my shit rigorous. Don't get it twisted, though—a queen will find the holes in a bitch's fishnets. They just won't try to kill you for being different.

Sometimes, at the video store, in the rock-and-cock section, I rent what the boys are doing, just to stay in touch. I love those dolls. I take those tapes home and watch assholes puckering. Leather straps. The pizza boy, the pool boy. Drama and attitude and then the cock shot.

I'm in a similar business. I do voice-overs for porn films. I'm an artist of sorts—a Foley artist for rock-and-cock movies. Split snatch, too. My voice goes both ways—male and female. My mind goes both ways, too. I've been at it for nearly twenty years now, ever since Richard failed me for the last time. In a sense, he and I are in the same business: talking dirty. But that was his choice. This is my survival.

I have appeared—if voices appear, and they do—in everything from *Fags in Love, Fags on Vacation* (1992) to *Mystic's Pizza* (2001). You've felt yourself while you've felt me doing Polish accents. Or anal discomfort. The old gag and sputter when it comes to oral. I do it all.

No one does it better, either. (I've twice won the porn industry's highest honor, the Hot D'Or, for Best Sound, Oral Division.) No one does it better because no one in the business I'm in believes what we do has anything to do with acting. But it does, because acting is convincing folks to feel something. And you've felt yourself while I made the sounds that made you feel something.

Just recently I did a scene where the woman—a skinny white girl who looked like she'd just been shipped in from Estonia—was getting spanked and rimmed by a trannie who may or may not have also (at least in the movie) been her uncle. The director couldn't get the money shot right. Not the close-up or the cum, but the sound of joy and pain that the girl onscreen needed to make while her uncle ate her ass, her face buried in a pillow, a few sparkles from out of nowhere on the small of her back.

So I searched what I had been once and when I could have made a sound like that, just to add a little reality to the scene. Background.

* * *

I went looking for it blindly, like a mole distressed by hunger. I tapped into a little memory of pain and confusion, the high drama of it. I'm in the kitchen with my mother and some of her friends. We are in Peoria, Illinois. The time: the late nineteen forties. I may have been four or five, I can't remember. I may have been standing in between my mother's legs. If I am, she has just washed my hair and is greasing it. She had to be doing something. She didn't just sit down and hold you. This was back in the day when grooming a child was as sincere a form of attention as a black mother could muster, mammy myths to the contrary. I am bearing the weight and sound of her circling hands working and working the grease into my scalp, the warmth, the grease, the murmur of voices rising and falling, fighting the need for sleep. The two or three other women in the kitchen are doing what women do: creating an atmosphere of domesticity that could shift, at any moment, into an atmosphere of violence. Snapping peas and then threatening to break some errant child's neck. The story they tell—it sounds like a round—is a story they like telling and elaborating on, when they can. It reminds them of when they were young and nothing had run out, least of all time. The story goes: Once, long ago, they knew a girl, very beautiful, who had a great love. He was handsome and had sworn his heart to this young beauty early on. Before they could marry, though, he was drafted into the service. World War II. He made it through, four years, and he came back home afterward, after saving all those Jews. He had a part in his hair. He was with his girl in her mother's kitchen, a celebratory dinner. His girl had curlers on; she was wearing a pair of pedal pushers. She was sitting on her mother's blue-and-white-enamel-topped table. To impress his love, the young man showed her a gun, something called a Luger; he had smuggled it out of Germany. The young man had assumed the safety was on, but it wasn't.

I remember thinking back then: So this is love: happiness burning on the stove while a section of the dead girl's flesh smoked, too. I wondered, then, where the fatal wound had been inflicted. Her chest? Her stomach? None of the women ever said. But as they talked, they provided the voice-over and the laugh track to my imagining the dazed and inconsolable lover being led away in handcuffs, the great outpouring of Negress sympathy that met him as his part grew in, behind bars. The girls who had known the accidental murderer and his dead lover grew into women, visiting him in jail, taking him fresh-baked pies with no files in them. They carried those pies and new gossip, tightly wrapped in their white scented handkerchiefs, right up to the grille, all in love.

Of course, underneath their sympathy, they visited him out of envy. By not shooting them all, he had indirectly denied them their tragic heroism; no one would ever talk about those women in the way he remembered and talked about that dead girl. All they'd been left to was cooking and eventual bitterness. They didn't even keep up with that man when he was released from prison; they couldn't put their fantasies on him in the free world, so they weren't interested.

I thought about all that. And then I went into the booth and did my part. And I nailed it.

There's this trend—have you noticed?—of boys who are into bare-backing. Fucking without a condom. Cum dripping out of that pink-brown hole, cum dumped there with no thought of the scum bucket dying. People tell me there are clubs devoted to this activity, people taking cum, others giving it. Most of the movies I've seen featuring this practice are set in Palm Springs, for some reason.

When I watch those films I look less at the men shooting shit into gaping holes than I do at the boys on the other end—something else to identify with. The men shooting shit—that's what men do. But what about the queens who walk away with the Condition because of the shit so to speak that's shot into them? It's the doll lying on her back, maybe acting, but I don't think so, saying, "Give it to me, Daddy, Daddy give it to me," that has me upset. Does that make them more fabulous? Their gayness more real? I say, are they actresses?

Maybe those barebacking queens are saying they literally put their ass on the line for a part. Acting is acting and I'm using what I've got and I needed to play the part of bottom bitch for whatever reason. Maybe they're saying, opening their assholes up: AIDS is my Oscar.

Those bitches dripping cum, eyes dead, but still looking for the cameraman's key light: that's what happens when you're an actress. All an actress is ever saying: Look at me, even as I'm dying.

Love is complicated, if it exists.

Stanislavski wrote that acting was an "if." And that "if" was synony-mous with intention. Let's say you're playing X. X must want something from Y. Trying to convince your stage or film lover that they must run off with you in order to prove that they do indeed love you, for example. That's the part about acting that has always confused me: my intention. I have never had one, other than to be an actress. I could never imagine wanting anything except the praise of the queens who loved me when I first started out, and who love me still. Me: a black, uninhabitable rock with maybe a couple of talking birds pausing on it in the middle of the sea.

Aren't the tech boys fabulous?

When I go to work I'm treated like the star they know I am. They get me a glass of water or anything else I need before setting me up in the booth, facing the screen. I put my script on a stand. The tech boys make sure my headphones are clear, free of earwax. I'm the Marni Nixon of the gash-and-gnash set.

There in the booth, I stand in front of the microphone until I feel I've found the voice I need. And when I do feel it, I give the cue to roll tape. A director is rarely, if ever, present nowadays. No need, no need. I've been doing this so long, no one can tell me how to do it more real than it needs to be. I'm an actress.

My friend Charles got me into all of this. There we were in L.A., in the mid-seventies, broke and brotherless, and Charles got me work doing some looping for a B movie he was in. Something by Roger Corman. They needed a girl to approximate the offscreen sound of Charles fucking a girl in a motel room. One thing led to another, I met one person and then another; I established a reputation. So far, I've survived. Porn shot on film and then on video; nice seventies pussy hair and then shaved, babylike snatch; Tom Selleck lookalike mustaches and butt-fucking against a black velvet scrim followed by what we've got now: barebacking in Palm Springs. I stick to what the audience needs, which doesn't really change all that much.

I like to mix it up, though. Throw in portions of myself—my thinking—into my characters' voices, when I can. The other day, I came across a tape I did some work on: *Mandingo Makes Manhattan* (1983). The film is a little riff on *Roots*. The protagonist is Kunta Kinte Johnson. He's black, naturally, and does a number of white or mulatto-looking women. The director asked me to supply a few of the requisite oohs and aahs for Kunta and the colored women. He wanted those oohs and aahs performed in the Negro style—all guttural, like a funky urban chorus. As it happens, I find Negro and Puerto Rican voices difficult to perform. Their performances—if that's the word—are so stilted. Not to get all Mary McLeod Bethune about it, but since those people are looked at in the wrong way most of the time, they can't fuck in a way that lends itself to the viewer's imagination. They're too self-conscious, too mindful of the camera. They act like people in a documentary.

Maybe they're too vulnerable to the whole enterprise. When you watch fucking, you want to be the one to take off the girl's (or boy's) clothes with your eyes, your imagination. What you don't want is for the fuckers to make you feel as if not only shouldn't you be stroking, but you should be in church, or contributing a little something to Planned Parenthood.

Rarely do the visuals in my work bother me, but something—a pile of sick—wells up in my stomach when I watch all those black and Latin people fucking. Maybe they remind me of my brother. Maybe they're not my type.

*   *   *

Of course, there are certain tonal facts about my voice that I can't ignore. I am a Negress. As such, I have a great deal of bass in my speech that cuts girlishness off at the pass. In addition, being a black American, I make of English what I will, since it's not, historically speaking, my first language. Or, to put it another way, I have made of English a form of American that other Americans don't speak, because they don't have the confluence of history and genetics that I do. It's interesting.

I think the best vocal interpreters of Gertrude Stein's work, for instance, are people like me, since we get her form and her brilliant, protracted insight that American makes no sense to begin with. It lies too much, just like her bastard son—artistically speaking, anyway—Richard Pryor.

I was able to infuse some of my disgust—similar to the disgust I feel about today's acting bitches, marriage, my brother—into *Mandingo Makes Manhattan*. In the film you see two blacks—a man and a woman, named Kunta and Re-Re—fucking. Re-Re is called Micro-Pussy behind her back, because she can't take all of Kunta's quite considerable dick. So: white sheets. Lube and pussy juice shining in the key light. Then you hear me. I say, as Kunta, pushing my dick into Re-Re, panting: "Can I go deep?" And then I say, as Re-Re: "No." But as Kunta you can hear me go deeper anyway. Playing Re-Re, I object: "I told you no. Hey!" They fuck some more. And then a kind of haiku laid out, as it were, in philosophical terms:

KUNTA: Nigger, I ain't going deep.

RE-RE: Nigger, how in the fuck you gonna tell me?

KUNTA: 'Cause I'm looking at my dick, all right?

RE-RE: You ain't in my pussy, either.

KUNTA: I am in your pussy.

RE-RE: No, I'm in my pussy. I can feel how deep you going, nigger.

KUNTA: No, your pussy is yours. I'm in your pussy.

RE-RE: So, I know how deep you're going, so back up. I'm serious.

KUNTA: Look, Re-Re.

RE-RE: Nigger.

They fuck. Then:

RE-RE: Come on, nigger, hurry up.

He comes.

It wasn't until I'd listened to this again recently that I thought how many of the feelings you'd like me to express about my brother are expressed there, depending on how you listen.

I love my work.

It provides me with certain necessities. This so-so apartment in West Hollywood (the walls are too pink, though; I'm not thrilled about the constant sunlight). The requisite car. Stamps to put on the envelopes to mail the bills.

On the job, technical problems arise from time to time—a glitch in the projection, audio wires crossed—but that interests me, too. The downtime provides me with more time to read. I am an actress, and, as such, much of life is made up of waiting, reading, looking for characters to imagine playing in the books I read while waiting to be told whom to be.

An actress's job description is this: the search for self through words, characters, and situations that are not your own. Another reason I could never be a star: I lack a fundamental interest in finding the phrases that fit my personality. Because that's what stars do: find the parts that define their personality further. Kate Hepburn is Jo in *Little Women*, that kind of thing. Had I been young enough in the eighties, or interested enough, when women were shoving yams up their twats while talking about the patriarchy or what have you—well, maybe I would have gotten somewhere, talking about a brother. But all of that was as distasteful to me then as my need for you to listen to all this is now.

I like metaphors. I like history. It plays tricks on my mind as I stand in the recording booth, watching whatever. Faces grimacing in some hotel room in Cleveland or wherever with no sound or the wrong sound coming out, waiting for me to correct them—those faces are bracketed in my mind with soldiers in the trenches in World War I, men dressed in green woolen coats, pith helmets, bandages tied around their calves, the gas about to disfigure their enemy's eyes, his mouth, melt the skin.

I don't know what makes my mind work that way, makes my eyes see the things it sees. I grew up with books—there were so many people, all of them talking, that reading was my only way out then.

You know the facts: me and my brother, Richard Pryor, were raised in Peoria, Illinois. I was born in 1938, a little bit before the war started, Richard in 1940, a year before Pearl Harbor. Our mother was a whore. Our grandmother ran a whorehouse. Our father loved them both. Pussy was the family business. There was so much pussy around, I used to wonder: Do I have a pussy, too? And: If I have a pussy, will that make me a whore? I used to sit in the corner of our grandmama's living room, playing with my titty and eating a honeybun, waiting for somebody to love me the right way, like anybody knew what that was.

I'm reluctant to talk to people like you, a reporter, because Richard talked to you all all the time. And the shit he didn't tell you he talked about in his act. Maybe that's one reason I became an actress: to be free in a different way than my brother was free, spewing his guts that way. My freedom comes when I have another name, a different voice. Same as when I was a kid. Everybody was involved in the real-life drama of living in that house; everybody talked and talked. Living there, I could barely hear myself feel. Books were my release.

Everybody said how white I was, reading the world. But after I was in the world, white people didn't believe how much I'd read; that's not what a black bitch is supposed to do. Heh. The stories, the characters I found when I was a little girl—they told me how I could live if I busted out of all that pussy and death.

I've decided to close the book on a real white woman, though. She's the enemy of sisters like myself. You know her. There are enough famous photographs of that writer dressed in linens and hats, that long face a kind of weeping willow of thought—Virginia Woolf, also known as Suicide Bitch.

In some of the pictures I've seen, she's surrounded by homos. I hear that. But what I can no longer hear is people in your line of work going on about her meaning. Her feminism. Her process of intellection. Her mean-spiritedness, which passes as a kind of high literary style. To me, her life and work taste as insulting as the toe jam not looked after before the foot is shoved in some unsuspecting lover's mouth. As a woman, I've tasted it. As a woman saddled with a famous brother, I know more about what she thinks she's writing about than she'll ever understand. Her name—don't make me say it again—sounds as ugly to me as you asking after Richard.

In *A Room of One's Own*, she writes a kind of fairy tale. She says, What if Shakespeare had a sister named Judith and the sister's brilliance went unrecognized because she had to take care of everyone else? Had to mother a father and look after the cutlery? Suicide Bitch probably made Shakespeare's sister up because she never knew a bitch—including herself—whose gifts were obscured by any living man. But I have. I've tasted nothing but what she thinks she's talking about. I am the contemporary Shakespeare's sister. Except instead of saying "Fear it, Ophelia, fear it my dear sister / And keep you in the rear of your affection / Out of the shot and danger of desire," Richard said something like, "My daddy told me once, 'Boy, whatever you do, don't eat no pussy.' I couldn't wait to eat a pussy." Did that destroy me? I survived. Suicide Bitch would never have the slightest interest in women like me, women who endure a brother's fame and emerge from its jaws mangled but intact. That would be too complicated for her reason.

But to continue. Buried in *A Room of One's Own* is this line: "It is one of the great advantages of being a woman that one can pass even a very fine Negress without wishing to make an Englishwoman of her." I took this to mean: Who gives a shit about a colored bitch; your invisibility is your freedom. I agree. I do voice-overs in front of actors who don't even know I'm there. But why does Suicide Bitch have to drag a Negress into it? Because that black bitch by definition tells a white bitch who she is.

Listen, my job depends on my physical invisibility but never my absence. My voices are real because I believe in them enough to apply my interior voice to their reason. I resent Suicide Bitch. I resent her talking about me as though I wasn't in the room.

In something else, about *Middlemarch* and *Jane Eyre*, Suicide Bitch wrote, "We are conscious not merely of the writer's character...we are conscious of a woman's presence—of someone resenting the treatment of her sex and pleading for its rights." She goes on:

> This brings into women's writing an element which is entirely absent from a man's, unless, indeed, he happens to be a working man, a Negro, or one who for some other reason is conscious of disability. It introduces a distortion and is frequently the cause of weakness. The desire to plead some personal cause or to make a character a mouthpiece of some personal discontent or grievance

always has a distressing effect, as if the spot at which the reader's attention is directed were suddenly twofold instead of single.

Looking at the kettle calling the snatch black, I blanch. If there's anyone we can hold at least partially responsible for the mealy-mouthed nonthink that permeates contemporary women's writing, let alone their lives—all of us Negroes!—it's her. Everything she ever wrote was infused with special pleading for her genius, her madness, her Leonard.

And anyway, what's an artist but a mouthpiece for his or her sensibility? Look at Richard. And actually, Suicide Bitch is just the kind of girl Richard would like—imagine Richard fucking Suicide Bitch! Talk about riding Miss Daisy! Talk about a joke that would play well under layers of voice-overs. I saw him with someone like her so many times: a homely white girl who grew even more smug under his hetero heaving. I hated the black girls who became enamored of Richard even more. They all had terrible voices, the kind of voices that made my ear ache with their flat whininess, their mean, competitive, cunty femininity. Those black girls, their talk was imitation talk. And the sound they were imitating—are imitating still, for all I know—was the sound of white girls whose hair and career they envied.

You see a lot of those types of black girls in Hollywood now. They're jumping out of airplanes every other second and then heading straight for the hills, looking for a male star who'll make them a star, too, while keeping their eye out for that white girl to hate.

Maybe Suicide Bitch would be too much for Richard. They were too much alike: one big "I" insisting on their reality. I'd like to fuck some truth into Suicide Bitch, if I could get it up. I could tell her a thing or two, while I humped her, about what Shakespeare's sister really felt like, my hot breath on her dead white face, saying: I lived, this is what happened, all of life is imagined and made into art so that I can bear it.

Aren't the old songs the best?

When we were little, Richard and I used to sit in Mama's yard and sing:

Salty dog, salty dog
I don't wanna be your Annie doll
Honey, let me be your salty dog
Candyman

Two old maids
Sittin' in the sand
One were a she
The other were a man
Salty dog
Candyman

Worst day I ever had in my life
My best friend caught him kissin' his wife
Salty dog
Candyman

The lyrics tickled our noses like sand. We laughed so hard when we came to "Two old maids…One were a she / the other were a man," because back then, when we were certain that time would never use us and spit us out, we knew we'd never end up being anybody's old maid.

We were sitting in the grass when we sang, and Mama wasn't technically our mother; she was our grandmother, our father's mother. Our daddy never had a chance with a mother like that. Even though she was a whoremonger, Mama was a woman of such enormous efficiency that she swept any ambition our parents might have had under the rug, like dust.

As I started to tell you before, in the nineteen thirties Mama—me and Richard's grandmother—owned one of the most popular cathouses in town. (She didn't close up shop until forty years later, when Richard hit.) She absorbed her children into the business. First she had Daddy working for her, running errands: picking up Kotex for the whores (there were about five girls who lived with us, aside from our mother and grandmother), finding doctors who would kill babies. By the time he was sixteen, my daddy was a baby pimp.

When he met our mother, he was in his early twenties. She was sixteen, a pretty girl he knew from around. He didn't even have to seduce her into giving her pussy up. The promise of his love made her do it. But Daddy didn't love her anymore afterward. She was always looking for the right wrong person to do that.

It was like growing up in show business. I never knew anything else. Daddy was the kind of man who was so stunned by his mother's formidable presence that he used to grind his teeth as she shaped dough into ovals on a Sunday. Other times she carried a knife around and he lived in fear of his own face. Often he looked like the fear you hear in Richard's voice, in one of his routines. Skittish, like he's telling a joke—on Mama. And she's waiting offstage to give him the back of her hand, by way of a little colored criticism.

Richard loved Mama. Her control. She was a star who dominated everything around her. I think he was hell-bent on becoming a star in order to duplicate her power, but he never had her inside strength. He thought that by imitating her image, he'd be a Mama, too, but he was always too lovesick for that, and not nearly as ruthless. He was much more like our real mother.

Richard went off to the army when he was eighteen, right after he found out that Daddy had been fucking some girl Richard loved. Daddy got that girl pregnant, but the girl lied and told Richard it was his. As I've said before, the business I'm in now—nasty talk—it's a family tradition. Lies, too. Daddy hated Richard as much as he hated his own mother. To him, his son was just another woman: charismatic and awful.

Eventually my brother came to stay with me in New York for a while, after I moved there looking for work as an actress. Did anyone tell you that? That was in the sixties. He got a few TV spots; he wore black pencil suits; he was a less-menacing-for-all-his-jocularity Bill Cosby. In the late sixties, right before he found his voice and blew up, he moved to California. And in the hope that his star would confer some star status on me, I followed him out there. For the record: he let me into his house for a bit, but not his career. I haven't seen him in more than thirty years. When we were kids, it was like we were married. Now I call him my wuzband.

*   *   *

As it happens, she wasn't wedded to anything. As it happens, she lived in a way that suggested she could pull up stakes at any moment and hit the road—to join a traveling circus, say, or do a little summer stock somewhere in America, dressed in spangled tights and a red tiara. In her sitting room—which is where the reporter conducted the interview—there were books, VHS tapes, a video player, a DVD machine, two chairs, and a sofa. The reporter sat on one of the chairs facing her. She sat on the sofa, his tape recorder between them. The furniture was of a type peculiar to Los Angeles, irrespective of class: white linen with a fine dusting of cat hair, even though there was no cat in evidence. It all looked as if it could be folded up and put in a box in an afternoon.

That was always the dream of the girl performer, no matter what her age: packing up and heading off to illuminate the darkness, a sparkler in each hand eclipsed by the brilliance of her smile. As it happens, Richard Pryor's sister did not smile. She sat with her feet arched, balancing the lower half of her plumpish body on her prettily painted toes, ready to spring for her suitcase.

As Richard Pryor's sister spoke, the reporter was aware of a peculiar sensation rising up in him. When Richard Pryor's sister said "Peoria," "house," or "when Richard and I were children," he stopped listening. He stopped doing the work of the reporter and instead ran with his preferred translation of Peoria: a green-and-brown landscape. Richard Pryor as a child, his nose bigger than his head, his sister's white cotton socks slipping down into her patent leather Mary Janes. There they were, Richard's older sister pulling their shared red wagon, Richard sitting in it, his little baby tits jiggling, a somewhat somnolent breeze wafting over their sweaty little bodies performing the perfect relationship of love: one being carted and the other carting. Thank God for the tape recorder. Otherwise, the reporter would have had no idea, after a while, what Richard Pryor's sister had to say.

He had been interviewing her for three days now. He'd been with Richard for much longer, two years or more. When he began his work, the reporter had approached his subject with the best intentions in the world. Acquaintances and friends of friends of Pryor's called to set up meetings, clamoring to be heard. They showed up for their interviews with eyes narrowed against the past, but dressed well enough for the mirror and an expense-account lunch. The interview "process"—strange word—was always the same for the reporter, no matter whom his subject was. But what made Richard Pryor different—and one of the reasons for the reporter's continued interest in him—was this: Richard Pryor had all but stopped speaking.

In the early days, people on both sides of the fence—family members and film producers alike—were "intrigued" by the project. There was much back-and-forth between the two camps. Each used the reporter as an intermediary, not least because he had read all the material and knew the players involved. He had many lunches with screenwriters who wanted to soak up his "insight" before they went in for a pitch meeting. But invariably those screenwriters were vetoed by one or another of Richard's kin—his wives or children or former schoolteachers—because they felt, for one reason or another, that the writer didn't have the right to take on their Richard,

whoever that was. Richard Pryor's life story was not his own but theirs, and
since he rarely spoke now, what objections was he going to raise about how
his family saw him, or saw themselves through him, in the refracted light of
his fame? The two or three—and then ten—producers who were attached
to the untitled Richard Pryor project would individually take the reporter
out to discuss the nonexistent deal, and to talk about the ways in which his
behavior was or was not helping the project move along. Perhaps he should
consider, they said, being a little more rock and roll, or rather gangsterish,
when he met with potential screenwriters? To give them a feel for what the
material could be, as opposed to just the facts, ma'am?

In the end, the producers went away. If only, they said, the conditions
his heirs attached to the project were not so risky, and—in the Hollywood
parlance—Richard Pryor not so "dark" a subject. Still, it had been inter-
esting for the reporter not to write, for a while, and just have lunch.

When I first began doing this kind of work, I looked into its history.
There's a link between the Foley artist and what came before: the
Japanese benji. I love shit like this. History no journalist can fuck
with. In the nineteen twenties, before sound came in, Japanese
movie-theater owners hired live orators to recite the dialogue through
megaphones. Some of those orators became as famous as the stars on
the screen. Listen to this bit of beauty from a book I cherish: *The
Talkies*, by Arthur Edwin Krows. It's from 1930.

The prime point here is that too much stress should not be placed
upon what is sound and what is picture. As soon as talking films

became a theatrical actuality, critics sought their standards in distinctions between these; but the artistic differences are not between sight and hearing as such. The truest, most genuine appreciation of art takes no cognizance of eye or ear. In admiring a fine statue no one thinks importantly about the physical fact that he sees it, or, in listening uninterruptedly to a beautiful symphony, is for a time aware that he hears it. The instant he is conscious of either, then his enjoyment ends.

That's what I'm talking about. My voice is equal to what you see. For some, what's heard during fucking is more powerful than watching the act itself. When I first started off, I had to do much more than voices; I had to put on rubber gloves and submerge my hand in a jar of lube while rimming a carrot in order to get the sound of penetration right. As my voice earned some demand, I didn't have to do so much incidental stuff. But in a sense, doing Foley for stroke flicks is the greater challenge, since the sound makes the surreality richer. The films you hear me in are about people pulling out at the deepest moment of connection.

I define that as the sound of love. It's also the sound of me loving and being abandoned by Richard.

On January 18, 2001, Adult Video News reported this: the institution, in the porn industry, of the Cambria List. The list is named after Paul Cambria, a lawyer specializing in the First Amendment. He represented Larry Flynt; the list was supposed to help the rest of the industry stay out of trouble during the Bush administration. Here's what it said, under the heading BOXCOVER GUIDELINES/MOVIE PRODUCTION GUIDELINES:

Do not include any of the following:
No shots with appearance of pain or degradation
No facials (bodyshots are OK if shot is not nasty)
No bukakke
No spitting or saliva mouth to mouth
No food used as sex object
No peeing unless in a natural setting, e.g., field, roadside
No coffins
No blindfolds
No wax dripping
No two dicks in/near one mouth
No shot of stretching pussy
No fisting
No squirting
No bondage-type toys or gear unless very light
No girls sharing same dildo (in mouth or pussy)
Toys are OK if shot is not nasty
No hands from two different people fingering same girl
No male–male penetration
No transsexuals
No bi-sex
No degrading dialogue, e.g., "Suck this cock, bitch," while slap-
   ping her face with a penis

No menstruation topics
No incest topics
No forced sex, rape themes, etc.
No black men–white women themes

Notice that nowhere on the list is there an edict against the voice—that is, there are no directives against the way the voice can and should be used. Of course, there's that reference to so-called "degrading dialogue"—e.g., "Suck this cock, bitch"—but when isn't need degrading? In any case, I get around that particular mandate by making it sound more like a question—"Suck this cock, bitch?"—or punk-ass pleading, and therefore more like love.

Sometimes it's fun to make shit up. Maybe as a way of getting at myself without having to go through all the boring pedestrian shit you want to hear, like where I was born and what it was like, having a brother. Cancer Bitch made shit up all the time. Acted in plays, acted in movies. I was her paid companion and half-assed dresser from 1961 to 1964, beginning the year I moved to Manhattan from Peoria. Cancer Bitch—that would be Diana Sands.

She and I were friends until her death. Who can forget her? She was tiny, with high, high hair that didn't necessarily make her appear taller but gave her a kind of heft she didn't have otherwise. Black hair, shaped like a pineapple; light came through the curls. Bee-stung lips, I guess you could call them. She looked like a light-skinned colored lady of a certain age no matter what age she was. And then there were her eyes—rent one of her movies and see them in close-up. No amount of pain you'd ever experienced could ever eclipse the sadness in them. She was always alive, even when she had cancer. Not just alive to the scene or character or camera she was playing to, but available to the alchemy that was happening right before you as you watched her watching, holding on to her character's life with her hands, a character she made live in her admirers' minds by doing what used to pass as an actress's work: taking the page and running it through her body, her mouth, her brain. And when you went home after watching her onstage, her character went home with you, too. She was that good.

She stole Jimmy Baldwin's man in '64. Most likely he handed his man over to her. Subconsciously. He was that way. I knew all about it. She had a role in one of his plays, *Blues for Mister Charlie*; Jimmy, he of the pop eyes and sense of duty toward the abstraction known as colored people, hadn't written her much of a part. Or, rather, it was too much of a part: as Yolanda, she was meant to play a slain civil rights leader's pregnant girlfriend. Yolanda had to deal with a lot of verbal histrionics.

Truth be told, Diana told me, what interested Jimmy more was Cancer Bitch's part in the drama of his relationship with Lucien. Lucien: Baldwin's Swiss piece carried over from Paris, where they met in the early nineteen fifties, in the days of cafés and such. And as is the case with most relationships in which queens fall in love with someone so pointedly different—which is to say someone who is essentially straight—Lucien loved Jimmy but didn't want him. You know the way: after the first seemingly tender kisses, the nose under the armpit, the shock waves of pleasure, toes curled, temples damp with perspiration and the thrill of the mind turning off, blind to any

ambition other than the tactile and the dreams it can lead you to—
after the first few times of that, Jimmy perceived—it took him a while,
as it takes many writers a while to see that truth has nothing to do
with their imaginations—that Lucien really wasn't in it, and could
take the romance away from Jimmy. Which he did.

We can not see things on purpose for just so long. Later, Cancer
Bitch asked Lucien how he could put his body in a situation that wasn't
exactly what he had in mind, meaning how could he separate his body
from his mind, what people laughingly refer to as their desire—how
could he put his body, which eventually became her body, in the way
of Jimmy's cock? After all, she didn't have a cock, or much of one to
speak of. And Lucien said, What makes you think any of those things
are separate? Jimmy loved me. But then I opened my eyes and there
you were. It's a wonder, the eyes and mind and flesh.

Actually, he didn't "just" open his eyes. Jimmy introduced them.
He had brought Lucien back with him from France with the secret
hope that his fame, which was significant for a writer, would somehow
keep Lucien in his fantasy of shared love. But it didn't work.

Blues for Mister Charlie was the old Jimmy exegesis on white on
black—the stage was, in fact, divided into "Blacktown" and "White-
town"—and Diana Sands, Cancer Bitch, was somewhere in the
middle of those towns, bringing to the hackneyed genre Jimmy's play
grew out of—a little Archibald Macleish, a lot of Clifford Odets—her
weird naturalism, colored at the very core. No other country could
have produced her. The head-snapping. The lies you tell to save your
children or get out of mothering them. The little laughter that is like
a bulwark against laughing outright in ridiculous white people's faces

because they might kill you if you did. All this Lucien saw in Diana when he attended rehearsals. He saw it without quite understanding what Cancer Bitch meant, because the only colored person he had known up to that point was Jimmy, and Jimmy had lived in France too long, had prettied his Negroness up, thrown L'Air du Temps over the hogmaws.

Jimmy thought he was directing the play—he shouted instructions at the actors over the (white) director's head, and the director didn't say shit; Black Power was a new and intimidating language— but really he was directing the path his life would take: to become the child to Lucien and Diana's parents. Truth to tell, that was all he wanted—someone in his play and someone watching the play he had written involved with each other. His real story was an old one: the terrible father, or rather stepfather—Jimmy never knew his biological father—and the mother whom he adored but resented because he couldn't save her from Daddy. I say, are all sons born to that? Mother cutting the carrots while Daddy's twisting her nipples in the dark, telling the little Mrs. that she had to ignore her son, the one who wrote so he'd eventually be acknowledged somehow, somewhere? And what did that mean to the little Mrs., especially with a Daddy Baldwin who couldn't provide anything but babies, not even the carrots? What kind of Mrs. is that? One who accepts the babies but no food to nourish them with? A stupid one? I say, is this a woman? Didn't she have any kind of imagination about what a Daddy is supposed to do? Let's not get into the fact that it was the times, her circumstances, she was black and poor, uneducated, blah, blah, blah. She became a Mrs. so she could have a son who would provide her with something.

An imagination. Who could move her into her true glory as a woman.

Is a blow to the imagination the same as a blow to the ego? Maybe to someone like Jimmy it is. To not believe, or have other people not believe, in what he had, made him redouble his own efforts to court Cancer Bitch himself, so Lucien could see how close to a girl Jimmy really was. If she was by his side, Jimmy thought, Lucien wouldn't be able to tell the difference between them. And whatever Lucien was willing to give up to Diana would be his, too, even just a little bit, which is never a little bit, not really, to someone like Jimmy, who was all heart and theatrical calculation.

Biography explains nothing, but it's fun to tell these stories.

In an essay titled "Notes on Black Movies," written in 1972, the film critic Pauline Kael observed:

> Peggy Petit, the young heroine of the new film *Black Girl*, doesn't have a white girl's conformation; she's attractive in a different way. That may not seem so special, but after you've seen a lot of black movies, you know how special it is. The action thrillers feature heroes and heroines who are dark-tanned Anglo-Saxons, so to speak—and not to lure whites (who don't go anyway) but to lure blacks whose ideas of beauty are based on white stereotypes. If there is one area in which the cumulative effect of Hollywood films is obvious, it is in what is now considered "pretty" or "handsome" or "cute" globally; the mannequins in shop windows the world over have pert, piggy little faces.

When I was starting out, there were even fewer black girls on screen than there are now. In the sixties, there was Gloria Foster, and Abby Lincoln, and Brenda Sykes, and the fabulous Judy Pace, who played the first black villainess on TV—on *Peyton Place*, starring little Miss Mia Farrow. What a voice Judy had! Snide and contemptuous and full of hard, cold luster. All those girls were fabulous, in their way. Glamorous and real, which is one definition of movie acting. Their naturalism didn't exclude their coloredness or femaleness. They didn't treat sex as a big deal, either; it was all integral to the inherent humanism of their behavior.

But by 1972, globally, like Ms. Kael says, Gloria, Brenda, Judy, Diana, and not to mention myself were out; movies shifted away from documenting the realism of human interaction to the by-now-predictable surrealism of black bitch in a head rag putting down whitey or an ineffectual husband.

You hear tell now of these actresses like Halle Berry—globally cute and acknowledged as such by picking up an Oscar for it. What Halle wants—what "actresses" of her ilk want—is to be living molds in a global idea of what men are supposed to want: perky-looking chocolate drops that taste like shit and are therefore naughty because black equals shit. Imagine what a black bitch who can actually act feels like when she sits in the cinema of today, recalling the ghosts of the past— Gloria, maybe, and a little bit of me? Imagine what Gloria—who played nearly two hundred characters in *In White America* onstage, back in the sixties—would have thought sitting through contemporary crap like *Juwanna Mann*. Imagine what I felt like looking at Halle with her tits out in *Monster's Ball*, telling some cracker to "Make me feel good." How could I have played that part without feeling my mama in the background, about to go upside my head because I'm declaring a need to a white man?

Or maybe the only thing separating us is my fat ass. Having Richard's face—or his having mine; remember, I'm older—has been a hindrance in my career; people see his fame in me long before they see what I can do as an actress. When people see me, they see Richard's hilarity. In the old days—the seventies—when there was no black performer bigger than Richard, I'd show up for some movie audition or another and the casting director would ask me to put a "Pryor spin" on whatever part I was up for. So I'd look up from the script and start cursing the room out. Then I'd throw the script down and walk out the door. That got me a few laughs, but fewer jobs.

Maybe some low blue lights here, or red. And many cigarettes leading to other cigarettes. Jimmy and Diana smoking and smoking in a bar in Harlem after a particularly frustrating rehearsal. Maybe a little discussion about the play, mouths sticky with cocktails, and Jimmy's black, black skin—an arm—resting on the table, Diana's light, light skin in a sleeveless shift made blue or red by the overhead lights, lights flickering through the holes in her pineapple hair. She's an actress. She says: Well, I don't know if my believability is up to the play. But what she means to say is she isn't sure if the play is up to her believability, the lyrical naturalism in her work, which made of each prop, each wearing of a costume, the very thing you would have worn yourself and done and said yourself, were you not in the audience yourself.

"Oh, baby," she said, "the part," she said a little tentatively, drawing her audience of Jimmy in, "it's a great part, that's not what worries me, what worries me—"

"Yes?" he inquired, never taking his eyes off her. The famous Negro concern overlaid with an analytical listening quality. "What's wrong, baby?" His mouth split, revealing the famous space between his upper teeth. She had a smile, too, and she used it.

"I'm not at all sure I get all of these characters; I mean, I'm not at all sure I'm accessing my character properly. Can we break it down?"

This was the kind of conversation his egotism could bear, since it was not "just" about his work, but about how his work had become her world and thus transformed her into someone he could recognize: a character expressive of his thoughts and feelings. Aren't actresses fabulous? They may know in their minds that they're acting, but their bodies don't show it.

In any case, in that bar, lighting another cigarette in his high faggot style of physical expression—talkative arms and hands that cut the air, leaning forward in his chair to his interlocutor, touching her shoulder with one arm and his heart with another—Jimmy said: Chile, chile, chile. Did I ever tell you about the time when I was a chile—this was when I was in the church—and I was preaching then, preparing one sermon a week? I stood before the people, a nigger Ezekiel, and I preached not because I had the word—I had many—but because I wanted to escape, and because I was in love.

The church was my escape. That is a convenient phrase. Wait. The church was and wasn't different from home. There was home, there was the church, and there was the street, all filled with black people. And how could you not look at them and see Jesus, his Jesus hair, the thorns in it wound tightly in nigger hair piled correct under a picture hat? Negroes high-stepping into eternity, not even seeing the blood dripping before their very eyes? Flies sticking to the blood, can't wash their face because the Jesus blood has burned a hole in it, Jesus rays of acceptance and sorrow over the acceptance coming out of the hole? You can't see anything else if you stay, and you can't not stay, because you're a child aspiring to be Jesus but yourself, forgiveness gouging out your face. But to say any of that is to be exiled by the very people you love.

Cancer Bitch didn't think about what he was saying much; some of it was bullshit that she could already find the holes in. His whole thing about exile, for instance; only famous people complained about all that, after they'd achieved it.

Cancer Bitch knew that no matter how many plays she appeared in by people like the man sitting in front of her—ugly in a way that made you feel protective of him; ugly in a way that made you think, Damn, could it be that I'm that ugly, too—she would never be famous like that; she didn't want fame bad enough. What she wanted was to act bad enough, and when did a bitch ever get famous from love? She had known people like Jimmy throughout her career—they started off as artists with something to say, and they ended up being some cause's voice, living to tell the story of people who needed them as opposed to needing to communicate something themselves. And the love and attention that their work garnered them—that love and attention stood in equal proportion to their insecurity, their feeling that they would be less without being known, that the next black bitch with a typewriter would supplant them. That's what drove them: the fear that they would no longer exist if they were on the level of Cancer Bitch. Or me.

Jimmy drank, I think, scotch in those days. He had many of them, sitting there talking to Diana. If I played her sitting there, in conversation with him, how would I do it? I'd work from the inside out, in that Harlem bar, uptown from where Jimmy, with his playwright's paranoia, thought Burgess Meredith, the director, was clobbering his play and so undermined Meredith's authority with You're white, you don't understand my characters; I didn't write this play for you but for my people who are up there on the stage, with their guts and hems showing, the long moan of the writer who has too much mouth left over after the nonwriting is done, so he can't leave others to the interpretation of it, and besides which, what Jimmy was fighting with was not so much his director as the knowledge, never faced, at least in the press, where he lived by now, that the play wasn't any good, that he had lost his way as a writer, producing work he was supposed to produce as opposed to the work he was the propagator of, mixing cotton fields and crepes, chitlins and coq au vin—this can appeal to a girl, especially if she feels sorry for you because you're ugly. And so I'd listen when he said, lighting another cigarette, a little column of white between his two dark columns of fingers, the same fingers that maybe had been inside of Lucien's mouth—

"And so I learned to perform, because if I didn't I would upset the needs of the people, the people all around me; I'd be called out as a queer, which is to say a living example of someone who didn't believe in them and their Jesus need, because after all there I was, godless, because I'm a queen, and a slave to my queen ways, dirty cuffs dragging in the gutters and bowed down like a dog waiting to be made upright by a word from heaven. Their church was a kind of revenge fantasy—things would turn out better in the next world because Jesus—who was God, too; we didn't make any distinctions between the two—would allow us to step on white heads to get there. We would win the moral war that our very presence in the world, in our slum, in the church, said we would win because we had worked so very hard at suffering.

"So they pushed out everything that was wrong with their world, which is to say people like me, so it wouldn't show up in the next. They didn't want any smart niggers to question how and why they had come to think of themselves as chosen in the first place. They'd bust your ass if you read anything besides the Bible, developed an imagination outside of their imagination, said a thought; because you said a thought, you were white. You sound white—that's what Daddy and some of my siblings said after I'd discovered a building of lies: the library.

I went to the library and came out white. Only my mother didn't punish me for reading, because I was her imagination waiting to happen."

Cancer Bitch adjusted her brassiere strap. It was maybe a little dirty; sweat from the rehearsal and a little baby powder coming down the inside of her armpits, little crumblings of baby powder like butts of wet chalk or pumice stone. She was a little uncomfortable. I say, is this a woman? Diana couldn't act any of this, but I can.

Women lie. An actress lies even better. I don't mean all of that "let's pretend" shit, either, although that's precisely what I mean, too. An actress will believe anything, including herself. They convince their bodies of something and then it exists.

For instance: It's Dover, 1943. Twelve seagulls circle four American servicemen who sit on a cliff. They are picnicking with four English women wearing flower-print dresses and cardigans made at home in front of an electric fire long before they knew the Americans, knitted by the Philco, a little red dot of music in the gloom.

Maybe one woman has red hair, and she longs for the Negro American soldier but is too shy to imagine anything but his tongue on the red tongue between her legs. Those are the clues a director or script might give, and a real acting bitch will say: Got it. And then she'll try to represent the foregoing.

I have never been to Dover, but I could play that place. I could also play that white woman. I could have red hair if I dreamed about it long enough. Long, flowing shit.

Despite her fear, the English girl—myself—went for a walk with the Negro American. They—we—went and sat somewhere near the cliffs, and he kissed her. I know that kiss; those were the first fat lips I ever licked. The kiss is a little dry because you're outdoors, and a little salty because you're near the sea. The kiss is not a kiss on the brink of catastrophe, like the beginning of every love story I've ever known, which goes from hope to boredom to disaster in an instant.

Later in the story, my best English girlfriend tries to fuck him, but I find out. I cry. I love to cry. (A producer friend of mine once described an actress as a woman who feels the need to cry in front of three thousand strangers. Too true!) As the red-haired English woman, I trusted too much. I loved the black American too much, and in a fit of anger I say to my former best English girlfriend: You should get cancer, bitch, and die. Maybe that last line isn't in character. You see, I need a director. If I had a director, he could show me where the hair falls on my shoulders and I could take it from there. As much as a bitch needs dick sometimes, she needs a director more, just as she needs a writer's language in order to be someone other than herself. I wish someone would hire me apart from voice-overs.

Journalism. Bullshit. If it's the "truth" about Richard you're after—haw haw—let me say up front that I'm perfectly aware why Richard is a success and why I am not and why I am not bitter, now, because I am able to understand it: he was able to perform some version of "blackness" and I was not. In the later films—before he got sick—when he was yukking it up in shit like *The Toy* and whatnot, he was a mass of colored buffoonery and feeling sporting a Jheri curl. If you look at him in that film and others, he starts to bear more than a passing resemblance to Flip Wilson crossed with Stepin Fetchit. That was always his thing—a kind of Negro nervousness that white people in particular were able to feel somewhat comfortable with, no matter how "transgressive" or whatever the fuck his humor was considered by journalists and reviewers and the like, since all he did as far as I was concerned was bug out his eyes in a sketch of colored fear. What a caution. I could never do that. So humiliating. How can you want to be loved so much that you make your race some kind of shtick? I am an actress. I could never wear the head rags and look up pleadingly at master as I dusted the doorstep where last the lilacs bloomed, hoping he wouldn't rape me again tonight in some shitty teleplay that becomes a hit on ABC, and what have you.

I'm not a sympathy-getting bitch, I told you from the start. You won't catch me telling a target liberal audience how we done suffered, and how my cunt was raped by America. And no one would believe me if I was cast in that part, anyway! I'm too much myself, too much of a mind that shows its thinking—which is what acting is, too—to be believed as unschooled in life, let alone books. That's hard for white people to accept, I'm sorry to say; they wouldn't know what a colored actress looked like who wasn't playing a slave. Nothing's changed. If a colored girl wants to be seen as an actress, she's gonna have to spread 'em. So what's there for me? Richard and Halle took it all. It's a shitty thought, but I've said it.

Actresses—they're women in search of a self, like all women. But at least a real actress like Diana or myself will admit it. An actress has her eye on you—an audience—while in her head she's looking for a way to get her proverbial Daddy to pay for a script she can play. No abuse is too great to withstand to make that happen. A black eye as the actress blackens the chicken. An acting bitch can even watch herself as her eye is being blackened, and plan what costume she's going to wear to go with it. An acting bitch can stand outside herself while working on the inside of her character, which is to say herself.

I say, isn't that something? Maybe Cancer Bitch didn't think like that after a while, given the cancer. But she never did stop acting. Maybe a better phrase is: She never stopped presenting herself. An acting bitch doesn't stop acting until God yells "Cut!" Toward the end—I saw this myself—Cancer Bitch was up in the hospital bed, shit stuck all up in her, liquid dripping every which way, maybe even out of her asshole, tube stuck up her ass like a plastic Daddy. Her hair was melting against the pillow. Black hair against a white hospital pillow, spreading against a sky of illness. And when she saw me—I had come to visit her—Cancer Bitch pulled the white sheet away from herself, exposing all those tubes, the liquid Daddy in her ass, and said: "Ain't this some shit?"

Metaphors sustain us. To talk about Cancer Bitch as she was—the tubes leaking, her ass—is beside the point. Or beside her point. She was an actress, and as such had a fundamental disrespect for "I." "I" doesn't take into account all the years a bitch spends on becoming something else. Find the character and you find her. That was Cancer Bitch's life work—to be something other than herself, in order to talk about herself in terms beyond the kind of shit that biographers encourage: no metaphors but the thing itself.

I blame Cancer Bitch's acting for making me an actress. To identify me solely as Richard Pryor's sister, to ask me what that's "like," is a question that strikes me as being as pornographic as my mouth. It's as greedy and innocent as a child asking his mother to describe what he was like when he was little. I am an actress. And as an actress I'm interested in Diana Sands and emulating the will she exercised to get over herself and into you, whoever you are. What force! By the time Diana said, "Ain't this some shit?" she knew what she was talking about: acting and dying.

I am an actress. We find truth—human truth—by pretending to be people we're not. That frees us to explore the metaphor of being. Okay, so you'll write that Richard did this, he did that. How will that resonate in the reader's heart beyond the thrill of gossipy revelation? And as to Richard's black celebrity: isn't that an oxymoron? What you want are stories about his black infamy, not a sister. Acting isn't funny, but being is. Richard was never an actor. All he did was put his being out there. People responded. He became famous. What he did wasn't as complicated as acting. Diana Sands was an actress. There are no jokes about her.

"I" is a sitcom. "I," at best, is a pratfall in slow motion. I am an actress, which is to say a woman who pretends to be something other than herself. Risking exposure and not. Richard would never do that. He could never be someone else's text. He'd always fight to be Richard instead of trying to inform the part—Hamlet, whatever—with the deepest parts of himself.

That's not what I do. Honor that. Honor the fact that you'll get more of what you want from me by allowing my "I" to speak through other characters, scenes, events. Allow me metaphor even though I'm not supposed to dally there, being colored or whatever. I know, I know, being colored, I'm not supposed to exist in the realm of ideas; my skin would dirty them up. The general audience expects my shit to be black and raw and "real"—like my literal shit. Like Richard's. Fuck you.

In fact, I blame Richard and his popularity for helping to formulate the audience's expectations whenever they see a black face onscreen, or on a book jacket: Aha! the viewer thinks. Here we have more officers in the race-class-gender bores! And with them come whores! Drifters! Pimps! Junkies! Grifters! At one time or another, Richard and I have been all of those things, but why not allow us the flowers, too? You can see them near the footpath I walked past the other day, years ago. This was in 1993. A man is leaning drunkenly against a crooked fence. Flowers at his feet. They call him Gary. Gary's not drunk, he's just on drugs. Sometimes his own existence is too much. But he can hold a job. He works at a crab house in Baltimore, separating the big and little crabs into different crates. Gary works in the crab house even though he's allergic to the things. The money he makes there is just enough for drugs; just enough so that he doesn't get too sick. It's the first selfish thing he's ever done, being a junkie.

Like all junkies, Gary is a baby; he lives in his mother's basement, so he doesn't pay rent. After he gets high, he likes to read his books: books on chemistry, religion, history. Book knowledge has made him feel funny ever since he was a kid, different from everyone else in his neighborhood, most of whom didn't read and grew up on drugs, including his former wife, Fran, who had a junkie's contempt for Gary from the very beginning and, also from the beginning, a distrust, a steady hatred for what he tried to give her before he started getting high: love, a bit of security, a home. Which is what Gary knew growing up, before drugs.

But Fran couldn't deal. Sometimes, when they were married, she'd grab his cock roughly and sit on it. He would have preferred inserting it into her lovingly, but that journey of love always disgusted Fran, especially since she knew that Gary was always worried about whether or not he was hurting her. Sensing his worry, Fran shat on it, and then she shat on his cock. Gary had a sap's heart and didn't know that the worst part of loving those who do not want to be loved is this: denying them the instant intimacy of fucking, leaving, and never seeing them again, so you live on in their imagination without the further burden of touch. Gary never realized that if only he'd thrown Fran onto a pile of empty crab shells from time to time, they'd still be together. Stunned by pain, she'd be too distracted to notice his love, which made her think of piles of sick. In the sick, there were chunks of options. That was the worst.

Gary let Fran have her own life. She had never had that before. Everyone she had ever known growing up—friends, family—lived a kind of predetermined existence: get up and drink and then scramble for the next drink; get up and snort or shoot, and then knock in the head of some old lady with just enough change in her purse so you can have the same day the next day, and the day after.

They got married in 1983, a few years after they graduated from high school. They were married—or rather, they lived together as Mr. and Mrs. McCullough—for eight years. Then Fran left. In the beginning, Gary gave Fran her own pocket change. After that, he gave her any number of other things: a nice house, a little boy, some nice outfits. In those years he worked security; he always had at least two jobs, plus he invested what he made. Gary thought he and Fran were living a love story.

Fran never thought so. By giving her everything he thought she should have and more, he opened up the world to her. She had the luxury of picking and choosing what she might like for herself. But what Gary didn't know was that no one likes living with options. It makes you feel motherless. Everyone looks for someone to tell them what to do. To resist or accept the perfection in that is one way to get through life. That is the work of an actress: No, I will not hold the teacup that way as I walk across the stage. Or should I? Why tilt my head just so to catch that light in this movie scene? But perhaps, dear director, you are right. I am less equivocal than most actors, because I am less interested in the game of approval than most. I never say to the director: If I do X, will you love me? Because I know they won't.

Directors used to hurt me. When I worked in front of the camera, I generally disagreed with any and all interpretations of my body, since their interpretations are just that—some white boy saying that the distribution of my weight on a given mark is wrong. When I was younger, I'd shift my weight from one leg to another, stick my left hip out, try not to be obtrusive, someone with flesh, even though I was being paid to be seen. It wasn't until many years later that I realized my being colored had something to do with my being off the mark; that is, the colored body is a kind of joke, like the kind Richard would tell about black pussy taking a walk in America. He'd say: Say there, labia too plump, clit too long, people drowning in pussy juice, better wrap that shit up and look for Jesus before I throw up. Richard would have said that in any number of his voices—it's the only way he could make a character, through his voices. Most of the voices he became famous for were just imitations of the people we knew while we were growing up; they weren't acting. I guess he used his body some, used it to show how ridiculous coloredness looks in the context of America; sometimes he could look like a coat hanger hanging on an empty clothesline blowing around in someone's front yard and you could see white people looking at the hanger from their living room window all scared and mesmerized. Or sometimes he could look like a hamburger on a griddle with bean sprouts and hairy tendrils sticking out of its burnt surface, assaulting Americans with fat and weirdness—their worst fears. In any case, what Richard was trying to show based on my telling him stories about the unequal distribution of my weight on the set was that by now it doesn't matter what coloredness looks like, or how it presents itself; it stopped belonging to its body a long time ago, after it was co-opted by Jesus, drugs, biographers, audiences who deluge you with their dreams and expectations—which are, in turn, defined by politics, weather, whatever—and whatever directors have to say about it.

To compensate, the colored spirit became bigger, as if that would protect us. We empathize with all bodies, not having one ourselves. We empathize with all audiences, always being one ourselves. That can be the making of an actress—accepting that one is everyone and no one. I've learned from a brother that, in the end, if you're colored, your fame makes not the slightest difference in terms of how you are seen or not seen by the world, let alone yourself.

A friend who edits books told me this story: Once, the music impresario Quincy Jones was running around pitching his life story to a bunch of publishers. His agent, Irving "Swifty" Lazar, was in tow. So Quincy is pitching his life story to a roomful of editors, and Swifty interrupts and says, "Why don't you tell that other story about your life, Sidney?" Meaning Poitier. Nothing's changed much, certainly when it comes to the Negro in Hollywood. If you're colored, you have to handle things for yourself.

That's what I did. I became myself when I began to tell directors that I couldn't agree with what was being made of me, since I knew they didn't know what to make of me. So let's start somewhere else, I'd suggest to these directors, like with the text, a little improvisation, some sense-memory exercises about a brother. As a result of my candor, I worked less in front of the camera, even less onstage, but when I did, I felt my pores open up when I missed my mark. I was alive to myself. Resisting the direction I needed, I became the character I needed to be—for myself.

Maybe it's better as a joke, though: the body dragging itself through experiences directed by a reality not your own. If Richard's life shows you anything, it's how white people can make you crazy by saying what you are: too fat, too lazy, too loving, too dangerous, too close, too political, too silent, too druggy, too talkative, too generous, too loud, too drunk, too strong, too sensitive, too cruel. That's what Richard's success is based on, a little bit if not a great deal: recounting what the body has seen and felt when certain people can't see or feel you at all.

The trouble with Richard, though, is that he became rich and powerful doing what he did, which contradicts the beauty he found in his nothingness. If you become well-known because of an act of invisibility, you're fucked, because your fame makes you part of the quotidian. You can't really make theater out of these contradictions unless you're an actor, which Richard never was. An actor can sort all of that out and make it clear to an audience just where the confusion begins and ends. Richard just lived in it—all colored and crazy. Add to that earning a lot of money for being yourself, which makes no sense to the colored soul at all—money as a reward for being nothing?—and you end up a nasty joke, a jogging matchstick. You know how it goes: What does this lit matchstick look like, standing upright and then moving across the counter? Richard Pryor jogging.

In actual fact, no one can handle vast quantities of power or fame. Richard couldn't. It nearly burned him alive. He was always looking for something bigger than himself to tell him what to do. We all are. Being an actress is one of the few jobs on earth that tells the truth about this need that exists in humans—to be told what to do. When we were little, Richard looked to me for that—I always thought that was because I was his older sister. But that's not it, not entirely. You can see it in children and their need to be disciplined. Children stamp on flowers to show the blooms who's stronger, and then look to their parents for their punishment. It's the limits we impose on children that help them define who they are.

Sometimes you can find direction in a marriage. At least, that's what Fran was hoping for. In order to become herself, or rather, be herself, Fran wanted to be told what to do so she could hate it. She was like that lyric in the song: "You know I do it better when I'm being opposed." She was my kind of actress.

For Fran, a day was not a day unless there was a little killing in it, some rip-offs of the jack-offs. In the last years of her brief marriage to Gary—1989 to 1991—she worked as an operator for the phone company, but she partied more than she showed up for work. Mostly she liked to stay at home, snorting whatever and spitting invectives at her kid, whom she would sometimes forget to feed.

Sitting in the split-level house Gary had bought for her a few years into their marriage (she had covered nearly all the floors in blue shag carpeting), she wanted something to happen—a firm hand across her face, say. Something more directly cruel than the bullshit Gary gave her, something to make their life together seem more real, beat-up, tangible. Gary did hit her once or twice when she filled the house with drug trash, but what was that to her when she knew his heart wasn't in it? He'd never go out into the world and do a little killing himself. And what kind of husband was that? She would have licked his stank fingers if there were little murders on the tips of them.

The truth of the matter is, Gary was fixed in his dual roles, as a success and as an underdog. He worked hard and did well not only because he wanted to take care of his wife and mother, but because he wanted to wrest from those women all the love they had stored up— the love that he perceived the world didn't want. It never occurred to him that some colored women can be foul, too, being human.

Think back to Richard and our Mama. Not our mother, who barely raised us, but our grandmother, who did. She was as ugly as red mud and as tall as a pile of buffalo dung. Richard attached love to that pile; he kept throwing himself onto it, never mind the filth. Gary was like that with any colored person who came his way, especially women, even though the people who knew him made him feel embarrassed by what his love could yield: not love in return, but competition. Generally speaking, people felt morally diminished by his concern—his goodness—and so, fearing that they could not better it, or even live up to it, were compelled to behave as badly as possible in his presence, borrowing money they could never repay, going after girls Gary found attractive, telling him lies, asking for help they didn't need, telling him he was an ass loaded with books, trashing his secrets. We were a quartet, Gary and Fran and Richard and I.

When Gary got his job at the plant in Baltimore, word spread that he wasn't really black. What black man in his right mind would want to be an overseer at a shitty company in a small town? He reminded his coworkers of the old days in the fields. They said he was just like a house nigger, a spy always asking after his coworkers' wives and children with trouble in mind. He was always lending the new guys money until the company cut their first check, or going to the hospital to visit other guys who got laid up on the job, bending down to smell the flowers he'd sent them on his own dime. What kind of human was that?

The problem with seeing all colored people as a tribe that he, Gary, some ghetto Jesus of infinite heart and thorns, wanted to bundle up, throw on the back of a mule, and take to the promised land with its water sprinklers, shag carpeting, and aboveground pools, was that his love would never make any of them different. Fran was the only one to join him in his promised land, and she hated it there. By being outrageous and foul and dressing her foulness up with perfume and wit, she made him differentiate between herself and the other colored people he wanted to love and save. She was an artist. She could stand outside of her sadness and comment on it with contempt. Hatred was her art. Gary had never known colored people like Fran when he was growing up; at least he didn't want to remember that he had. He kept coming back to his dream of saving her in the way one always comes back to one's desire, which is always riddled by absurdity.

From the first, Gary had been thought absurd, especially by his daddy, who learned to distrust his son when it became clear he had a heart; that turned Mr. McCullough's stomach. But since his father liked the taste of his own bile—a daddy taste, or rather, the acid of son-hate that defines Daddy as a smell—Gary thought he was giving his father what he wanted just by existing so he could have someone to hate.

As a boy, Gary thought he could save his mother, who worked so hard for him, by making money, helping her around the house, being different than a daddy. As the youngest McCullough in spirit if not age (he had two younger siblings), Gary would jump out of bed first, his heart beating fast and his mouth wet with the desire to do good. Daddy always felt little Gary was trying to show him up by making the beds, sweeping up, taking the sour laundry to the wash, but he wasn't; he was just working toward a certain repetition he wanted for the rest of his life: his mother having a look at how he had tidied up (even dusting her alabaster Jesus, and her bust of John F. Kennedy), taking him in her arms, pressing his head into her warm bosom, and then saying those two words of love: "Oh, my!"

Even as a grown-up, so-called, Gary thought: Maybe if women like my mother are not loved in the world, they can give me more of what they've stored up. Maybe if I make one more bed and some extra cash, they'll put a wedding ring under my pillow. Who's to say that if Gary had been filled with enough Oh, my!s as a child, he wouldn't have worked so hard to hear it? But his mother loved him and his father couldn't.

Maybe absence is all we hear. It's the shell we can't pry our ear away from. Gary was human, despite his goodness, and so he fell in love with its lack in others, fell in love with Fran, who, like his father, made him believe what others said about him: that his care was a covert bid for attention, a shitty star turn. Fran made him ashamed of his own nature, and made him feel that all the girls in high school were right for having exclaimed, as he approached: "Here comes the leech!"

Now, at thirty-one years old, he wasn't any different. He was sitting at the kitchen table. It was five o'clock in the morning. He was looking for a clean plate to eat an egg on. He couldn't find one in the pile of filthy dishes Fran had stacked in the kitchen sink. He had no woman to wife him. He saw a roach crawling over the pots filled with Fran's hair chemicals and old macaroni and cheese. In his heart, Gary couldn't believe that that roach wasn't a love bug after all.

Where had the time gone? he wondered. Perhaps, he thought, this wasn't enough for Fran: the sour breath of morning. She didn't even stir when he got out of bed. (He had time to sleep for only three or four hours; just enough time to get the poison of dreams out of his head.) She'd never even made him a lunch, let alone gotten up and fixed him an egg.

There was a certain beauty in that, he reasoned, boiling his own eggs. He toasted some about-to-go-bad bread. Wasn't there a beauty in her bad moods, too? Wasn't that love enough, he thought, seeing love in the bugs feeding on her dirty pots in the way he always wanted to feed on her?

Talk about roaches! Imagine my brother as Kafka. Imagine Richard as Kafka or his roach. Those are the parts he could play. Richard and Franz had the same nose and fears—the Jew and the Negro. At the end of that story, after the roach in fact and at last dies, a bug to martyrdom, the family—the roach's parents, and his sister, Grete— leaves for the countryside. As they travel away from the city, the air grows sweet. Kafka writes:

> It struck both Mr. and Mrs. Samsa, almost at the same moment, as they became aware of their daughter's increasing vivacity, that in spite of all the sorrow of recent times, which had made her cheeks pale, she had bloomed into a pretty young girl with a good figure. They grew quieter and half unconsciously exchanged glances of complete agreement, having come to the conclusion that it would soon be time to find a good husband for her. And it was like a confirmation of their new dreams and excellent intentions that at the end of their journey their daughter sprang to her feet first and stretched her young body.

I could play that sister, if I had a brother who would play Kafka.

I could play the horror of her young flesh as it promises to grow old. Her innocence, even in the face of her brother's dead feelers—so stiff and cold—is the real tale. We can survive anything, if we make it up.

Fran shut the door. She took off the trench coat she had thrown over her bra and panties. She threw the coat over the banister. It was a

Thursday, around two or four. (This was in 1991, two years before Gary was leaning drunkenly against the drunken fence.) She had just gotten rid of her kid again. He was seven. His birthday had passed days before. September. That month also marked her eighth year of marriage to Gary. This was the longest she had ever been with anyone. She had stayed with Gary largely because he paid for her drugs; now she didn't even care about that.

She had put on her raincoat to go to the door—many afternoons, when she got up, she'd go to the front door half dressed, looking for someone to take her child away. She'd throw her raincoat on over her bra and panties and wait until a teenager—they were more irresponsible; she liked that; danger lurked wherever they stood—passed by. She'd let the pimply kid see her tits a little bit, like they were the promise of something to come, and then she'd beg the kid to take her little boy up the road for a burger. She'd say there were a few dollars in it for him if he did. She didn't say her tits were his if something happened to her little boy on the way home, but that's what she hoped for.

She couldn't face it again: hitting that bedroom and all that would ensue, crawling back into bed and the chemical migration to some other place. What would be the point in starting all that up again now, when Gary would be home soon? Asking her, again, to crawl out from under Morpheus? He was always bugging her to be a wife. She didn't know how to do that. She stood at the kitchen door. Dull, dull, dull. Dull dirty dishes, dull flies on stiff, dull dirty dishrags. Her failure at domesticity didn't turn her on like it had in the old days, when she began her descent into fucking everything up. That was five years ago now. Then it had been thrilling to watch Gary get mad, or rather, complain, since she thought it would lead to other things—namely her challenging him and not winning. But she could not drive him to bloodlust. So all she was left with was her failure.

What did it matter that she was in a better house, in a better neighborhood? It was like she told Gary when they moved in: "What am I supposed to do here? Twirl around baking cookies? It ain't me, Gary." He didn't listen. She knew that the minute his back was turned, she'd be inviting dope fiends in—her sister and brother, Scoogie—to fuck it up and make it more like the kind of home she had grown up in. After a while, she didn't even care when Gary came home to watch her destruction; her siblings and friends went on in front of him, blowing blow in each other's depressed and giddy direction.

She moved toward the sink. If you can't beat 'em, join 'em, she thought, stretching on a pair of yellow rubber gloves. But the congealed grease and dead hair in the burned once-enamel pot she'd used to rinse the relaxer out of her hair turned her stomach, making everything in her bra feel queasy. And anyway, the gloves were cracked, dry from disuse. They made her hands clammy. But she didn't take them off when she returned to the kitchen table, annoyed that the smell of Gary's customary breakfast—hard-boiled eggs and toast—eaten hours before, was, for her, more awful than all the things she had done to foul up the kitchen put together.

She was an actress, fond of props. They gave meaning to the scene. She sat back down and enjoyed the image she had of herself, dressed only in her bra and panties, hair half-done, wearing a pair of cracked yellow gloves. The gloves were a distinctly domestic touch, and therefore useless, which interested her.

*　　*　　*

You ask about my brother's fame—what that was "like." It's the same for all of them, the ones who eventually make it. They have the same generator. It's fueled by hysteria and self-interest. Their hysteria is based on a kind of screaming insecurity about whether or not people will take an interest in their self-interest, which the public often interprets as a kind of love, thinking, How could anyone withstand that much self-regard, it must spill out into the world just for me, a sharing of their private self (or selves), how brave!

And how brave, too, that what would be so embarrassing for the rest of us—singing, acting, dancing, telling jokes—would be the thing that would make the performer feel so present and available. Surely that is a gift. And it is. But there's something else that goes along with that (I know this because I can look at it now, not being a star, but being related to one): their self-interest isn't satisfied onstage. All the world's that for them, and every living room and every mother and all of a sister's love are swallowed up and eventually pissed on because you can't love them enough. Stars like my brother don't feel convinced of other people's concern and fidelity until God yells, "Cut!"

Like Richard, Gary was fucked from the first because he was a star growing up in a neighborhood that hated him for it. Unlike Richard, he lacked the core of self-interest that would have made his charisma pay. What interested Gary about his allure was using it to make other people feel like star attractions, especially women. He encouraged them to overwhelm him with their charisma, but a lot of women— his mother, girls in high school, Fran—were confused by his desire, because they had been raised to be an audience for men. Gary was fucked because it's awful for women to be told they're stars when they've been raised not to believe it.

At first, Fran thought Gary's desire for her to be seen was just what she wanted. In their high school, Gary was one of the few boys who wanted to talk to Fran. Her confusion about his interest interested her for a while, so she pursued it.

When she was fifteen, she would go by the candy store where Gary worked after school, making sandwiches. An elderly Jewish couple owned the place. Some people thought the Jew people, as the colored people called them, were using Gary as a front to make the store feel more Negro friendly, but really everyone knew they only hired Gary so the colored people would feel friendlier toward them. Not rip them off so much. That's how bad the neighborhood was getting.

When Fran would go by the store, Gary would be wearing a starchy linen apron tied high above his waist. If it was summertime, as it was now, Fran would be wearing shorts, knee-high tube socks, and Candies, bergamot plastering her bangs to her forehead. For Fran, Gary's interest in her was like trying to learn a foreign language at a late age: frustrating and pointless but maybe there was something to it.

One summer day, near the end of the school year—they were sixteen now—she walked into the store and went up to him and said, "Hey." Gary looked up from the hoagie bread he'd been slathering mayonnaise on. He said "Hey" back. Then he put his mind back on his work. Fran looked around at the cans of wieners and beans and saw nothing in them but dust on top of the lids. She was thinking about how to steal something she didn't want. "So how long you got to work here?" she asked, fingering the cellophane packaging wrapped around some pink and white Sno Balls. Gary was over near the store's cookie and candy section.

"Till eight. Then I stay to help them lock up."

"Oh," she said, less than mildly interested. She pulled one of her socks up; the elastic was loose. When she stood up again, she caught Gary looking at her tits or bra straps. That made her think about trying to act modest, because girls should, she'd heard that somewhere, but what did modesty mean when everything was so obvious, like dust on old cans of Chef Boyardee macaroni and such?

"So what you doing after work? I mean, after you lock up?" She scratched the back of her knee, still staring at him. He cut the sandwich in half.

"Homework; I mean, nothing."

"So, you want to hang out a little bit? It's nice out. You know Olivia?"

"That's the girl from your class? The one who beat her teacher up?"

"Yeah," Fran said, not bothering with the hurt in Gary's eyes. She was more interested in ignoring the Jew people who were staring at her, this girl who was taking up Gary's time. Gary wrapped the sandwich in wax paper, then put it in a brown paper bag and carried it to the front of the store, where the Jew people were waiting on a customer. Gary was back before Fran could shake the memory of the mayonnaise sticking to the wax paper. Upon returning, he offered her a little smile. Mayonnaise teeth. "I don't know if we should, Fran," he said. "That was an old lady she hit."

"So?"

"So if we went to her house, wouldn't that be bad? Like agreeing with a bad idea she had once?"

"Bad for who?" Fran asked. "That old white lady was getting on Olivia's nerves. I'm surprised it took her that long to get around to knocking her down. I would have fucked her up more, and before."

Gary bent his head low, started wiping bread crumbs off the counter. He didn't like that kind of language. Fran was the best kind of actress: one who wouldn't take direction from some director who believed he had a right to her, no matter how nice he thought he was, or could be.

After he agreed to at least walk her over to Olivia's, she pulled on his heart a little more by stealing a package of Ring Dings. She didn't hide them in her shirt or socks. She just crushed them in her left hand, like a purse she kept forgetting to throw away. She didn't even want the cakes. What she wanted she got when she walked out the door with that mess in her hand: the look of incredulity on Gary's employers' faces as she sashayed past them, defying them to stop her for not paying. What Fran didn't see and never would was Gary motioning to his employers that he would take care of it, pay for the damage. And he did.

Opening the door to her house, Olivia—small, busty, doe-eyed—let her smile of greeting curdle noticeably when she saw Gary standing there. "What you bringing him up in here for," she said. It wasn't a question, but a command. She eyed Gary, who was standing a little behind Fran. Fran didn't say anything at first. In that moment, she felt less like a woman than a wall he couldn't scale. Or write his name on.

"Gary," Fran said, after a while.

"I can see that. Why?"

"'Cause I want him to be here. I didn't want to walk over by myself."

"Why?"

"'Cause I didn't want to walk over here by myself."

"Does this look like a hotel? I can't be having all these people in my house, Fran."

"Shut up, girl. Nobody's trying to make you feel like anything." Fran didn't turn back to see if Gary was following her up the three white steps—an architectural detail germane to Baltimore, but who cared?—where Olivia stood sentry, but he did. Fran pushed past her. Gary followed. Olivia sighed, less annoyed than exasperated, and maybe something more. "I thought it was just going to be us," she said, closing the door after them.

"It is just us. Gary's just tagging along. What you got?"

"Enough for us. Nothing extra."

"That'll be fine. Gary, you don't do this shit, do you?"

They were in the living room now. Along one wall was a pink sofa made up in crushed pink velvet. It was covered in plastic. There were two pink chairs on the opposite wall. They were made up in the same fabric as the sofa, but the plastic the chairs were covered in was older, cracked, slightly yellowed.

Gary didn't know what Fran was referring to, but he shook his head no. They sat on the carpeted floor between the sofa and the chairs, in front of the living room table. The furniture looked as if it was reserved for grown-ups, or wakes. Olivia didn't have to tell them that. The table was littered with the signs of Negro respectability:

doilies, a tall bowl filled with plastic fruit, a little hymnal. Gary sat across from the two girls. Fran fingered a doily on which a bowl of fruit rested, as if she was trying to recall where she had seen one before, a lace thing that felt as if it had been dipped in wax. For some reason it disturbed her, these artifacts of someone's idea of home.

"How can we spread our shit out with all this bullshit out?" Fran said, in a sudden fit of pique. She swept Olivia's mother—that is, her mother's bowl and hymnal—to one side of the table. The bowl partially obscured Gary's face. But he could see Olivia take a little brown envelope out of her pocket, tap it against the table's edge, and put a line of white powder down on the table. She handed Fran a little cut-in-half straw. All of this they did in silence. Gary watched it all in silence, too: Fran snorting up the mysterious substance in one nostril and then another; rubbing her nose; and just like an actress becoming the substance she imbibed.

She shivered; she laughed; she looked at Gary as if she had never seen him before. She stood up and stretched her arms out wide. For Gary, there was no other woman in the world, except at home. Fran hugged herself, asked Olivia for a little music. But before Olivia had a chance to get up off the floor, or put the straw down, Fran had turned the radio on herself. Optimism. That's what Fran looked like, dancing to the song that said: "Skip to my lou, my darling. / I'd love to be the man who shares your nights. / My name is Romeo if you'll be my Juliet. / Let's pretend I'm the shoe that fits you perfectly."

Fran was dancing alone and not alone; the world, the man singing on the radio, the station's antenna, the airwaves, the sky bouncing with sound no one could see, were with her. It was the first time Gary had ever seen her attached to anything. He had never seen her clutch life before, unless she was stealing something from it that didn't matter to her much, like a cake or a boy.

Fran closed her eyes and extended her arms toward Gary in a way he'd dreamed of seeing one day. Now that day had come. But if he reached for her—reached for it, whatever "it" she represented—would every dream be fulfilled? And if they were, what would he be then? A boy without longing? How could he recognize himself otherwise?

There was the question of his body, too. If you prefer looking, and confer stardom on the thing you're looking at, you don't want to look at a different movie, one that features us instead of you.

"He won't dance 'cause he's a faggot," Olivia said. "Ha ha, didn't I tell you? A faggot or white. He can't dance." Olivia giggled, and Fran giggled, too, but drily. The weight of their sudden hatred weighed on Gary. He made a move to rise to Olivia's challenge, but the floor pulled him back. Maybe he was white. He could be anything. In any case, there was no room on the dance floor. It was filled with female meanness, the thickest substance known to man.

"Go white boy, go white boy, go!" Olivia started chanting in time to the bright beat, the singer's voice on the radio running at a clip underneath her. The singer was asking, "Will you be my Juliet? / I want to be the shoe that fits you perfectly." They were dancing around him now. He could smell their girl bodies and drug scent. Fran pushed the table away from Gary; it was anchoring him and she wanted him to float free, too, near where the song was playing, near where she was, in the air. Pushing the table aside, she knocked some of Olivia's mother's fruit to the floor. It didn't bounce. Olivia, bending down to pick it up, said: "Girl, be careful. Banging shit up."

"Leave it."

"But she's going to kill me; it was a gift—"

"I said leave it."

Olivia drew her hand back, stood up again, and looked down at Fran, who was squatting in front of Gary, rocking on her heels, legs spread. Fran looked up at Olivia as if to say, "So?" Which was what Olivia looked to Fran for in the first place: a dare. And the threat of punishment—if you do or don't do this, this or that might happen—that gives the dare its spark.

Satisfied, Olivia turned to the radio and started flipping dials. Fran turned back to Gary. She asked him: "What you want to do?" He didn't take it as a dare, but it was. Fran laughed. "Come on, now, you gonna let all of this spoil and go to waste?" There was no music, just static, but she was rocking on her heels as if the static had a beat. That's what drugs made you hear: happiness and static. He thought: I wish I could hear it. Gary closed his eyes.

He was always waiting for love to be what he thought of it: an event informed by niceness, divorced from appeased egos, hatred, and pornography. Love would be his rescue one day, laying him down on a field of daisies, making him and his love lambs of Jesus.

He heard one of the chairs go crunch, followed by another of Olivia's giggles. She said, from across the room: "I told you he was a faggot." Opening his eyes, Gary found Fran standing above him. She was slapping her right thigh with her hand. She wasn't as interested in corroborating Olivia's statement as she was in going where the drugs were taking her: to the irritating realization that she didn't know what

Gary was, since if there was to be no fucking, his perceived rejection of her preceded Fran's eventual rejection of him—and nearly everyone else. She couldn't face that. She wanted to do another line, but it had to be in front of someone it might make a difference to. Fran walked over to Olivia and said: "Get up." The radio was picking up reception from two stations simultaneously. Fran's voice was hard against some man crooning crossed with a woman's voice out of a commercial.

"What?"

"I said get up."

"Girl, get out of my face."

"I'm not in it. But it's about to get the back of my foot if you don't."

Olivia gave a helpless little cry, struggling for a laugh. "But why— you could sit on the sofa, over there." Fran stared her down. The radio played on; out of it came all the sounds that fall between love and advertising. Olivia got up, reluctantly; as she did so, the plastic made a depressed, whoosh-y kind of sound. Fran sat back in the seat, pulling Olivia toward her. Olivia opened her mouth and closed her eyes, like a baby baffled by its own hunger. Fran made her wait a while before she kissed her with her eyes open, looking to see whether or not envy would hurt Gary's heart. But she had miscalculated his optimism; to Gary, she was still the most beautiful woman he had ever seen. He was reveling in his senses being dwarfed by her movie moves, and its soundtrack: the radio playing between two stations, and the ladies slowly lapping tongues.

Fran pulled her mouth away first. She said to Gary: "Now you can leave. But you know I'll be rolling up in that store to take what I need again. Bitch." Gary understood what Fran meant: she was coming back to the Jew place, and for him; he was what she needed. She was coming back—one of the sweetest phrases ever. He tried not to smile, all in love, as Olivia shut the door behind him.

Another Kafka. In "Conversation with the Supplicant," the unnamed male narrator attends a church where a woman he loves goes to worship. One gets the sense that the narrator is not particularly religious; the young woman is his religion, inaccessible and therefore deifiable. In the church, the narrator notices, among the other supplicants, a young man who seems to take a particular interest in our narrator's comings and goings. They strike up a conversation. One could take the narrator's interlocutor as his double: the mystical voice to the narrator's all-too-human reason.

> The young man standing opposite me smiled. Then he dropped on his knees and with a dreamy look on his face told me: "There has never been a time in which I have been convinced from within myself that I am alive. You see, I have only such a fugitive awareness of things around me that I always feel they were once real and are now fleeting away. I have a constant longing, my dear sir, to catch a glimpse of things as they may have been before they show themselves to me. I feel that must have been calm and beautiful…" Since I made no answer and only through involuntary twitchings in my face betrayed my uneasiness, he asked: "Don't you believe that people talk like that?"
>
> I knew I ought to nod assent, but could not do it.

In other words, the narrator cannot agree or rather acknowledge the liminal, least of all in himself—the only "real" there is.

The scariest moment in *Psycho* is not when the people are getting hacked to death, but when Vera Miles, searching for the sister who is lost to her, walks into a bedroom and is taken aback by her own reflection in a floor-length mirror. I sometimes wonder if I am lost to Richard forever. Richard and I didn't see each other much after he became Richard Pryor in the seventies, because we couldn't see each other. That is, we see each other too clearly, and then past the actual seeing. I wonder what it would be like if I didn't have to wonder what he thought. It can make you lonesome, knowing that you're out there as another person with another name but still yourself and yet unavailable to yourself, traversing the trail of the lonesome pines littered with family memories. The way Richard and I are like now is like this, I reckon: being colored and walking into a restaurant full of white people and finding another colored person there. Genetics, politics, I don't know what, makes you seek that black person's eyes out as a way of acknowledging, yes, here we are, for good or ill, kind of together. Maybe I'm looking for a conversation among the supplicants. Invariably, the only other colored person in the restaurant doesn't want to acknowledge your presence, let alone your mind. So they turn away. Being Richard's sister was like that, sometimes. He'd look at me as if I were the only black person in the restaurant. And sometimes I was.

*   *   *

Gary felt that way all the time—like a supplicant—even without a sister. Skinny and strung out on his love for Fran, and the terrible responsibility he undertook when he decided to honor and obey her, he truly didn't have anyone to talk to. Certainly not his mother. From the beginning, Fran and Mrs. McCullough tolerated one another for Gary's sake, but there was no love lost between those two women he did it all for: the savings, the mortgages, pushing his sickening dick to the side so they wouldn't have to deal with it if they didn't want to. He understood that. They didn't want to hear about his love of other women, being women. And since he was interested in little else, he became conversant with himself—a supplicant who would have understood Kafka's tale of love, even if I don't. "He remarked that I was well dressed and he particularly liked my tie," Kafka writes at the end of his tale. He goes on: "And what fine skin I had. And admissions became most clear and unequivocal when one withdrew them." Maybe that's what Gary felt when he left Olivia's that night, the night of Fran's drug show: by leaving, he'd be able to feel those two girls clearly and unequivocally. Absence makes the heart think about what it's feeling. And since this is a DVD world, where the story line is not equal to the star—I blame Richard and his kind for all that star-over-the-story stuff—maybe Gary would matter more to you now if Richard played him. I could coach him in the part: Gary, walking home from Olivia's, a supplicant talking to himself, wanting nothing more than to withdraw his feelings from himself so they existed in a world made perfect by his absence from everything.

Richard could play that. Part of his charm, if you want to call it that, was his ability to look defeated by the attention he craved.

His persona, onstage, in movies, and elsewhere, was interesting, if you want to call it that, because you could never be quite certain if he wanted you to look at him or if he wanted you to look away. Like Kafka, like Gary, Richard couldn't play a pimp but he could play a pimple. Like Gary, once Richard understood that the women he craved loved to compete with him and one another for the rather dubious prize of head bitch of the Richard Pryor universe, he collapsed inside, became a stranger to himself, since he couldn't imagine he was much of a prize. Add colored to that kind of feeling and maybe you're totally fucked.

And like Richard, Gary thought his mother was above that kind of bitch shit, and so revered her. Neither Gary nor Richard could see it any different, because they couldn't feel any different than how they felt. This was their strength and their tragedy.

Gary found out that his mother was just another woman when he brought Fran home for the first time. He and Fran had been dating for about two years by the time that happened. They were about to graduate from high school, Gary still cutting sandwiches in half. He gave Fran money on the side. Immediately upon asking her home to Sunday dinner, he was apprehensive about it. But he could not say why.

Of course his mother knew Fran by sight and reputation. She knew Fran's entire family and blamed them for the dirt and drugs that were remaking their community. In the early nineteen eighties, East Baltimore was swelling up in the middle and oozing slime on the sides; it was fat with the drug traffic that had been dumped there because God knows why. When Gary was a child, the white children only came to his neighborhood if their mother told them to collect Mavis, her runny-nosed kid, and her bag of cleaning supplies. Now the white kids had red-rimmed eyes and runny noses themselves, looking to die a little, too. Rock and roll, fashion, drugs—white people will follow your colored ass into everything. The McCulloughs tried to keep their white steps white, but fools like Fran's family were all too happy to get sick on those steps, thereby proving how ridiculous the effort to keep them clean was in the first place: what was the point of living in nigger heaven if you kept trying to scrub the clouds?

It was a Sunday in spring, fleecy-clouded. Even though Gary had been going out with Fran for two years and change, he hadn't fucked her yet. Fran didn't care as long as he kept giving her pocket change, and anyway, what was it to her, his old dick, the fact that it made him feel like a stupid interloper in her presence? He was too mother-soft for her anyway. There were plenty of hard motherfuckers around. She wasn't even boy crazy unless the boys were crazy. If she did have to fuck Gary one day, she reasoned, she could get high first. She knew he was dick-soft that first night at Olivia's, but she didn't care. Drugs made her hard enough for the both of them. Maybe all she meant for him to be was a brother.

So while Gary cut sandwiches, she dealt drugs. There was so much money to be made, you had to be stupid not to develop some angles. Fran'd take little schoolkids into someone's hallway and get them high on a variety of glues she'd mixed together and charge them fifty cents a pop. Or she'd buy bennies she got on Gary's straight dime and drop them in her older sister's hand for a dollar. She bought shoes with her money, too, but she didn't wear any of her new shit when Gary dragged her over to his mother's house for her first visit. Nor did she get high. She didn't want that woman—a mother—to know who she really was. In any case, getting high would have been redundant, she thought, once she got a look at his mother's Technicolor Jesus. It was such a trip.

"You like my Jesus?" Mrs. McCullough asked her, by way of an opening gambit. There was a pitcher of lemonade and three tall glasses on the kitchen table, with little rings of liquid sweat underneath them. Fran was standing in front of the stove, facing the kitchen windowsill. Jesus was standing on it. Gary sat across from his mother, not looking anywhere at first, and everywhere, as one does when one looks at a movie.

"He's all right."

Beat.

"I'm glad Gar brought you home for a Sunday, Fran. After church is the best time for visiting."

"Huh," Fran said.

"Don't you find it so, Gary?" Mrs. McCullough asked, turning to her son. Gary twisted in his chair, not looking at either woman. There they were, together, because of him; the realization prickled his skin with sweat and made him feel trapped and slightly sick.

"Gary?"

"Yes, Mama?"

"It's nice that you could bring Fran over on a Sunday."

"Yes, Mama."

"Fran, why don't you sit down, honey. You're making me nervous."

"Oh, I'm all right."

Beat.

Mrs. McCullough got up, brushing one of the wet glass rings off the table at the same time. It was something to do, and having done it she couldn't figure out what to do next, so she sat down. The kitchen was small enough without another woman standing up in it.

"Do you go to church, Fran?"

"No." Pause. "Ma'am."

"Oh, your mother—"

Fran cut her off.

"She just never—"

"I see."

"Pardon."

"Your mother."

"She just never mentioned him. Jesus and all. Too many kids, I guess."

"Well, it would be a shame if she knew what she was missing and still didn't do it. He is a comfort. And the church! People just enjoying being together in His name. People like us. Like me and Gary. We go together all the time. Of course, Gary's daddy never gets to church, because he works so hard every day, doing something or another. Like today. He won't be here for supper." She turned to Gary. "He's working."

"Oh."

Gary thought he could say something, just on principle, but if he did, then the attention would be on him instead of the women, his two stars. So he shut up before he had a chance to speak. In this way, he was becoming a man.

"And you've lived here for how long?" Mrs. McCullough asked, knowing the answer. She was staring straight into the side of Fran's head. Fran couldn't stop looking at Jesus. If she wanted Him so much, Mrs. McCullough reasoned, then she might as well go on and take him, since she was in a taking mood.

"I don't know," Fran said. "A long time. Always over on Fayette."

"And how many of you are there?"

"You mean in my family?"

"Yes."

"Five."

"And I bet you're the baby!"

Mrs. McCullough knew as well as anyone that Fran's younger sister, Denise, had been the baby. But she had burned up in a fire. Fran didn't want to talk about that.

"I am now," Fran said. She fingered Jesus' long, shoulder-length plaster of paris hair.

"He's got good hair," Fran continued. "Does he always look like this?" she asked, turning to Mrs. McCullough, who said: "He looks like the person you imagine."

"I think he could be black."

"I mean, he should look like love," Mrs. McCullough said sharply.

There it was; there was no taking it back. She didn't equate blackness with love. Coloredness was so trying, why add love to it? And anyway, what did Fran know about praising anything? My son, my Jesus. Mrs. McCullough knew where Fran lived, all right; that's what accounted for her flat, trashy affect. It was due to her family tradition, too, and its legacy of smells. When she closed her eyes for a moment, as she did now, Mrs. McCullough could smell and then see Fran's parents smoking reefers while their children ate boogers, their nappy hair looking like hairy boogers on top of their idiot heads with their slack jaws underneath, dribbling snot from their flat, ashy noses, snot being what they fed on from generation to generation. And besides being nasty, Fran's family was tearing down the McCulloughs' neighborhood. Mrs. McCullough knew they were doing it out of nigger boredom and neglect. If that was the kind of love that Fran came from, what did she know about the Good, which was to say Mrs. McCullough's son Gary, who was, after all, herself?

Mrs. McCullough said: "Well, let me get my plates on the table. You children must be starved."

She got up. As she walked to the corner of the kitchen where the dishes were stacked, standing in neat rows, she rubbed Gary's head. It was a mother's gesture, an acknowledgment of this fact: if she had accomplished anything in this world by way of bettering the species, Gary was it.

Looking on, Fran felt something nasty-tasting well up in her throat. But it was too late to look away and not be sick. Mrs. McCullough called from the corner: "Honey, would you put a fire under those pots?" That first word, like Mrs. McCullough's gesture of ownership moments before, caught Fran off guard and turned her saliva to tin. She did not know what that kind of female meant by anything. Words and gestures that are inexplicable to us annihilate the self, since we cannot prove we exist in a language we do not understand.

Fran was never one to be overwhelmed or discouraged, though. If being a girl in the presence of a boy-loving mother put her at a disadvantage, she wouldn't show it. Just to contradict everything, she took Mrs. McCullough's "Honey" as her own. She walked over to the stove. She turned the gas on when she was certain she was in Mrs. McCullough's and Gary's line of vision. She could tell, as they set the table, that they were surprised she was standing at the stove; they kind of flinched. But since Fran was a guest and they were colored, they didn't make any remarks about it. Then Fran did this: she pulled a leaf of collard greens out of Mrs. McCullough's big stew pot, ate it, and said, a star fully aware of her audience: "Needs more salt."

That's the worst thing one black bitch can do to another: say your shit needs any kind of seasoning. It's not we don't ever do it to one another, but being colored we never talk about it. That would be grandstanding. Mostly, competition and need stay in our hearts, until they kill us. That's just how our bodies work. Look at Richard, a perfect example of Negro genetics: all fucked on MS and living to crack jokes about it. What would Richard say about Fran looking into Mrs. McCullough's pot? He'd pretend he was Fran, and imagine getting all up in Mrs. McCullough's face with: "That your son over there? Was, I should say. He's mine now. Come on over here, baby, and say good-bye to Mama." Then, raising his voice, Richard would say: "I said come over here and say good-bye to your Mama—bitch. And bitch, say good-bye to your son, otherwise known as your wuzband." Richard could get away with stuff like that onstage because we don't say it in life. He was our id. Fran didn't know from a stage, but to her, everyone was an audience. And like any star, she was annoyed when other people didn't perform their parts in a way that complemented her own—or, worse yet, upstaged her. Mrs. McCullough as the Mother. Was that role greater than her own? She wouldn't know how to play that. And Gary letting Mrs. McCullough pat his head like a dog. What kind of performance was that? After leaving the Mother's home, she took Gary back to her own so-called home and made him fuck her.

They did it, after a fashion, in Fran's dirty room. Cranberry polyester sheets. The TV was on. I say they did it after a fashion, because it didn't feel real to Fran. When she'd been with a girl like Olivia, Fran did her in the boy way. She could even hate her in the boy way. But Gary was too gentle, using his fingers instead of his business when other guys would, you know, just hit it. He wouldn't even have known what she was talking about if she brought all of that up—other guys and such. If she did, maybe he'd go back to his mother. That would be worse than his hands.

Fran was quite the little performer, though, I can tell you. What she projected was a kind of Geraldine Page–like meanness. By the time she got to Gary, she'd been so evil for so long that she'd reduced her parents to sniveling roommates. She'd never quelled her desire to be a child, which is to say an actress, overtaken by a power greater than her own, told when to have the glass of milk and turn the light off: life as a stage direction. But now Gary was showing her what was inside her own body by pushing up against it—fear, which her meanness masked. He was using his mouth now. She could tell because fingers don't breathe. He was offering her what he presumed she wanted: love. Exhaling it all over her wet.

Most showgirls, I can tell you, are interested in the audience member they can't get at, the guy in the third row riffling through his program while you're pouring out your heart. Richard was that way. Even when he played stadiums, he could spot the guy in the fourth tier who wasn't amused and work on him. Be an audience member that withholds and that tap-dancing bitch will beat the boards forever. Most showgirls, they'd get steamed if you told them they weren't particularly giving out of makeup. That wasn't Fran's fear—that someone like Gary would say she wasn't giving. She didn't mean to be. What she feared that afternoon was that he would make her play a part he thought was perfect for her: the supplicant's beloved. Before, boys had handled Fran like a passing moment descended from a larger moment starring them and the first woman they hated: Mother. Their hatred worked on Fran like the guy in the third row works on a performer: as the only lack of attention worth having. No matter how difficult or hard those boys thought she'd been when they were together, she was with them for their lack of attention. And now Gary was giving her nothing but.

He spent more time on her than any boy she'd ever known. That pushed her cowardice to the fore, plus her panic over not knowing how to act in relation to this slurping writer intent on making her play the role he'd written for her. His mother had been too much; now he wasn't even reading a script—her script—that she could follow. Her instinct was to drag him out of that dark mess—she could only imagine what he saw down there—but fear gripped her stomach before she could act. Gary pushed harder. So hard, in fact, that she believed she'd relieved herself. She wondered if her meanness, fear, and cowardice—shaped like bullet-shaped turds—were smashed against the cranberry sheets. She would not roll over and take a look. She didn't know how to act. She couldn't do anything, least of all see if she'd shat. In any case, Gary would have scooped her shit up, wrapped it up in Kleenex with a bow, and put it in her purse had he known that's what she was looking for, instead of the happy ending his imagination insisted upon.

I can tell you that despite what was in her mind, she would have won the Hot D'Or Award for her performance that afternoon anyway. Sometimes the camera is less interested in what's in your mind than in how you use your head. Eventually she got used to Gary's probing what she hated, because she could get high while he did it. Eventually the drugs she liked helped her not only bear the tedium and horror of their life together, but cultivate it. Billie Holiday once said that she knew she didn't want to be on junk anymore when she couldn't bear to watch TV. The flat sameness of it, you know. That's what Fran introduced into her marriage to Gary, almost from the first. An affectlessness—when she wasn't being evil—that was meant to squash Gary's Walt Disney approach to marriage. Are we happy? I don't care. Isn't our newborn baby a champ? I don't know. Isn't it amazing we got out of the old neighborhood and into this new house? Let's call it love. I don't care.

I have here the short article you wrote about Fran and the woman who eventually played her, in 2000. Now why can't I have that? I was up for the same part. So what if Miss Alexander is younger than me by some twenty years? I feel a certain resentment about the Diana Sands comparison you make, saying Miss Alexander reminds you of Cancer Bitch. I felt Fran when I read the book. So much so that I could make her backstory up. All I get is being a sister to celebrity. What am I supposed to do with that? Write children's books about Kwanzaa and hope my brother dictates a five-hundred-word introduction that would sell it? Write a memoir that betrays family secrets? Or produce a documentary with, let's say, Prince's sister, about star brothers who overwhelm their equally gifted, barely lauded siblings? That's what you want to hear. I am an actress. Maybe I could have done something different in this life, different than talking dirty to get you to be interested in me. I couldn't have worked harder on Fran. Everything I've told you about Fran—it wasn't even in the movie or the book. I know her so well, I could make her up and it would still be nonfiction.

An out-of-work actress is a terrible thing to see. They're always acting bright, ready, and available, because they're trying to seduce men—writers, directors, and so on—who can claim them and put their bodies and imaginations to work. Longing to be claimed, an out-of-work actress is always trying not to show her true desperation. They act more "girlish" than they would ordinarily, just to get some dick interested. That kind of girlishness always comes out as brittle tasting. You can smell their fear: about getting old, tits falling, work drying up. If you're not working, you can take classes, think about plastic surgery, do stuff that makes you think you're doing something. But what if you're an actress with no kind of access to show business? Auditions and the like? Take it from me.

An actress is a liar. An actress's soul is whatever you're paying her to shape it as at the time. Why do men fall for it? I can spot an actress a mile away—and then avoid her. I don't suppose it's because men like you find some general truth about women under the tits and feathers, is it? Look at all those men around Mary Tyrone—her two sons and husband—drinking themselves to death, waiting for her to be different, waiting for her to become less of a junkie and more of a mother. Why did they do that? Why did Gary? Can't Mary's sons and husband see that actress, junkie, mother—it's all the same? That all those roles are fueled by self-regard and self-pity? What kind of hope do men find underneath all that acting? Are you hoping that one day she'll stop acting and love you as herself forever? You might as well give that idea up. A mother doesn't give that part up until God yells "Cut!" Neither does a junkie. Neither does an actress. The hope you all have that women will act differently—somewhere, somehow—is just that: your hope. Actresses are themselves, if only they had one. Women are themselves, if only they could stop acting.

IT WILL SOON BE HERE

THE WALL SURROUNDING memory misremembered is clean and wide and high, similar in effect to the wall one finds in certain airports in other countries, clean and wide and high like that, banking in or letting go those who want to remember clearly or don't. Passengers coming or going in the field of memory are a tangle of arms and legs, hands, hearts, hair and minds that—if you do not stand too close or listen too carefully—speak a shared language, remarkable in its oppressive loneliness, its denial: What a horrible memory, and so forth. Regardless of where many of us believe we land—in that field encumbered by not too much baggage or entirely too much—we all come from the same place, which is a road rutted by experience so banal, nearly remarkable, that memory tricks us into remembrance of it again and again, as if experience alone were not enough. What are we to do with such a life, one in which we are not left alone to events—love, shopping, and so forth—but to the holocaust of feeling that memory, misremembered or not, imposes on us?

Against that wall, which is clean and wide and high, we fall disastrously at times, when we can no longer be—quite—the fascist-minded custodians of our past that we'd like to be, as in: I don't remember, I can't, and so forth. In censoring our past we censor ourselves—a not remarkable observation; nor is the idea that the will to censorship begins, like some weird music, in the home, heard most acutely by the children, or the queer children someone's mother must love most. Not remembering, or misremembering one's childhood is a way of allowing oneself the notion that the past does not exist, that it was not lived through in quite that way, that somehow it did not make one different than the rest, as in, I was the one in hellish bliss wearing my mother's garters behind the closed door, not being a boy; or, I was in my childhood bed with her and our legs were entwined and young ladies are supposed to keep their legs away from one another, and closed, and so forth.

Some of us regard these memories as accidents, which is for the best if what we want is to forget them. But we condemn ourselves to self-disgust if we insist on not remembering, because memory's always there, no matter what.

Something else happens in the process of falling, again and again, against the clean, wide, and high wall of misremembering or not remembering at all. With the blood that eventually appears as the result of this repeated violence to the self, one attempts to write one's name—with a finger, or nearly broken tongue—but can barely make it out after doing so, it's just too late, as in, That is the way my parents spell my name, I believe, but I cannot pronounce it, and so forth.

For as long as my memory can remember, I existed characterless, within no memory at all. Or if I did exist it was in remembering the text of someone else's life—that is, in the devouring of biography. If there was a general rule to my thinking then it was: This is someone else and it is not me so I will remember this because of that; or: The subject's having done this means that I need not—no life bears repeating; or: This takes me out of what I am—a self. It was never, ever about a self that belonged to me—that is, myself—which for so long I dreamt did not belong to me, because it didn't. Or maybe doesn't still.

Here is his story: Once upon a time there was this boy who did not have breasts, but he saw them on nearly everyone in his family, men included. Often he would bury his face in his mother's breasts, feeling no distance and great distance from her and them all at the same time. This was before he spoke much; his mother was in the distance of speech—brown like that, and all engrossing. They lived in this world just on the other side of speech, where reflection lives inside of reflection, until one day this boy, who in looks and manner had often, favorably, been compared to a girl, was in the subway with his mother. While there, this boy and his mother saw two people they recognized from their neighborhood: an older woman who was the mother of a son too, and who was always accompanied by her son, as she was now, underground, except that her son's appearance in this instance was all different. Almost in direct imitation of his mother, the son was dressed in black shoes with princess heels, and flesh-colored hose through which dark hair sprouted, and a lemon-colored linen shift with grease spots on it, and a purple head scarf, and bangles. He carried a purse with no straps, out of which he removed, after little or no consultation with his mother, a compact and lipstick to dress his face, too. As the boy and his mother looked at their neighbor and son, the boy's mother sort of brushed his eyes closed for an instant with the back of her hand and said something he had never heard before but thought he know the meaning of. She said, "Faggot." This boy never forgot that other boy who wanted so to look like his mother. He did not even forget him after the terror of memory reinstigated this memory—something he had censored from his family because of the way in which his mother had used the word *faggot* in the filth of that underground station, where someone was exercising the courage inherent in being himself.

Here is a terrible memory: The boy who was favorably compared to women was thought to be the same by a man he did not know. This man covered his mouth in a hallway that stank and stank. He removed this boy's trousers without removing his own, but this man opened and opened his zipper. When he opened his zipper things were very dark and stank and stank in there and felt larger than awful, terrifying and familiar. This man's hands went to parts of this boy's body the boy himself had never known. There was something that hurt him very deeply; there were his trousers down around his ankles and there was this man's hand on his mouth, which was as big as the memory of what his mother had said once in the underground station, and was saying again in his ear or maybe the man was. Together this man and the boy's mother said the word, *faggot*. For a while this was all the boy remembered, besides the pain and the smell, and his body disappearing. That was the motive behind his body disappearing, and turning all of this into a dream, which it wasn't.

We often pretend that the profound shame that accompanies our resistance to remembering is fleeting, as though being revisionists of our own past made much of the difference, as in, "Actually I believe my childhood to have been quite happy. We had a dog, a psychiatrist, a house…" and so forth. But for the child, the queer child some mother must have loved most, this revision of history takes place even before there is a past to be had—it takes place simultaneously with the realization that the parent may pull the following out of his wig or hat: "You are no son/daughter of mine." To whom do we belong in this ruined kingdom we all want to belong to, regardless of how wrecked, how stultifying? To be central and apparently loved, one will do a great deal, even exercise, continually, the courage of shutting up, the conviction that yes I am just like you and everyone else or at least exhibit the desire to be. At home, in the face of the parent, self-censorship as the entry fee into the ruined kingdom of their existence, of lies and lies again, means a good-bye to the memory of all the cocks and cunts and hearts and minds that we embrace in our mouths, and our hearts, too, but spit out before we give ourselves the chance to name them. If you choose this, all of those others who fly but fall so disastrously against the clean and wide and high wall of memory misremembered may choose not to remember you, too, as the boy who will not love the other boy because he has never loved a boy whose skin was somehow like mud to him; or who will not love anyone because that love means to remember a hate that consumes his heart; or produces such a memory of the mother saying, "What if your father saw you like that?"; or interferes too profoundly with being something other than himself, which is a Jew and beautiful. There are many stories like this one, but only one, too. Such as the story about the Latvian who died, a white girl no one will ever forget because she not only told the people she cared for they were beautiful and valuable, she told her colored brother, who remains her writer, too. Our recourse in reinventing the love affair with no love, or a surfeit of it, the memory misremembered or tossed altogether, is learning how to write our name—in blood or whatever—on that clean and wide and high wall which only learning to admit oneself to one's home, recumbent with memory, can destroy.

THANKFULNESS BECAUSE OF:

Walter

D.A.T.

Deborah Treisman—the years, David Remnick—for his Malcolm admiration and Pryor love, Junot: heart.

Profound gratitude to Brent Sikkema, Jean Godfrey-June, and Alexandra Shiva for their beautifully open doors, true hearts, and true shelter.

Then: Ang, J.C., Mr. S.R., and Mrs. S.C.R., George and Gary, Khandi—her voice—and Annie-pants, Miss Phipps, PM Doig, Miss Sarah, Miss Soah, and Miss C.K.N.Y.C.—for the conversations, and saying what needed to be said, for growth.

Love and endless thanks to: Phil Mariani, Ida Panicelli, the late Joe Wood, Tina Brown, Deb Garrison, Gary Smith and the American Academy in Berlin, Bob Silvers, the ever present Barbara Epstein, Thelma Golden, Vendela Vida and Dave Eggers—editors who said the word every writer needs to hear: Yes.